RULE OF LAW IN LATIN AMERICA:
THE INTERNATIONAL PROMOTION OF JUDICIAL REFORM

Rule of Law in Latin America: The International Promotion of Judicial Reform

Edited by
Pilar Domingo and Rachel Sieder

Institute of Latin American Studies
31 Tavistock Square, London WC1H 9HA
http://www.sas.ac.uk/ilas/publicat.htm

Institute of Latin American Studies
School of Advanced Study
University of London

British Library Cataloguing-in-Publication Data
A catalogue record for this book is available
from the British Library

ISBN 1900039 39 7

© Institute of Latin American Studies
University of London, 2001

Printed and bound in Great Britain by Biddles Ltd
www.biddles.co.uk

CONTENTS

Acknowledgements

This book originated in a conference entitled ***Issues in Judicial Reform in Latin America: International Organisations, NGOs and Rule of Law Construction*** convened by Rachel Sieder and Celia Szusterman and held in November 1999 at the Institute of Latin American Studies, London. The editors gratefully acknowledge the support of Augusto Varas and the Ford Foundation for this endeavour and also thank all the participants in the conference, and particularly Julio Faúndez and Fiona Macaulay, for their critical input. The collaboration of USAID, IDB and the World Bank is gratefully acknowledged, as is the support of the administrative staff at the Institute of Latin American Studies.

Notes on Contributors

Christina Biebesheimer is Attorney and Senior Officer in the State, Governance and Civil Society Division of the Sustainable Development Department of the Inter-American Development Bank, where she works on projects related to modernisation of the state, focusing in particular on justice system reform, public sector management reform and the strengthening of civil society and democratic institutions. After graduating from the University of Iowa she studied at the Universidade Clássica de Lisboa, and received her JD from Harvard Law School. She is the co-editor (with Francisco Mejía) of *Justice Beyond Our Borders* (Baltimore, 2000), an examination of successful judicial systems and practices outside Latin America as possible models for countries of the region.

Thomas Carothers is vice-president for studies and co-director of the Democracy and Rule of Law Project at the Carnegie Endowment for International Peace in Washington, DC. He has worked on democracy and rule of law programmes in many countries for a variety of organisations and has written extensively on democracy aid and democratisation, including *Aiding Democracy Abroad: The Learning Curve* (Washington, DC, 1999).

Maria Dakolias is the Acting Chief Counsel of Legal and Judicial Reform in the World Bank's Legal Department. Since joining the Bank in 1992 her work advising and managing legal and judicial reform projects has spanned Latin America, the former Soviet Union, the Middle East and Asia. Her recent publications include 'Attacking corruption in the judiciary: a critical process in judicial reform' (with Kim Thachuk, *Wisconsin International Law Journal*, vol. 18, issue 2, 2000), 'Judicial Reform: A Process of Change Through Pilot Courts' (with Javier Said, *European Journal of Law Reform*, vol. 2, issue 1, 2000), and 'Court Performance around the World: A Comparative Perspective', in *Yale Human Rights & Development Law Journal*, vol. 2, 1999.

Pilar Domingo is a lecturer in the Department of Politics, Queen Mary, University of London. Her research focuses on democratisation, rule of law and judicial politics in Latin America. Recent publications include 'Judicial Independence and Judicial Reform in Latin America', in Andreas Schedler et al. (eds.), *The Self-Restraining State: Power and Accountability in New Democracies* (1999) and 'The Politics of the Mexican Supreme Court', in *Journal of Latin American Studies*, vol. 32, issue 3, Oct. 2000.

Luis Salas is a Full Professor in Florida International University's College of Health and Urban Affairs and has been the Director of the Center for the Administration of Justice since its creation in 1984. He has directed legal reform projects totalling over $15 million dollars and is one of the foremost experts on Latin American justice systems. He has conducted technical assistance, training and evaluation consultancies for USAID and other international donors in many Latin American states.

Margaret Sarles has been head of Democracy and Human Rights for the Latin America and Caribbean Bureau of the US Agency for International Development since 1996. A political scientist, she was formerly Chair of Latin American and Caribbean Studies at the Foreign Service Institute (US State Department) and has taught at various universities in the United States and Brazil.

Rachel Sieder is Senior Lecturer in Politics at the Institute of Latin American Studies, University of London, where she teaches courses in comparative politics and human rights. She publishes widely on Central America, human rights, indigenous rights and peace processes. She is the author of *Derecho consuetudinario y transición democrática en Guatemala* (Guatemala, 1996) and has previously edited *Central America: Fragile Transition* (Basingstoke, 1996) and *Guatemala after the Peace Accords* (London, 1998).

List of Figures

List of Appendices

Pilar Domingo and Rachel Sieder

During the last fifteen years the efforts of international donor organisations to strengthen democratic rule and market economics in Latin America have increasingly led them to view the rule of law as a critical aspect of governance and a central focus of policy concern. Across the region the rise in common crime and corruption dominate popular concerns, and confidence in the ability of national judiciaries to tackle these problems is low or non-existent. Widespread recognition exists that reform of the region's weak and ineffective judicial systems is vital in order to advance a range of objectives, including democratic governance, economic stability, respect for human rights, social justice and citizen security. However, despite general agreement on the need for reform, there is often little consensus on quite what is meant by the 'rule of law' or on how it can best be advanced.

This book draws together contributions from academics and practitioners who work in the area of justice reform. Specifically it includes different perspectives on rule of law promotion from the World Bank, USAID and the Inter-American Development Bank (IDB), the most significant international donors in Latin America in the field of justice reform. After more than a decade of reform and the disbursement of millions of dollars, how are these donor initiatives to be assessed? The contributors to this volume raise a number of questions about current efforts to promote the rule of law: how new is the recent international interest in rule of law promotion and judicial reform? How do international organisations go about developing their reform agenda? What specific objectives are prioritised in the reforms? How do consultation processes with local counterparts and target populations operate? What kind of mechanisms are in place, if any, to ensure that reform projects are followed up and monitored? How do international organisations relate to national governments? And how do they relate to each other in the area of justice reform?

Thomas Carothers' introductory essay critically analyses the issues at stake in international rule of law promotion. Carothers traces the evolution of international interest in Latin America's justice systems from the focus on justice administration during the early transition processes in the 1980s to a broader consideration of rule of law in the 1990s. He identifies four main areas of concern that drive contemporary international justice reform initiatives: democracy enhancement, human rights and social justice, economic development and international law enforcement. These areas overlap to some extent in practice, but they may also conflict with one another and be perceived very differently by donors and recipients. Carothers argues that the multiplicity of donor objectives behind rule of law reform is an inescapable fact of the policy domain. What is required, he maintains, is an awareness of the different agendas and perspectives at play.

In chapter two Luis Salas locates the main themes and problems of justice reform within a broader historical perspective, examining the evolution of justice reform programmes since the law and development movement in the 1960s to contemporary concerns with democracy and rule of law promotion. Salas reviews the different areas of international co-operation in justice reform. He also provides a highly critical assessment of the way in which international donor organisations carry out their reform programmes. Acute lack of transparency in the design, procurement and implementation of justice reforms, together with the absence of inter-agency co-ordination are identified as some of the factors which consistently undermine the effectiveness of judicial reform. Salas concludes that if donors continue to lack transparency, pursuing misconceived and poorly implemented programmes to support the rule of law, they will contribute little to ameliorating the acute crisis of citizen confidence currently affecting Latin America's justice systems.

Margaret Sarles from the United States Agency for International Development (USAID) records the experience of that organisation in justice reform. USAID was involved in some of the earlier reforms carried out under the law and development movement in the 1960s. With the transition to elected democracy across Latin America in the 1980s it was the first international organisation to be actively involved in justice related reform initiatives. Sarles' chapter sets out the different areas of judicial reform in which USAID has been most active, indicating how USAID has expanded its reform agenda from an early preoccupation with democracy and human rights to take on broader concerns related to access to justice, judicial independence, institutional strengthening, training and regional network facilitation, and tackling corruption. The chapter also identifies some key limitations and weaknesses in the implementation of justice reform programmes.

The chapter by Maria Dakolias addresses the work carried out by the World Bank in the area of justice reform. Dakolias emphasises the shift in attitude that occurred within the Bank during the 1990s, which has led to increasing attempts to build bridges between reform programmes and civil society. The chapter reflects a growing awareness of the need for broader 'ownership' of judicial reform processes within specific national contexts. The benefits of more participatory reform processes are discussed through the example of World Bank reform initiatives in Ecuador. Dakolias hints at shifts in the reform agenda of the World Bank, as it moves from initial concerns with efficiency and facilitating market rule towards a greater consideration of democracy-related issues, such as improving access to justice.

In chapter five Christina Biebesheimer explores the experience of the Inter-American Development Bank in justice reform during the 1990s. The IDB's strategy has incorporated a number of aspects, including strengthening justice-related institutions, law reform, research and consensus building through consultation and NGO participation. Like the World Bank, the IDB has involved itself primarily with civil law reform and until recently has been reluctant to engage with criminal law issues. Biebesheimer identifies a number of areas that the IDB needs to address in order to strengthen and improve its reform strategy. These range from increasing the scope for civil society participation, to improving the benchmarking and monitoring procedures of reform projects.

In their concluding chapter Pilar Domingo and Rachel Sieder draw together some of the lessons to be gleaned from the experience of international donor programmes to advance judicial reform in Latin America. They also map out areas for future research and conceptual clarification that could contribute to a better understanding of justice reform and the role played by the international community in these endeavours. Domingo and Sieder argue for a closer questioning of common assumptions regarding the relationship between rule of law, democracy and the market. In addition, they argue, as the discourse of donor organisations increasingly advocates more participatory reform processes, a critical analysis of what is meant by the term 'civil society' is essential if we are to begin to understand the successes and failures of internationally supported reform initiatives in the justice field.

CHAPTER 1

The Many Agendas of Rule of Law Reform in Latin America

Thomas Carothers

Introduction

In recent years the broad but suggestive notion of a 'rule of law agenda' has emerged in Latin America. Throughout the region, the problematic state of law and legal systems and the challenge of their reform are at the forefront of national policy agendas. To name just a few of what could be a long list of examples, in Argentina the public and the politicians engage in frequent, heated debates over corruption in the courts, police and other major legal institutions. In Colombia, the ability of the core legal institutions to withstand the pressures resulting from the civil conflict is a pressing concern. In Chile, the Pinochet case has brought to the surface buried questions about legal accountability for past human rights abuses. In Guatemala a surge in ordinary crime since the mid-1990s is obliging the government to respond to intense public dissatisfaction with the criminal justice system. In Venezuela, the courts, and the whole framework of an independent judiciary, are under siege as President Hugo Chávez refashions the political system.

Attention to the rule of law — how to repair it, achieve it or spread it — is rising both within most Latin American countries and among a growing number of international actors with interest in the region. Programmes of assistance or cooperation to promote the rule of law in Latin America began to spread in the 1980s and multiplied rapidly in the 1990s. A wide range of international actors, including bilateral aid agencies, the multilateral development banks, international institutions (including the United Nations and the Organisation of American States) and private foundations, are now involved in such work.[1] It has become hard to take more than a few steps within the legal sectors of most Latin American countries without coming across externally-funded programmes for the reform or strengthening of major institutions in those sectors.

Invoking the rule of law as a goal of national policy or of international cooperation typically provokes broad consensus. It is rare, after all, for any domestic or international actor to be against the rule of law as a matter of principle or to deny its fundamental importance. Yet it is evident that the term means different things to different people and that it is such a broad concept as to be capable of covering many different activities. This chapter examines the various components of the rule of law agenda in Latin America as interpreted

---

[1] Thomas Carothers (1998) pp. 95–106.

and acted upon by the external actors that sponsor assistance programmes explicitly aimed at rule of law reform. It starts by tracing the two early sources of rule of law aid in the 1980s and then analyses the four main clusters of rule of law work that blossomed in the 1990s. It then considers the points of divergence among these different clusters in order to understand the extent to which the rule of law agenda for aid providers is in fact one agenda or many.

The rise of rule of law aid: the 1980s

North American and West European efforts to promote legal reform and development in Latin America date back at least as far as the law and development movement of the 1960s or — if one looks harder — to law reform movements in the first half of the twentieth century or even before.[2] The rise of a broad field of rule of law assistance in the 1990s, however, grew out of two more recent developments — the human rights movement of the late 1970s and '80s and a set of US aid programmes initiated in the mid-1980s that focused on the administration of justice in Latin America.

Human rights activists from within and outside the region fought hard in the late 1970s and the 1980s to call attention to the gross human rights violations committed by authoritarian regimes in Latin America. When elected governments returned to power in the region across the 1980s, the human rights movement devoted significant attention to the issue of what is now called transitional justice — helping new governments and newly-opened societies decide whether and how to hold wrongdoers accountable for past abuses. And as serious human rights abuses persisted in some countries even under elected governments, human rights activists continued to exert pressure for governments to do better.

The human rights movement did not characterise its agenda in Latin America in the 1980s as that of promoting the rule of law overall. Human rights activists focused intensely on trying to stop very specific, immediate wrongs, such as torture and political murder. They worked in opposition to many governments and were far removed from the cooperative NGO-government relationships that are now common in the rule of law field. Although the human rights movement was highly charged politically, it operated from a strong legal basis and raised the profile of law and legal institutions as a cause of external attention and internal reform in the region. As such it paved the way for the current nature of rule of law aid in the region.

The other stream of rule of law work with direct ties to contemporary rule of law aid was a large-scale set of assistance programmes sponsored by the US government aimed at improving the administration of justice in the region.

---

[2] On the law and development movement see James Gardner (1980); David M. Trubek and Marc Galanter (1974), pp. 1062–102.

The first group of these programmes arose in Central America in the mid-1980s. They were soon followed by undertakings in the Caribbean and in several countries in South America, primarily Colombia, Peru and Bolivia. By the end of the decade the US Agency for International Development (USAID), the main US agency behind these programmes, was at work in more than ten countries on administration of justice programmes and had already spent upwards of US$100 million in the area.[3]

The US decision to initiate work in this domain was originally prompted by the calamitous condition of the criminal justice system in El Salvador and the inability of that system in the early 1980s to track down the perpetrators of some of the most notorious political murders in El Salvador, such as the murder of the four churchwomen from the USA in 1980.[4] Under pressure from the Democratically-controlled House of Representatives and a sceptical public, the Reagan administration needed to show some human rights improvements in the Central American countries to which it was providing increasing amounts of military aid. When US officials turned to the legal and judicial systems of these countries for help on this front they found that they were not up to the task and decided to provide aid to help strengthen them.

The administration of justice programme quickly expanded beyond El Salvador and took on a broader democracy promotion rationale. The Reagan administration made the promotion of elected civilian governments part of its anti-leftist strategy in Central America and cast its policy rhetorically in sweeping pro-democracy terms. The administration of justice programme expanded as a democracy promotion programme, operating from the basic assumption that an independent, effective judicial system is an essential part of democracy and that promoting better administration of justice is fundamentally pro-democratic. Within the overall domain of the administration of justice, the US programmes of the period concentrated on criminal justice. They underwrote criminal law reform and the training of prosecutors, judges and police as well as other activities. The focus on the criminal side reflected the aid providers' view that improving the treatment of citizens who come in contact with the criminal justice system (such as reducing the numbers held in detention without charge) was a key to helping the fragile states of the region become more responsive and accountable to citizens, and thus more democratic.

Multiple agendas: the 1990s

At the end of the 1980s, rule of law aid was getting underway in Latin America, although only a few external actors were yet involved and most Latin American governments were still only starting to take a real interest in the sub-

---

[3] See José Alvarez (1991) pp. 287–332; and Thomas Carothers (1991) chapter 6.
[4] See Margaret Popkin (2000).

ject. By the end of the 1990s the field had expanded enormously with many more external actors engaged, more programmes under way, and interest in rule of law rising throughout the region. At the risk of some oversimplification, the current universe of rule of law aid programmes divides into four major activity categories (see Figure 1.1).

By far the largest category is that of efforts to improve the functioning of the major state institutions directly involved in the making, implementation and enforcement of laws — the courts, prosecutors, police, public defenders and prisons. One can also include in this category legislative strengthening programmes, which have become fairly numerous in the region, although they are part of a broader democracy agenda that focuses on political process goals (such as stronger party systems), somewhat distinct from rule of law concerns.

Two relatively limited categories, at least in terms of the attention devoted to them, are programmes to fortify bar associations (such as encouraging bar associations to establish ethical standards for lawyers) and to improve legal education (such as by setting up clinical law programmes in law schools or revising law school curricula).

A fourth, large category are efforts targeted at non-governmental organisations (NGOs) that can contribute in diverse ways to rule of law reform. This includes training of journalists in how to cover legal matters, support for NGOs that use legal advocacy to achieve social and economic objectives, support for NGOs that seek to foster citizen interest in rule of law reform, aid for human rights groups and help for legal aid clinics.

Almost all of the many different rule of law aid programmes in Latin America fit somewhere into this overall 'menu'. Looking closely at the many activities in the region it is possible to identify four main clusters of rule of law assistance, with each centred round a different underlying motivation. These four clusters are rule of law work carried out to advance democratisation, economic development, human rights and social justice and international law enforcement. Two of these four clusters, rule of law programmes for democratisation and human rights/social justice, evolved from the above-described initiatives of the 1980s. The two others, relating to economic development and international law enforcement, arose principally in the 1990s.

A significant amount of rule of law aid in Latin America is carried out under the rubric of strengthening or consolidating democracy. The United States and other external actors (including Canada, the Nordic countries, the United Nations and even the Inter-American Development Bank, which unlike the World Bank bases its rule of law work on a political as well as an economic rationale) have expanded the initial operating assumption of the US administration of justice programme — that democracy requires an independent, effective judiciary — to the much broader notion that the rule of law generally is critical to democracy.

Figure 1.1: The Rule of Law Assistance Domain

Solid line = primary focus dotted line = secondary focus

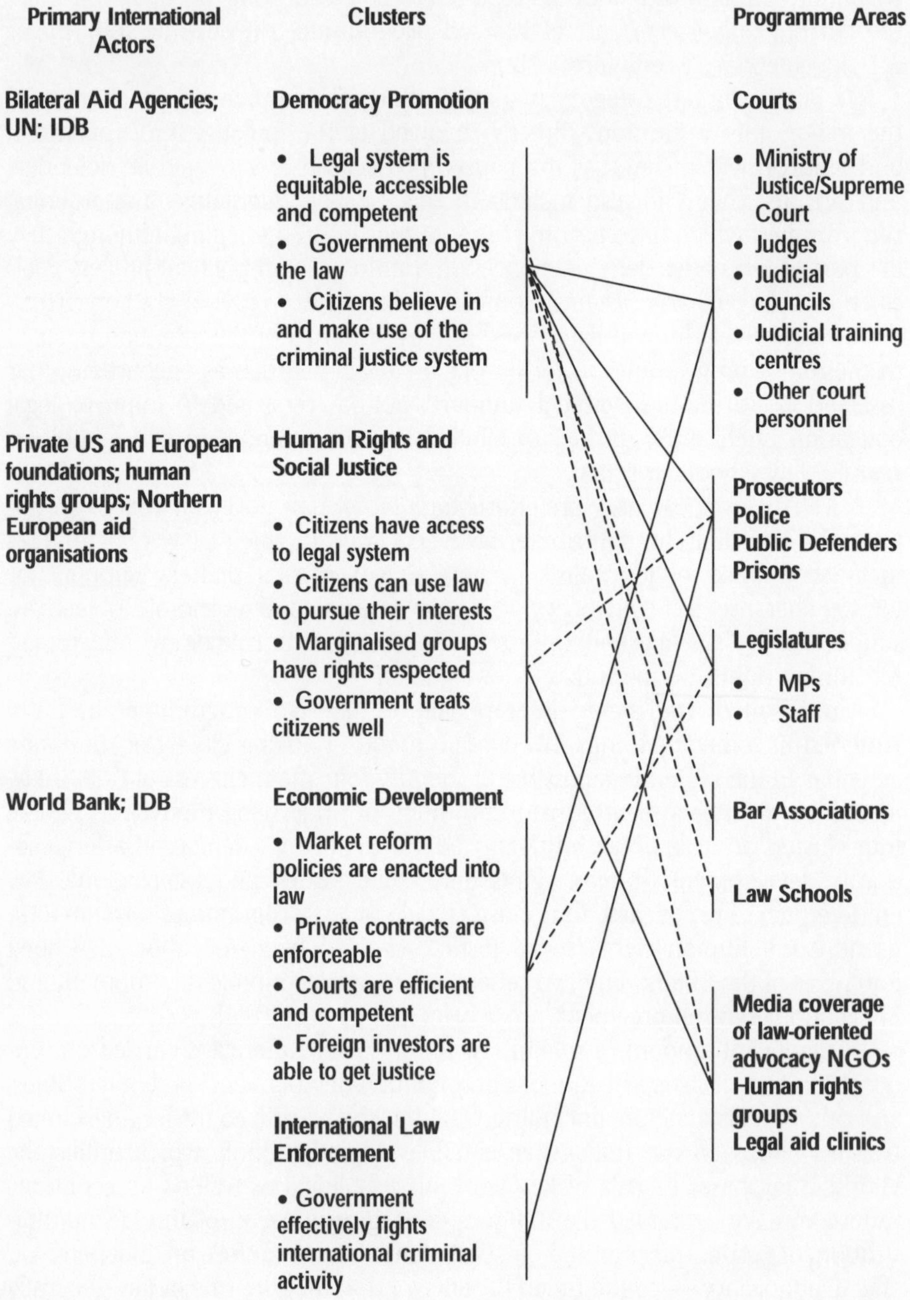

Primary International Actors	Clusters	Programme Areas

Bilateral Aid Agencies; UN; IDB

Democracy Promotion

- Legal system is equitable, accessible and competent
- Government obeys the law
- Citizens believe in and make use of the criminal justice system

Courts

- Ministry of Justice/Supreme Court
- Judges
- Judicial councils
- Judicial training centres
- Other court personnel

Private US and European foundations; human rights groups; Northern European aid organisations

Human Rights and Social Justice

- Citizens have access to legal system
- Citizens can use law to pursue their interests
- Marginalised groups have rights respected
- Government treats citizens well

**Prosecutors
Police
Public Defenders
Prisons**

Legislatures

- MPs
- Staff

World Bank; IDB

Economic Development

- Market reform policies are enacted into law
- Private contracts are enforceable
- Courts are efficient and competent
- Foreign investors are able to get justice

Bar Associations

Law Schools

International Law Enforcement

- Government effectively fights international criminal activity

**Media coverage of law-oriented advocacy NGOs
Human rights groups
Legal aid clinics**

This view takes it as axiomatic that the rule of law is necessary to ensure respect for constitutional order, the separation of powers, individual liberties and other cornerstones of democratic political systems in Latin America. Rule of law programmes rooted in pro-democracy objectives draw from all different parts of the overall activities menu but they have tended to emphasise the strengthening of core state institutions, especially those involved in criminal justice. They have given minor attention to bar associations and legal education. They have gradually begun to reach the non-governmental side, particularly in countries such as Peru where the possibility of making progress with the state institutions was particularly unpromising during the 1990s.

The alarming surge in crime in the region during the 1990s gave new urgency to criminal justice reform and external efforts to support such measures. USAID, as mentioned above, had begun work with criminal justice systems in the 1980s in many countries. Yet this work was not so much driven by the objective of reducing ordinary crime as by that of improving the treatment of citizens at the hands of the system. In response to the crime surge of the 1990s, rule of law assistance aimed at the criminal law system has increased in quantity and begun focusing explicitly on the goal of crime reduction. Such work fits naturally under a broader pro-democracy rationale given that citizens of many Latin American countries cite rising crime as one of the major negative aspects of life under democratic rule.

A second major cluster of rule of law work revolves around economic development objectives. Here the multilateral banks, especially the World Bank, are the dominant external actors, although some bilateral aid agencies link their rule of law work to economic goals as well. Interest in promoting the rule of law as a tool of economic development evolved in two phases. As the multilateral development banks began to push for structural adjustment policies and other market-related reforms in the region in the second half of the 1980s and the early 1990s they discovered that law reform — such as the writing or rewriting of banking laws, bankruptcy laws, tax codes and antitrust laws — was a necessary element of their agenda. Accordingly they began to give greater attention to law in their projects and to consider more systematically the role of law in development.

A broader phase of interest in rule of law aid as a form of economic development assistance unfolded in the 1990s. As market reforms in the region moved beyond the initial relatively rapid stage of macro-policy reforms to the slower process of institutionalising reforms it became evident that merely rewriting key economic laws was of little use if the legal system was incapable of actually implementing and enforcing them. The World Bank and the IDB began to work on judicial reform in Venezuela, Bolivia, Peru, El Salvador and elsewhere, hoping to improve the efficiency and competence of courts. Their growing involvement in judicial reform connected to their broader emerging interest in governance. By the mid-1990s the multilateral development banks had publicly embraced the view that promoting transparency, accountability and anti-corruption in the public sectors of developing countries was essential to deepening the market reform process. Strengthening judicial systems and the rule of law overall fits naturally within this ambit.[5]

The assumption or rationale connecting rule of law to economic develop-ment is generally rather loose and broad: multilateral development bank representatives assert sweepingly that a well-functioning rule of law is critical to economic success. Although it is clear that most economically successful countries do have a more effective rule of law, the actual relationship between the development of the rule of law and the development of a successful economy is much less certain and has become the subject of much new research.[6] The World Bank tends to emphasise the importance of foreign investors receiving reasonable treatment by the legal systems of the countries where they invest and private domestic actors enjoying sanctity of contracts and other basic elements necessary for regularity and predictability in business life. In corresponding fashion, its rule of law programmes focus on the updating of commercial laws and improving the efficiency of the courts, with emphasis on the commercial work of the courts. They do sometimes reach other elements of the overall menu, such as legislatures and legal education, but usually as complements to their main priorities.

The third cluster of rule of law work relates to human rights and social jus-tice. It is an evolution and expansion of the human rights work of the 1980s. As democratisation took hold in the region, the agenda of domestic and inter-national human rights groups shifted from primary attention to gross abuses of political and civil rights to a more multifaceted agenda. This includes women's rights, indigenous peoples' rights, anti-poverty and other socio-economic issues relating to inequality and marginalisation. Within this agenda, law is seen as a tool for advocacy by or on behalf of disadvantaged groups. Efforts to promote legal access, legal aid and legal advocacy skills among the relevant groups are therefore paramount. For external actors sponsoring aid of this type, this usu-ally means directing assistance at NGO advocacy groups or other non-governmental organisations.

Private Western foundations, notably the Ford Foundation, as well as nu-merous Nordic aid organisations, are leading actors in this domain. Such work often goes under the expanding rubric of 'civil society development' rather than rule of law work per se, with the category of civil society aid rivalling rule of law aid both for its fashionableness and capaciousness. Although growing out of the progressive side of the international aid community, the idea of

[5] See World Bank (1995); Edmundo Jarquín and Fernando Carrillo (eds.) (1998).
[6] Richard E. Messick (1999) pp. 117–36.

supporting legal advocacy by grassroots groups is being mainstreamed by the aid community as a whole. Under both civil society and rule of law rubrics, for example, USAID now assists NGO groups in various Latin America countries working for women's rights, indigenous peoples' rights, wider legal access and other core elements of what the progressive side of the aid community has long thought of as its own special domain.

The fourth cluster of rule of law aid arises from international law enforcement concerns. In the past ten years international drug trafficking, money laundering and other types of transnational crime have become matters of serious concern in many Latin American countries. Among the tools that the United States and other external actors employ to help combat these problems are rule of law aid programmes. Their hope is that training prosecutors and police, and in some cases judges, will give Latin American governments better means of fighting dug-trafficking and related ills. The aid programmes based on international law enforcement goals reach many of the same institutions as those carried out under the democracy or economic development rationales but usually with a somewhat different focus. A police training programme sponsored by the US Drug Enforcement Administration, for example, is likely to seek to increase policy operational capability, where police training as part of a democracy project will emphasise human rights standards, community policing methods, or similar topics. In parallel fashion, a training programme for prosecutors that is part of an international crime reduction effort may teach prosecutors how to build cases in drug offences or how to meet international extradition standards, whereas prosecutorial training as part of a democracy promotion effort will focus on other things.

In short, by the end of the 1990s the rule of law agenda in Latin America had expanded in many directions to cover a wide range of issues. Although the four clusters identified above are somewhat separate from each other they can all (with the possible exception of the international criminal enforcement side) be seen as linked to the central task facing Latin American governments: successfully completing transitions to democracy and a market economy. Rule of law strengthening, it is hoped, will advance the two main elements of the dual transition challenge, deepening democracy and facilitating market reform processes. Aid providers also hope that it will ameliorate some of the main negative social conditions that are seen as side effects of the attempted transitions — the increased crime, social dislocation and marginalisation of disadvantaged groups. Rule of law strengthening is thus embraced as an elixir for transitions that have been attempted but not yet achieved.

The ubiquity of the rule of law as a topic in current policy debates relating to Latin America is not due only to its close relationship to the transition agenda. The rule of law appeals broadly across political and intellectual lines. The right, left and centre can all find what they want in the concept, or interpret it in a manner favourable to their interests. Scholars, civic activists, legal practitioners and government officials can all find reasons to embrace the concept and assign part of the task to themselves. Like the equally ubiquitous concept of civil society, it is a mellifluous ideal whose pan-ideological or post-ideological quality is unusually well suited to the post-cold war era.

Competing elements of the agenda

It is clear that the four clusters of rule of law aid in Latin America overlap substantially and draw from the same overall menu of assistance programmes. At the same time, the different clusters are not always mutually reinforcing, and in some cases compete or even actively clash. Assessing the areas of tension that exist among the different parts of the rule of law agenda requires analysing some of the relationships between the various clusters.

Consider first the relationship between rule of law aid carried out for democracy promotion purposes and rule of law aid that serves an economic development rationale. Such undertakings often reach the same institutions, particularly court systems but also legislatures, bar associations and law schools. Though they frequently work with the same institutions, they sometimes pursue different objectives within them. Judicial reform projects born out of a democracy motivation, for example, often focus significantly on increasing judicial independence to encourage the separation of powers and the deconcentration of political power. They do so by facilitating reforms of judicial selection methods and judicial career rules. In contrast, judicial reform projects developed from an economic development rationale pay primary attention to increasing judicial efficiency. They seek to help courts process cases with a higher degree of organisation and efficiency, through help on administrative methods, personnel training and, in some cases, infrastructural improvements from equipment donations to the building of more courts.

These are different relative emphases, not a sharp division between the two types of rule of law programmes. Democracy-oriented programmes do also often devote some effort to fostering greater efficiency while economically-oriented ones sometimes address the issue of judicial independence (although the World Bank, for example, often shies away from the issue, determined to avoid anything that might be construed as political). The programmes developed from the differing motivations of democracy and economic development can certainly be complementary with regard to rule of law reform. Yet they are not always fully compatible and points of tension arise in practice. To take just one small example, an emphasis on judicial efficiency (coming from an economically-oriented programme) can clash with an emphasis on judicial access (coming from a democracy-oriented programme) — increasing access to the courts may heighten delays in already backed-up courts.

It is not only in judicial reform where the economic and political perspec-

Who really benefits from loans? especially if they are short term & real change w/in governal systems is a long term process?

tives may lead to contending approaches. In attempting to strengthen legislatures, the economic development imperative may point to a need for greater technical competence and speed whereas the democracy promoters, though not oblivious to those issues, may stress the need for greater representativity. Again, the different goals are not always mutually reinforcing: greater representativity achieved by opening up a legislature to diverse interest groups may impede efficiency and even technical rigour in the drafting of laws.

Another area of difference between rule of law efforts in the democracy and economic development domains concerns the substantive legal focus. Economically-oriented programmes usually emphasise commercial laws and the commercial side of courts' work. Democracy-oriented programmes tend to concentrate on the criminal justice side. Reasonably persuasive arguments can be made that improving the commercial side can have beneficial political effects and that strengthening the criminal justice side will have positive economic effects, but economic developmentalists and democracy promoters are nonetheless drawn to the different sides. Improving the rule of law across different substantive domains can be complementary endeavours, but interests do sometimes diverge. Economic developmentalists intent on improving the functioning of a legal system for economic elites sometimes push for measures — such as special access courts for high-stakes business litigation or narrowly targeted alternative dispute resolution mechanisms -that can mean resources being shifted from justice for the many (a democratic imperative) to special justice for a few.

The relationship between rule of law programmes rooted in democracy concerns and those deriving from a focus on human rights and social justice should in principle be strongly complementary. Greater respect for basic rights, a stronger civil society and improved treatment of marginalised groups are all pro-democratic elements. On the whole, democracy-based programmes have taken a top-down approach, aiding major state institutions, while those from the human rights and social justice arena work naturally with the non-governmental sector. There is some tendency toward synthesis. Democracy promoters have increasingly attempted to incorporate bottom-up components to their rule of law programmes, such as supporting NGOs that seek to generate public pressure for judicial reform. Programmes designed to bolster human rights and social justice are starting to engage governments as well as NGOs.

Despite the concordance in principle between democracy on the one hand and human rights on the other, divergences do arise. Some human rights and social justice activists argue that democracy promoters, by working directly with the state institutions, lose their ability to be hard critics of flawed institutions. In police reform, for example, they warn that once an external actor becomes a cooperative provider of aid to a troubled police department, that actor ends up downplaying the police's problems. More broadly, proponents of bottom-up approaches to rule-of-law assistance express the concern that purely top-down approaches can put external aid providers in the position of legitimising governments that claim to want reform but are really not interested in it. Sceptical that impulses for deep-reaching reform are likely to come from governments as opposed to citizens, human rights and social justice activists are wary of formalistic democracy aid ending up as a mere palliative.

There also exist basic philosophical differences about the nature of justice between some democracy promoters on the one hand and human rights and social justice activists on the other. Reduced to essentials, the difference is between an emphasis on process versus result or form versus substance. Individuals operating from a social justice perspective tend to believe that justice is achieved in a society when certain substantive conditions are met, such as a particular level of economic equality. Those operating from a democracy perspective, by contrast, tend to view justice in terms of fair legal process for all citizens. This difference can manifest itself in subtle but real ways in aid programmes. A democracy-based programme and a social justice-based programme might end up supporting the same NGO advocacy group. The democracy programme would do so in the general belief that citizens' advocacy is in principle good for democratisation while the social justice programme would do so because it agreed with the specific objectives of the group.

The most obvious and open conflicts within the different clusters making up the assistance efforts aimed at furthering international law enforcement goals and those based on either democracy or human rights concerns. A frequent area of dispute, at least in the US policy domain, is aid to police or other public security forces. Various US government agencies work directly with the Colombian and Peruvian security forces, for example, to strengthen their core operational capabilities and increase their ability to fight drug trafficking. These activities provoke sharp disagreement from US human rights groups and at least some queasiness among US democracy promoters. Although the most frequent conflicts arise over police work, similar divisions also sometimes occur with respect to judicial aid. In Colombia in the early 1990s the US Justice Department and USAID helped support the establishment of special judicial bodies, known as 'faceless judges', to help Colombia's beleaguered judiciary prosecute high-profile drug traffickers as well as leftist rebels with less fear of retaliation. This effort was criticised by US and other human rights groups on the grounds that anonymous judicial proceedings invited the abuse of due process rights.

Though the most visible, these conflicts over aid to police, prosecutors and judges are not the only conflicts between rule of law activities based on law enforcement goals and those carried out by democracy promoters or human rights activists. US law enforcement agencies have been urging some Latin American and Caribbean governments to modify their criminal justice laws to lock away drug offenders for long periods and criminalise every part of the drug trafficking process. This provokes a negative response from some judicial reform and criminal justice experts. They worry that such changes will be counterproductive both by overburdening courts with relatively minor drug cases (as has happened in the United States) and turning small-time participants in the drug trade into hardened criminals by putting them into bad prisons where they are shaped for life.

In addition to these various divergences among the different clusters of rule of law programmes there are two more general sources of tension that cut across the whole domain. One is the tendency of different aid providers to try to import their own models and for those models to conflict with one another. Aid officials habitually insist that they do not try to impose their models on recipient countries, but in fact they often do, especially in the rule of law field where formalistic approaches are ever present. The civil law–common law divide is wide on some points and becomes a line of division, especially when the US aid providers push for favoured aspects of the American system, such as oral proceedings.

Two typical examples of conflicting models arose in Guatemala in recent years. When Guatemala set out after the 1996 peace accords to reform its police force, both the Spanish and US governments strove to be the main international partner for that effort. Spain won out, with US officials complaining bitterly among themselves that the Spanish 'Guardia Civil' model was inappropriate for Guatemala. The US police trainers carved out a small role as advisers to a special investigative unit in the Guatemalan police within the broader, Spanish-designed project of reorganisation. In other words, they carved out space for their own model within the larger framework of the Spanish model. The second example concerned the prosecutors' office. For several years USAID sponsored a project to help the prosecutors' office carry out an internal reorganisation following a US-proposed model based on the precept of replacing a highly hierarchical structure with a relatively horizontal one. After several years of work in this vein the United Nations offered the prosecutors a new aid programme. UN consultants from South America advised the prosecutors to adopt a more hierarchical structure, to replace the horizontal one that they had just instituted.

A second cross-cutting tension concerns the question of whose interests the aid programmes serve. Donors project the idea that their programmes are designed with the interests of the recipient countries foremost in mind. Yet in some cases questions arise in the recipient countries as to whether aid programmes are not in fact mainly serving the interests of the aid-providing countries. The most obvious area within the rule of law domain where this issue surfaces is with aid relating to international law enforcement objectives. There is considerable doubt in many Latin American circles about whether

US aid efforts to help Latin American governments fight the drug trade are genuinely in the interest of Latin American societies as opposed to the United States. But the issue comes up in other areas of rule of law work. The efforts of the World Bank and other aid organisations to reform legal systems are viewed by some Latin Americans as efforts to smooth the way for North American and West European trade and investment in the region, which some critics view as more advantageous to those on the giving rather than the receiving end of the relationship.

Conclusion

The rule of law agenda in Latin America encompasses multiple component agendas. Within the growing world of international aid to support rule of law reform, at least four major agendas are at work — promoting democracy, supporting economic development, furthering human rights and social justice and combating international crime, particularly drug trafficking. In addition, each of the component agendas is viewed differently from the donor and recipient perspectives. The various agendas overlap substantially but also have important areas of divergence and they sometimes clash. The multiplicity of the rule of law agenda should not be seen as a problem in and of itself, an irregularity resulting from bad planning, poor communication or bureaucratic competition. It is an inevitable result of the fact that the rule of law agenda is a broad concept, with ties to many parts of the task of transition in which most Latin American countries are engaged. As such, the existence of multiple rule of law agendas will continue to be a feature of the Latin American policy domain and of international aid to the region for the foreseeable future.

CHAPTER 2

From Law and Development to Rule of Law: New and Old Issues in Justice Reform in Latin America

Luis Salas

> These newly developing nations need our help — not only our money and ma-
> chines and food, but also the great capital of knowledge accumulated by our
> professions... In the next decade there will be foreign law schools by the dozens
> that will need teachers of constitutional law. Governments of the newly
> emerged nations will need legislative counsel and legal advisors without num-
> ber. American lawyers by training and tradition should be equipped for this
> public service. Refrigerators and radios can be easily exported — but not the
> democratic system. Ideas of liberty and freedom travel fast and far and are
> contagious. Yet their adaptation to particular societies requires trained people,
> disciplined people, dedicated people. It requires lawyers.[1]

Thirty-seven years after Justice William O. Douglas made this statement, and
following almost two decades after the demise of the law and development
movement, there has been a significant[2] resurgence of the concept of foreign-
sponsored legal assistance programmes in Third World countries.[3] Several
factors have contributed to the reemergence of the newly titled 'Rule of Law'
(ROL) movement: the collapse of the former Soviet Union and the emergence
of numerous new democracies; almost universal adoption of the free market
economic model and its linkage to democratisation; the rise of multinational
enterprises and globalisation; and the development of human rights movements throughout the world.[4] At the core of this new law reform movement is
a belief in the inevitability of global economic integration and the evolution of
legal systems to meet the challenges of the new neo-liberal market economies.

Originally, law reform was solely a US enterprise, beginning with law and
development and administration of justice. Today, governments, international
organisations, private foundations, law firms and non-governmental organisa-

---

[1] Justice William O. Douglas (1962) pp. 909–13, 909, 913.

[2] Since 1994 the World Bank, the Inter-American Development Bank and the Asian
Development Bank have approved or initiated more than $500 million in loans for judicial
reform projects in 26 countries while USAID has spent close to $200 million in the past decade.
Richard E. Messick (1999) pp. 117–36. The Lawyers Committee for Human Rights reports that
as of July 1999, the World Bank and the IDB '... had approved or had under consideration 30
judicial or legal reform projects in 17 countries in Latin America and the Caribbean. At that
time, loan amounts approved by both banks for the region amounted to more than $302
million.' Lawyers Committee for Human Rights (2000) p. 2.

[3] David M. Trubeck, Yves Dezalay, Ruth Buchanan and John R. Davis (1994) pp. 407–98;
Jacques deLisle (1999) pp. 179–308.

[4] For one of the best reviews in this area see: Julie Mertus (1999) pp. 1335–389.

tions are involved in a law reform effort that dwarfs the prior initiatives. Many of these programmes present the loftiest of goals but few, if any, take into account the lessons of the past.[5]

I. The Law and Development Movement

In the 1960s, US academics at leading law schools (Harvard, Wisconsin, Stanford and Yale) provided the ideological basis, and much of the manpower, of what became known as the law and development movement.[6] The underpinnings for the movement could be found in the post-World War II 'modernisation' theory put forward by US economists, political scientists and sociologists.[7] Development, under this model, was an inevitable consequence of a process of 'social differentiation that would ultimately produce economic, political and social institutions similar to those in the West. The outcome of this process would be the creation of a free market system, liberal democratic institutions and the rule of law.'[8]

US legal scholars took their law reform message to developing countries in the belief that adoption of a US-style legal system would cure many of these countries' ills. Both due to their own backgrounds as academics and their belief in the centrality of the legal profession to the reform effort, many of the law and development projects focused on the improvement of legal education by the incorporation of interdisciplinary courses and adoption of the US casebook method of law teaching.[9] Projects were also designed to encourage the creation of legal services for the poor.[10]

Law and development projects were part of a broader US foreign policy democratisation agenda that included legislative reform, improvement of public administration and public safety. The most controversial democratic

---

[5] For criticism of the current wave of projects, especially the World Bank, see: Patrick McAuslan (1997) pp. 25–44. See also Joseph Tome's 'Comment' to the foregoing article on pp. 45–50.

[6] Much has been written about the movement. Among the most important works are: Sammy Adelman and Abdul Paliwala (eds.) (1993); C.J. Dias et al. (eds.) (1981); Elliot M. Burg (1977); Anthony Carty (ed.) (1992); James A. Gardner (1980); John H. Merryman (1977); Brian Z. Tamanaha (1995); David M. Trubek and Marc Galanter (1974); David M. Trubeck (1990) pp. 4–55.

[7] David E. Apter (1987).

[8] Brian Z. Tamanaha (1995) p. 471.

[9] See, for example: Keith Rosenn (1969); James A. Gardner (1980); Dennis O. Lynch (1981). Reform of legal education projects received support from the US government as well as private foundations. The Center for Study and Research in Legal Education (CEPED), for example, began in 1966 with the support of the US Agency for International Development (USAID) and sought to improve legal education in Brazil. Projects were developed in Costa Rica by USAID, and in Chile and Colombia by the Ford Foundation. The Staffing of African Institutions for Legal Education and research (SAILER) project was funded by the Ford Foundation, the Rockefeller Foundation and the Peace Corps and supported visits by US law graduates to African universities. See: James A. Gardner (1980); and David M. Trubek and Marc Galanter (1974).

[10] Committee on Legal Services to the Poor in the Developing Countries (1974).

assistance project involved upgrading the capacity of foreign police agencies to combat crime and curb potential revolutionary movements. The 'public safety programme', as it became known, was active in numerous Third World countries with the financial support of USAID and usage of US police consultants.

Law and development had a short life and by 1974 David Trubek and Marc Galanter were announcing its demise.[11] Critics focused on the naïvety of reformers who placed too much trust in the impact of the US legal system; underestimated the opposition from an entrenched legal culture; ignored the economic and political impact that reforms might have on the interests of elites and were ethnocentric in their approach. The ethnocentricity of the law and development proponents was represented by their assumption that foreign legal models would inevitably evolve into a similar model to that found in the United States. As a result, projects avoided comprehensive reform and focused on limited systemic changes — for example, legal education, on the assumption that adoption of US-based legal education techniques would inexorably contribute to the aspired legal reforms. They thus focused on formal rules while ignoring informal justice systems or the impact of non-legal actors in dispute resolution.

While these factors justified much of the disillusionment of US academics, they do not totally explain the rationale for the donors' abandonment of law reform as an integral part of development. Latin America, during the late 1960s and early 1970s was facing rising discontent, emerging revolutionary movements and harsh criticism of the USA from the left. Thus, it is not surprising that the law and development projects, often based in universities and staffed by US academics who openly advocated adoption of US legal models, would come under attack. Even in countries as moderate as Costa Rica the law reform project was criticised and ultimately expelled from the University of Costa Rica Law School by a vote of the faculty. Legislative reformers were also attacked for interfering in national political issues. Meanwhile, the democratisation initiatives also came under attack by the press and the US Congress following revelations of human rights abuses directly arising from the public safety programme.

At the same time as the end of law and development, many of the predictions of modernisation advocates failed to materialise as countries turned to military regimes, with the stagnation or collapse of economies and a further expansion of the gap between rich and poor. The early 1970s saw the demise of modernisation theory and the political development it had promised.

Tamanaha summarised the results of the failure of modernisation theory and the collapse of the law and development movement as follows:

The demise of the modernization paradigm was followed by an embrace of its

---

[11] David M. Trubek and Marc Galanter (1974).

ideological opposite. Stated in the broadest terms, this led to (1) blaming all the ills of developing countries on the imperialism of the West; (2) touting socialism over liberalism; and (3) arguing that the cultures of developing countries had to be protected against the encroachment of Western values, especially by preserving local customs or ways of life from the expanding reach of state law. Among many scholars who focused on law and developing countries, this resulted in a 'state law bad,' 'folk law good' attitude.[12]

With the passage of time, the outcomes of the law and development movement have been reconsidered. The goal of devising systems of law whose aim was primarily protection of the individual against abuses by the State was laudable, even if the strategies used were flawed. The law and development movement's greatest contribution may well be in the lessons learned from the experience. Whether or not a learning process really occurred is a major challenge facing the current 'rule of law' reformers.

II. Administration of Justice[13]

Following the demise of the law and development model, foreign donors (and primarily the Unites States Agency for International Development, USAID) abandoned justice reform as a tool of development. Agency leaders and field personnel were left with a sour taste in their mouths and rejected anything that harked back to the law and development and public safety programmes. Little did they know that justice reform would become a centrepiece of US democratisation policy,[14] especially in Central America, by the mid-1980s.

The new justice reform initiative began in response to Congressional criticism of human rights abuses in El Salvador during the 1980s. State Department officials argued that the impunity that characterised the Salvadorean justice system was largely attributable to defects inherent in the legal system and could be remedied by its modernisation. In 1984, USAID funded the 'El Salvador Judicial Reform Project'.[15] This project marked the first time since law and development that the United States provided foreign assistance to a law reform and police project and faced a great deal of internal opposition from within USAID, which saw itself being dragged into the justice reform field in one of the most controversial countries in the region.

Pursuant to recommendations of the Kissinger Commission on Central America,[16] and on the heels of the El Salvador programme, Congress funded a

---

[12] Brian Z. Tamanaha (1985) p. 481.

[13] For one of the best treatments of this period see: José E. Alvarez (1991).

[14] For a review of US democratisation policy see: Thomas Carothers (1991).

[15] Lawyers Committee for Human Rights (1989). Originally the project included: establishment of the Revisory Commission for Salvadorean Legislation (CORELESAL); establishment of a Judicial Protection Unit (JPU) to protect judges, witnesses and jurors in human rights cases; and creation of a Special Investigations Unit (SIU) to investigate important cases.

[16] National Bipartisan Commission on Central America (1984).

Central American justice reform initiative, which later became known as the administration of justice programme.[17] The original programme included Central American countries, with the exception of Nicaragua and the Dominican Republic. Later awards expanded the scope of the project to include Guatemala and to incorporate six South American countries (Venezuela, Colombia, Ecuador, Bolivia, Peru and Uruguay). A similar regional justice improvement effort was also funded to assist countries in the English-speaking Caribbean with a grant to the University of the West Indies.

By 1987, AID Missions began to develop their own bilateral projects. The most comprehensive and complex of these was the $16 million 'Strengthening Democratic Institutions' five-year project implemented by Georgetown University in Honduras. This was the first, and last, project to attempt to include a variety of diverse public sectors under one umbrella project.[18] Other bilateral projects, targeting the justice system, were also implemented in Argentina, Bolivia, Chile, Colombia, Dominican Republic, Ecuador, El Salvador, Guatemala, Haiti, Panama, Paraguay, Peru, Uruguay and Venezuela.

There were significant differences between the law and development programme and the administration of justice initiatives. First, law schools were not the primary implementers of the programmes.[19] Instead, grants were awarded to Washington-based consulting agencies.[20] Second, primary reliance was placed on the usage of non-US experts with Latin Americans eventually becoming the most prominent group of advisors. Third, projects stayed away from legal education and no assistance was provided to Latin American law schools. Fourth, law drafting, with minor exceptions,[21] was avoided. Fifth, the United States government was alone in its reform strategy,[22] with foundations and other foreign governments funding competing projects. Sixth, the US saw government agencies as the primary local partner in these projects and involvement of non-governmental organisations was severely limited. Seventh, public legal assistance was almost ignored by the early projects. Finally, US planners viewed reform of the justice sector as a systemic enterprise in which

---

[17] José E. Alvarez (1990). For a review of US democratisation policy during this period see: Thomas Carothers (1991).

[18] The project included assistance in the electoral, legislative and judicial sectors.

[19] The major exception was the USAID-funded Harvard law school project that began in 1987 and ended in 1990 (Guatemala/Harvard Criminal Justice Project). Harvard abandoned the project in 1990 because of the Guatemalan Government's failure to prevent widespread abuse of human rights. Statement of Philip B. Heymann (1990) pp. 59–60.

[20] Checci and Co. Consulting was the primary recipient of early grants through an 'unlimited quantity contract' for administration of justice. Chemonics International and the National Center succeeded Checchi for State Courts as primary project implementers.

[21] The major exception was the CORELESAL project in El Salvador, which had the vague charge of reviewing all Salvadorean legislation.

[22] Unlike the law and development programme which involved important partnerships with private foundations such as Rockefeller and Ford.

all of the actors in the system had to be included in the reform. Law reform, by itself, for example, was seen as a useless effort without a complementary reform of the institutions that implemented it.

Critics of the effort focused on the 'meagre' demonstrable results of these projects, especially given the large amount of funds expended.[23] They paid special attention to the human rights record of these countries and were especially disparaging of the police assistance furnished by the International Criminal Investigative Training Programme (ICITAP). Subsequent analyses of country-specific projects also questioned results, with El Salvador being the focus of much of the criticism. Human rights issues were of primary concern as well as questions about the legitimacy that a justice assistance project awarded to judicial systems that were seriously under question.[24]

Perhaps AOJ reformers most underestimated the number of political barriers that would be encountered, reinforcing the view that these reformers, like their law and development counterparts, were naïve. A clear example was the attempt to depoliticise judiciaries by establishing merit-based judicial selection processes. This was rightly viewed as a primary obstacle to the achievement of judicial independence and many of the projects sought to draft laws and regulations to create unbiased policies for the selection, promotion and removal of judicial personnel. In Honduras, for example, this was identified as a primary goal of each of several bilateral projects over more than a decade. Local justice officials gave lip service to the goal, requested resources for evaluation of personnel policies, engaged in numerous personnel studies and received substantial training and technical assistance to achieve the goal. Twelve years after the assistance began it is still far from being realised.

III. Rule of Law

The collapse of Communism in Europe, the economic reforms taking place in China and other Asian economies, along with the globalisation of economic markets, have spurred the renewal of the law reform movement, now under the title of Rule of Law.[25] Even some of the most ardent critics of law and development jumped on the bandwagon of the new law reform initiative, concluding that these countries no longer have any alternatives to the adoption of a democratic neo-liberal market model.[26]

---

[23] In a meeting sponsored by the Washington Office on Latin America the participants severely criticised the El Salvador, Colombia and Guatemala projects, claiming that there was no demonstrable improvement in the systems of these countries. Washington Office on Latin America (1990).

[24] Lawyers Committee for Human Rights (1989).

[25] Thomas Carothers (1998); John V. Orth (1998) pp. 71–82.

[26] David M. Trubeck (1996), cited by Carol V. Rose (1998) p. 124.

Governance

Much like law and development, the new law reform effort is not an isolated initiative and cannot be understood without relating it to international efforts to improve 'governance' and eventually to achieve democracy, all within the context of free market economies. Under this strategy, the emphasis of international agencies has shifted from simply improvement of governments to the much broader concept of governance. While the shift in terms may appear subtle, it is significant and affects how law reform is conceptualised.[27]

The prior emphasis on improvement of the public sector focused on the efficiency of government institutions. Under the broader concept, governance includes public and private actors who manage a country's overall affairs at all levels. 'It comprises the mechanisms, processes and institutions through which citizens and groups articulate their interests, exercise their legal rights, meet their obligations and mediate their differences'.[28]

While there are subtle differences between all definitions of governance, all of them emphasise the participatory nature of the term and the necessity of public and private sector adherence to the rule of law. They all share a rejection of the rule of law as simply an adherence to established laws and refer to the term within the broader concept of democracy, differentiating between rule of law and rule by law.[29] Rather than focusing on the powers that law awards to government's ability to regulate conduct, '… It establishes principles that constrain the power of government and oblige it to conduct itself according to a series of prescribed and publicly known rules … Adherence to the rule of law entails far more than the mechanical application of static technicalities: it involves an evolutionary search for those institutions and processes that will best facilitate authentic stability through justice'.[30]

Critics of the governance model point out that governance is very similar to the concept of democratisation since they both presuppose that the liberal economic model is a necessary component of democratisation.[31] This new economic model rests on notions of privatisation of government assets, shrinking of the state, drastic reduction of the public budget and integration of the national economy into international capitalism.[32] Since a primary objective of financial institutions is stabilisation, democratisation and governance require a peaceful transition from authoritarian rule, which can only be achieved by compromise with ruling classes and those responsible for the prior oppres-

---

[27] For a fuller explanation of this concept, from a donor's point of view see US Agency for International Development, 'Democracy', http://www.info.usaid.gov/democracy/.
[28] United Nations Development Programme (1995).
[29] Neil J. Kritz (1996).
[30] *Ibid.* p. 588.
[31] Ellen Meiksins Wood (1995).
[32] Robert Fatton, Jr. (1999).

sion.[33] The need to avoid conflict requires that authoritarian figures be protected and even included as key decision-makers in the transition. The legacy of authoritarianism 'contributes in making the "constitution of tyranny" an integral part of the new regime.'[34]

b) Rule of Law

One of the problems of the new rule of law movement is to find some agreement between users of the term as to its precise meaning. In its most basic form, the rule of law can be defined as a system in which democratically elected governments set forth a set of laws that are clear, publicly known and applicable to everyone. In the case of criminal law, for example, it encompasses the principles of the presumption of innocence, non-retroactoactivity of laws, the right to a fair and speedy trial before an impartial arbiter and the right to counsel. Safeguarding these rights is a set of institutions, especially the judiciary, that exercise independence in their decisions and act in an efficient and impartial manner in accordance with the dictates of national norms. Of these, perhaps the most important is that '... (t)he government is embedded in a comprehensive legal framework, its officials accept that the law will be applied to their own conduct, and the government seeks to be law abiding.'[35]

While there are some variations, there is fairly general agreement as to what variables should be examined to determine whether a particular country or a specific practice is in compliance with the rule of law.[36] One of the most comprehensive catalogue of these variables was issued by the Organisation for Security and Cooperation in Europe (OSCE).[37] They include: a representative democracy; governmental compliance with the requirements of the law; civilian control over the military and law enforcement; an independent judiciary; publication of all norms (in the case of legislation, after public debate); effective means of redress of grievances and review of administrative actions; protection of the freedom of lawyers to represent their clients; and a detailed set of procedural guarantees for criminal cases.[38]

There are significant differences between prior justice reform efforts and the current initiatives. Unlike the law and development and administration of justice (AOJ) movements, the new rule of law reform is not dominated by the United States. Instead foreign donors (Canada, Spain, Germany, Japan,

---

[33] For some of the best works on the 'third wave', see: Charles E. Lindblom (1990); Samuel Huntington (1991).

[34] Robert Fatton, Jr. (1999) p. 211.

[35] Thomas Carothers (1998) p. 96.

[36] Robert Fatton, Jr. (1999).

[37] The organisation was formerly the Conference on Security and Cooperation in Europe.

[38] Conference on Security and Cooperation in Europe (1990); also Neil J. Kritz (1996) p. 590, Julie Mertus (1999) p. 1357.

Sweden) and international organisations (European Union, World Bank,[39] Inter-American Development Bank,[40] UNDP[41]) are taking the lead in many reform initiatives. A major actor in the rule of law movement, almost totally absent from the AOJ and law and development periods, is the multinational law firm that is playing a significant role in law reform worldwide.

While there have been significant efforts to downplay ethnocentricity, it is almost inevitable that it creeps in as the bulk of implementing agencies and technical assistance consultants have their roots in Western legal thought, especially the USA. Naïvety is also a feature common to all of these movements. Rather than simply technical factors, the main obstacle to achievement of the rule of law, as with political democracy, is the lack of political will of local leaders to subject themselves to the scrutiny of an independent court system.

IV. Implementation Strategies and Programmes

When the United States was the only international donor involved in law reform, the identification of strategies and law reform programme objectives were clearer. The large number of international agencies now involved in justice reform projects makes such a clear definition almost impossible. This section will outline some of the major law reform strategies and the problems inherent in each. They can be grouped into three types: normative; institutional development; and comprehensive reform.[42]

---

[39] Although the World Bank had funded some discrete projects, its first major justice project was the $60 million 'Venezuela Judicial Infrastructure Project' approved in 1992. The Bank was originally reluctant to enter into this field and the World Bank's General Counsel restricted its participation in Rule of Law initiatives to activities that could be justified as having a direct and demonstrable implication for economic development. Thus, the World Bank's earliest activities focused on improvement of court operations and strengthening legal frameworks that facilitated private investment and economic stability. For a review of the World Bank's evolution in this field see: Lawyers Committee for Human Rights and Programa Venezolano de Educación-Acción en Derechos Humanos (Provea) (1995).

[40] Counterpart regional banks, such as the Asian Development Bank, have similar, if not more aggressive, law reform programmes. The IDB began to fund justice reform projects in Latin America in 1994 and focuses on modernisation of laws; access to justice; alternative dispute resolution (ADR); administration; human resources and logistical support. It currently has projects in Argentina, Bolivia, Colombia, Costa Rica, Ecuador, El Salvador, Honduras, Paraguay and Peru.

[41] The Regional Justice Project of the Bureau for Latin America and the Caribbean constitutes UNDP's initiative in this area. The objectives of the project are to propose and implement coordination activities between UNDP and other international agencies; to foster the exchange of experiences at the national and international level; to support the design and implementation of regional and national justice policies; and to provide information in the areas of access to constitutional justice, legal security of investments, rehabilitation of juvenile offenders and access to justice for pretrial detainees. UNDP (1999). It has also begun to publish a journal that appears annually: UNDP, *Justicia y Sociedad.*

[42] Carothers speaks of three types of reform projects: law reform; strengthening of law-related institutions; and increasing government's compliance with law. Thomas Carothers (1998) pp. 101–2.

a) Normative change and law drafting

One of the most attractive reform endeavours for foreign donors has been law-drafting. The amount of foreign law that is currently being transplanted to 'emerging democracies' is overwhelming, often with little regard for the culture of the receiving country and its capacity to implement the reform —[43] regardless of the fact that critics of past efforts of legal transplantation have focused on the failure of reformers to take into account the culture of the receiving country.[44] While many US academics may have concluded that the finalisation of the law and development movement also signalled an end to legal transplants, they were wrong to start with and have become even more so since.

The primary donor impetus for Latin American code reform was provided by USAID.[45] The priority of US-funded code reform efforts in Latin America has been modernisation of the codes of criminal procedure due to the negative impact that these antiquated codes had on human rights and a growing popular demand to combat rising crime rates. Other donors have attempted to reform commercial codes but none has yet involved itself in modernisation of civil procedure.

Reform of criminal procedure is now the rule rather than the exception in Latin America, with many countries shifting from an inquisitorial to an accusatorial model similar to those found in common law countries. Among the lessons learned thus far are that: 1) law reform must take into account local conditions, especially legal culture and prevailing vested interests; 2) wholesale reform of a country's normative framework is foolhardy;[46] 3) law reform must be part of a comprehensive justice reform strategy that relies on objective assessments; 4) implementation of the reform is as important as law reform, or more important; 5) law reform will never succeed in an environment in which

---

43 Robert Brown, for example, predicted that the large amount of foreign law being imported into Russia will renew the debate over the law and development programme, Robert Brown, Jr. (1995). Ann Seidman and Robert Seidman (1996) commented on the '(l)awyers and legal academics, mostly from the United States, jetted hither and yon on drafting missions, their briefcases like pigskin treasure chests bulging with draft bills'.

44 See: David M. Trubeck (1990); Maria Dakolias (1995). For a review of the argument over the transferability of law see: Philip M. Nichols (1997) p. 1245. Nichols summarises current thought on the transplantability of law as follows: 'Culture and law are closely intertwined; law can be transplanted, but there is a significant risk of rejection that is tremendously increased if the law does not comport with the culture of the recipient country'.

45 While the law and development movement devoted a great deal of effort to law reform, the administration of justice projects initially avoided it, fearing similar results of those of law and development. However, project planners failed to understand the emphasis of Latin Americans on law revision as the foundation of justice reform. By the late 1980s, criminal procedure and other law drafting reform became commonplace. For a review of USAID's law reform experience see: Linn Hammergren (1998a).

46 This was attempted in El Salvador, through CORELESAL, and failed.

poorly educated and compensated judges are selected for political reasons and in which there is limited judicial independence and corruption.

(b) Institutional development and limited or sector-specific reforms

All development projects usually target specific reforms rather than focus on comprehensive reform strategies that address sector-wide issues. While court administration, improvement of infrastructure and information systems all remain high on the reform agenda,[47] some new initiatives are being introduced while other areas of need remain largely ignored.

1) Public legal defence and access to justice

Although Rule of Law projects have provided substantial assistance to the improvement of courts and prosecutorial agencies, they have largely ignored initiatives to improve access to justice for the poor. Access to justice is a key theme in all development initiatives yet seldom does one find these lofty goals translated into actual project initiatives. In the few instances in which the problem of access, especially for the poor, has been addressed it has been in the form of assistance to legal services, especially the provision of a legal defence in criminal cases.

Even though USAID has targeted criminal justice reform as its main Rule of Law initiative in Latin America it has seldom focused on the right to counsel as a key project component. In those instances in which it has, it has encountered reluctance on the part of local officials to assume supervisory or financial responsibility for the establishment of such a service. In the extreme examples, El Salvador and the Dominican Republic, donors were compelled to even pay the salaries of public defenders for a period of time. Not unexpectedly, in both instances, the government failed to assume these costs once USAID assistance ended, although they eventually did so.

Recently, USAID has targeted public legal defence (in Nicaragua, for example) as a key component of justice reform projects, although these tend to be the exception rather than the rule. Other donors, on the other hand, have stayed almost totally out of this field. It is rare to find any projects or key components of major initiatives that support legal services for the poor or disadvantaged. Exceptions have been pilot projects to furnish legal services to women, small businesses and indigenous populations.

---

[47] Law enforcement assistance is the most controversial justice reform area. While governments (primarily the United States, Spain, Germany, Sweden and Taiwan) were leaders in this field, international lending agencies (primarily the IDB) have now become involved, as the question of preventing social violence has become more acute in the region.

2) Alternative dispute resolution

The introduction of alternative dispute resolution mechanisms (ADR) has become one of the most attractive Rule of Law Reform strategies for international donors '… because it offers alternatives to the delays and corruption that characterise the judicial system.'[48] Although the civil procedure codes of most Latin American countries have provided for arbitration and mediation, these have seldom been used.

While it is still too early to evaluate the success of these intervention strategies, the immediate results are mixed. In Costa Rica, a USAID programme introduced arbitration and mediation but after funding ended, the courts failed to assume operational costs while the juvenile agencies accepted its use for family law cases.[49] In El Salvador, mediation was introduced in the juvenile delinquency code but was heavily criticised because it permitted conciliation between the victim and the offender and applied to all types of cases, regardless of the severity of the offence. The result was that in some cases involving violent offenders or gang members associates of the offender would threaten the victim and compel conciliation. In Honduras, an IDB San Pedro Sula Chamber of Commerce arbitration programme received a great deal of notoriety but after several months had failed to receive many cases. In Argentina, on the other hand, mediation has become institutionalised and is being administered by the Executive to handle a large number of civil cases.

Among the reasons for the failure of ADR to work in some countries is the reluctance of the bar to refer cases for fear of losing their fees, which usually depend on the number of pleas filed or appearances made. Judiciaries have also been reluctant to adopt ADR for fear of losing control over the cases and/or merely repeat the process due to a reluctance on the part of one of the parties to accept the result or the non-binding nature of the arbitration.

In many countries, donors have failed to gauge the legal culture and the reasons why ADR had not been used in the past, even though it was permitted. In others, donors have concluded that ADR may be used in any legal field without considering the appropriateness of the reform to the particular country. In almost all countries, donors have overestimated the degree of local support for the reform and underestimated the level of potential opposition or apathy toward such practices.

ADR is a fairly new initiative for developed countries. Donors have made this reform central to many Rule of Law projects due to the appeal of bypassing the traditional court system. However, given the weakness of Latin American judiciaries and a complementary effort to unify court systems by

---

48 Maria Dakolias (1995) p. 200.
49 The Ministry of Justice is now establishing ADR centres but it is too early to tell how successful these will be.

incorporating Executive-run alternative courts,[50] ADR may have the effect of weakening judiciaries further and impeding the unification effort. The future of ADR is still to be determined, but further evaluation and review of experiments is needed before introducing these reforms on a broader scale.

c) Comprehensive reform issues

Development planners emphasise the need for preparation of reform policies within the context of an overall development plan for the sector based on assessments and evaluative data. Although all major international agencies favour such a planning process, it seldom takes place and specific reforms, sometimes grouped together without any linkages between component parts, are the rule rather than the exception.

In reviewing AID's administration of justice projects, the General Accounting Office criticised AID's over-reliance on specific technical reforms in lieu of addressing fundamental systemic flaws.[51] Surprisingly, USAID had funded comprehensive assessments of the judicial sector in all countries eligible for assistance in the mid-1980s with the goal of using them as tools for identification of reform areas, analysis of facilitating and inhibiting factors, determination of political will and overall planning guidance. Nevertheless, project designers routinely ignored them in their drive to fund easily manageable projects with little risk and measurable objectives. Although the World Bank and the Inter-American Development Bank have both stressed the need for in-depth assessments, these have seldom been carried out or have been limited to quick trips by consultants. Thus it is not surprising that World Bank and IDB project designers have also ignored the existence of prior assessments funded by other international agencies and have chosen to place their faith on their own quick and suspect reviews.

The project preparation process does not end with the identification of problems and determination of a strategy to solve them. It is crucial that local authorities become stakeholders in the process and agree on the nature of the problems and the solutions. This requires extensive discussion and vetting of strategies. This is especially difficult in the justice sector since, unlike other areas of the public sector, there is no-one entity that can speak for the entire system and the primary counterpart, the judiciary, is often the least experienced public institution in project management or planning.

Any assessment of the state of the justice system in Latin America will conclude that achievement of judicial independence is central to the Rule of Law. While all projects identify this goal as primary in their projects, there is little

---

[50] Latin American Executives have often tended to place politically sensitive legal areas (i.e. agrarian, labour, military, administrative, fiscal and others) outside the scope of the traditional court system by establishing exclusive jurisdiction in the Executive Branch.
[51] US General Accounting Office (1993)

consensus on how it is to be attained. Technical reforms can go a long way to making the legal system more efficient or accessible but until national elites see a benefit in supporting a strong and independent judiciary, foreign assistance projects will have little long-term impact. Hundreds of judges may be trained, for example, but the training will come to naught if, following a national election, the victorious party removes them and new judges are selected based on party affiliation.

Although the history of Latin American judiciaries is characterised by sub-servience to the Executive,[52] there are positive signs of change. In the Dominican Republic, for example, the public held the judiciary in low regard and blamed it for much of the weakness of democracy in that country. Follow-ing the 1996 national election, advocacy groups demanded that the new Supreme Court members be subjected to public review of their qualifications. As a result, hearings for their selection were televised before a wide audience and a public vote resulted in a Court with much popular support. USAID's support of some of the NGOs that participated in this process was instrumen-tal in the success of this initiative. In Guatemala, the Constitutional Court ruled that the attempt by President Serrano to consolidate power in the Executive by abolishing the judicial and legislative branches was unconstitutional. Although these are exceptions, they offer positive signs for the region. Whether international agencies are wise enough to identify these openings or to support these initiatives is to be seen. The payoff, however, is much greater than any technical reform.

Peru provides an unfortunate example of an instance in which donors overlooked clear signs of a lack of commitment to judicial independence in favour of approval of a large justice reform initiative. In 1992, President Fuji-mori staged an 'autocoup' resulting in the elimination of the Congress and a purging of the judiciary.[53] It was justified on the grounds that the judiciary and the legislature were corrupt and only radical change could overcome eco-nomic stagnation and terrorism.[54] The autocoup was followed by several efforts at judicial reform yet critics have pointed out that none of them in-volved depoliticisation of the judiciary.[55] The war against terrorism also

---

[52] See Keith Rosenn, (1987) pp. 1–36.

[53] For a review of the Peruvian justice system and efforts at its reform see: Linn Hammergren (1998).

[54] See: Steven Levitsky (1999); Maxwell A. Cameron (1997); and Cynthia McClintock (1996).

[55] One of the first involved the establishment of the Council of Judicial Coordination, with the goal of reforming the administration of justice, which Congress established under the leadership of a former naval officer. The appointment of a former military officer drew criticisms from the Supreme Court, concerned that the courts might be militarised and aware of the power of the Council to appoint or remove judges due to its close ties to the President. Charges were also levelled that the Executive stacked the Constitutional Tribunal in order to uphold legislation that permitted President Fujimori to run for a third term. Following the end of the hostage crisis

justified the maintenance of military tribunals, under the leadership of 'faceless judges', in which due process rights were seldom respected.[56]

International donors and lenders largely ignored the actions of the Peruvian government and continued to provide justice reform assistance. The United States, for example, donated over $8 million dollars during the period 1993-1998.[57] The World Bank, on the other hand, in 1996, announced a $22.5 million dollar justice reform loan '… to help finance an innovative and far reaching project to reform the Peruvian judicial system'.[58] This amount was added to $9 million from the Peruvian government and a $1.4 million dollar Technical Assistance Grant from the Inter-American Development Bank. In designing the project strategy, planners recognised 'political interference and political instability in the project environment' as one of five project risks.[59] The strategy sought to overcome the politicisation issue by: 1) supporting the National Judicial Council's (Consejo Nacional de la Magistratura) moves towards adoption of a merit-based system of judicial selection and removal;[60] 2) some project activities would be conditional on the establishment of judicial tenure; 3) training to further a culture of judicial independence; 4) support the development of a civil society constituency favouring judicial reform; 5) other project activities, for example, court administration, would indirectly contribute to eliminating political interference in the judiciary.

The rosy assumptions of the project designers[61] appear to have been flawed from the start. For example, in 1998 of the country's 1,531 judges, only 574 had permanent appointments, having been independently selected. The remaining 957, including 19 of the 33 judges of the Supreme Court, had provisional or temporary status only.[62] In order to strengthen its hold on the Judiciary, the government created two specialised chambers of the Supreme

---

in the Japanese Embassy, Congress dismissed the three Court members who had voted against presidential reelection.

[56] Maxwell A. Cameron (1998) analyses the autocoups and Fujimori's judicial policies.

[57] US General Accounting Office (1999).

[58] World Bank, Press Release, 'World Bank Helps Pioneer Judicial reform in Peru', News Release No. 98/1555/LAC, 7 December 1997.

[59] The others were: a) medium-term sustainability; b) a lack of inter-agency coordination; c) weak institutional project management experience; d) resistance to change from persons with vested interests in the current system. World Bank, Project Announcement, Project ID PEPA40107, November 15, 1996.

[60] Project designers claimed that the Council members 'enjoy widespread recognition in the legal community for their objectivity and transparency'.

[61] We need only quote the words of Izumi Ohno, World Bank Task Manager of the Judicial Reform Project, who said: 'There is a strong consensus in civil society in Peru on the importance of judicial reform and a corresponding interest and resolve to participate in its reform process. The project harnesses these positive forces and the firm commitment of the government of Peru'. World Bank (1997).

[62] United States Department of State (1999).

Court, staffed by provisional and temporary judges, to assume jurisdiction over some of the most sensitive cases.[63] Congress then enacted legislation transferring the power to select and remove judges and prosecutors from the Council to the Judiciary and the Public Ministry respectively. All seven members of the Judicial Council resigned in protest, and disbursement of the World Bank loan was suspended pending the restoration of the Council's authority.[64]

While the World Bank's decision to terminate this project is to be commended, the assumptions of political will and its assessment of the government's commitment to depoliticise the judicial system can only be characterised as naïve at best. At worst, it demonstrates ignorance of the most obvious political facts as regards funding a project.

Further instances of poor political judgement include a decision to award a multi-million dollar justice reform loan to the government of Carlos Andrés Pérez following an attempted military coup that invoked the politicisation of the judiciary as a primary justification.[65] The World Bank relied on the Judicial Council even though it had been criticised for its degree of politicisation and lack of action in curbing judicial corruption. What it will do in the light of the recent resignation of the President of the Supreme Court following the Court's acceptance of the Constituent Assembly's assumption of a primary role in 'purging' what they claimed to a corrupt judiciary still remains to be seen.[66]

V. Implementation issues and problems

While all project design documents support the loftiest of goals and set forth what appears to be a sound implementation strategy, it is in the implementation that the success or failure or a project is most often determined. This section analyses some of the most critical implementation issues faced by international agencies and national judiciaries.

---

[63] This chamber assumed control over tax, customs, and narcotics crimes previously under the jurisdiction of the tenured judges of the Lima superior court.

[64] The Executive Committee of the Judicial Academy also resigned in protest. Their replacements extended the period of training for new judges from six months to two years, a move seen by some as ensuring the continued reliance on temporary judges.

[65] The fact that the coup leader is now the President of Venezuela and is engaged in an overhaul of the Judiciary, through constitutional reform, is a curious coincidence.

[66] In the first half of 1999 the Constituent Assembly declared a 'judicial emergency' and assumed extraordinary powers to review the conduct of all of the country's judges. Several judges have already been dismissed. Following the Supreme Court's acceptance of these extraordinary powers, the Supreme Court President resigned declaring that the rule of law had ended in Venezuela. Tim Johnson, 'Venezuelan panel takes control from Congress', *Miami Herald*, 31 August 1999; 'La presidenta del Supremo venezolano dimite y da por enterrado el Estado de derecho', *El País*, 25 August 1999; Irma Alvarez (1999) (1999a).

a) Transparency, corruption and ethics

All donor agencies have made impressive statements about their commitment to combat corruption, especially in the implementation of their own programmes at the same time that they have recognised the need to improve transparency in their transactions and to develop accountability measures to gauge programme success and financial correctness. Corruption, however, is not limited to financial gains but rather extends to a broad range of conduct.[67] This section will deal with procurement practices, access to information and its impact on countries and civil society.

1) Project procurement

Rule of Law programmes are seldom, if ever, awarded to local NGOs and the bulk of projects are awarded to governments or to large institutional consultants whose long-term commitment to reform in this area is limited by the availability of funding. In the case of loans to countries, the implementing agencies are usually government or implementing units established by the lending institution. Local procurement rules are followed so long as overall lender regulations are also complied with. In instances of outright donations, with USAID being the primary actor, project implementation is usually the result of a procurement process. In either case, technical assistance, commodities and training support are usually components that are awarded to private firms through a complicated and often obscure procurement process that favours large multinational firms.

The initial stage of any project is the design stage in which a variety of critical technical and policy decisions are made. Donor agencies often contract technical experts to assist in this phase of project development and usually bar them from participating in future procurement bids in order to prevent the use of advantageous insider information and to avoid conflicts of interest. This, however, does not prevent the technical consultants from revealing insider information to potential future bidders or even from participating in future bids as individual consultants.

Once the programme is approved and funded, most agencies will publish notifications and invite potential bidders to participate, although in many instances closed bids are used and notifications are sent to a limited number of

---

[67] The World Bank has defined project-related fraud and corruption: (i) 'corrupt practice' means the offering, giving, receiving, or soliciting of any thing of value to influence the action of a public official in the procurement process or in contract execution; and (ii) 'fraudulent practice' means a misrepresentation of facts in order to influence a procurement process or the execution of a contract to the detriment of the Borrower, and includes collusive practices among bidders (prior to or after bid submission) designed to establish bid prices at artificial, non-competitive levels and to deprive the Borrower of the benefits of free and open competition', para 1.15 of World Bank (1999a).

firms. USAID is the only major international agency to post solicitations on the internet,[68] while the World Bank and IDB have bidders rely on poorly disseminated information, usually influenced by a firm's locus at the donor's home office, Washington. The World Bank, for example, places solicitations in a monthly United Nations publication ('Development Business') that monitors projects in the pipeline of the World Bank and publicises opportunities to bid as they arise.[69] The cost of the subscription varies from $445 to $695. IDB, on the other hand, relies on its own monthly publication ('IDB Projects') to inform of upcoming procurement and business opportunities.[70]

In addition to the difficulties in obtaining information on upcoming projects, potential bidders must meet demanding financial and project management requirements, which restrict bids to major international donors who have the financial capability and implementation experience to meet bidding requirements. In other instances, the donor agency restricts bidding to nationals or firms from the donor agency. For example, European Union contracts are usually awarded only to European firms or individuals while others establish de facto restrictions by placing language or other requirements that limit the field to nations from the donor country.

As can be seen above, most of these procurement processes are designed to favour large multinational contractors and often favour ease of contracting rather than technical expertise or merit. USAID, for example, has begun to rely more and more on issuing blanket Indefinite Quantity Contracts whereby one large firm bids on meeting future requests for services from the international donor for a specific period of time. This mechanism permits the local donor agency to bid contracts to a limited number of 'qualified' firms rather than sponsoring a costly and complicated open competition.

---

[68] As well as placing their applications online USAID allows potential bidders to subscribe to a periodic update service that notifies them by email of upcoming opportunities (USAID-CBD-L).
[69] Each month *Development Business* publishes the World Bank's Monthly Operational Summary (MOS), which is a summary of projects under consideration for financing by the World Bank as well as a description of recently approved Bank projects. It also includes a list of the categories of goods and services to be procured. *UN Development Business* is available by subscription in print or online. It is the only business publication providing comprehensive sources of information on opportunities to supply goods, works and services to projects financed by the world's leading development banks – the African, Asian, Caribbean, Inter-American, and North American Development Banks, the European Bank for Reconstruction and Development and the United Nations System, featuring the World Bank.
[70] *IDB Projects* contains a listing of individual projects being considered for possible financing by the IDB (also known as the project 'pipeline'). Paragraphs describing each of these proposed operations are broken out by country and by sector. By checking these listings, interested suppliers can track the progress of projects as they move through successive stages of preparation. In many cases the executing agency contacts provided in each of these short descriptions prove to be the single most important piece of information the Bank can provide, affording a chance for prospective bidders to learn about the context in which tenders will be carried out and allowing for marketing of products and/or technical expertise.

Judicial systems in Latin America are usually ill prepared to manage their own budget, not to speak of meeting strict and complicated financial management and procurement guidelines of donors. In these instances, donors have resorted to establishing local implementing units and conditioning initial disbursement on meeting certain project management guidelines. Once these management and financial oversight guidelines have been met, conditionality usually ends and little implementation oversight is required by the donor. This is especially true in the case of international banks; due to the fact that the funds are the product of a loan to be repaid by the national government; a reluctance to offend governments with much larger loans in other sectors; and a lack of in-country technical staff to exercise quality control over projects.

Once a project has been awarded, it is rare to find any updated information about the progress of the project or to obtain copies of reports or evaluations. ICITAP, for example, arguably one of the largest recipients of USAID Rule of Law funds, has never published, or made available, any of its technical reports or evaluations.[71] In other instances, even when projects have been terminated for political or other reasons, no subsequent information is supplied to the public. Availability of important publications is often restricted, except to the most persistent researchers, or its cost is prohibitive.[72]

2) Preventing corruption in international agencies

It is only in the last few years that international development institutions have begun to focus on corruption, especially as it involves implementation of their own projects. One of the most publicised efforts has been that of the World Bank, which concluded that: '... we cannot hold our clients to a higher standard than we hold ourselves. Corruption in all its forms is a crippling tax on the poor. Is corruption within the institution a widespread problem? We do not think so. But in an organisation that disburses about twenty billion dollars annually, we would be naïve to believe that there is none'.[73]

Following Bank President James D. Wolfensohn's call for greater internal oversight of projects,[74] the World Bank established an Oversight Committee on Fraud and Corruption responsible for reviewing all allegations of fraud and corruption received by any member of the Bank Group and then determining

---

[71] When the Center for the Administration of Justice requested such reports from a former director, they were informed that much of the material was classified or simply not made public.

[72] One of the most blatant examples are four monographs prepared by Linn Hammergren which lay out the experiences learned by USAID over its many years of managing Rule of Law Projects. Dissemination of these works has been poor, at best, they have not been publicised and can only be acquired by purchasing from a vendor.

[73] Anti-Corruption Knowledge Resource Center, 'Preventing Corruption in Bank Projects and Keeping our House in Order'.

[74] See: James D. Wolfensohn, 15 Oct. 1998 letter to all staff, 'New Measures to Combat Fraud and Corruption', http://www.worldbank.org/publicsector/anticorrupt/newmeasures.htm.

when and how an investigation should be conducted. To help facilitate the filing of complaints, the World Bank has also set up a twenty-four-hour telephone hotline that may be used by Bank staff and the public to denounce cases of fraud and corruption.[75] In addition, an 'Ethical Guide for Bank Staff Handling Procurement Matters in Bank-Financed Projects' was issued although it apparently only applies to permanent staff during a period in which international donors are relying more and more on outside consultants.[76] Other measures instituted by the World Bank are the hiring of additional procurement specialists, contracting independent projects audits (although only 20 audits were commissioned in between November 1998 and November 1999, a small number given the Bank's portfolio), and instituting new procedures for debarring contractors from future World Bank projects (although they have only reported eight debarments during 1999).[77] The World Bank has reported that since 1997 about 15 allegations of fraud and corruption were investigated by the Investigations Unit of the Internal Auditing Department, two staff members were terminated for misuse of $110,000 in trust funds, and one civil law suit resulted in recovery of funds from a former Bank member and an outside consultant.

USAID relies on its Inspector General's Office, with an annual budget of $30 million to investigate cases of financial mismanagement as well as corruption and fraud. The USAID web page now includes information on how to contact this office and on filing complaints by mail, email or telephone.[78] Unfortunately, the IDB offers little information to the public on the means of contacting their counterpart office or apparent encouragement to do so.

While the foregoing relate to issues of fraud in international agencies' projects, donors and lenders have had a more difficult time in defining unethical conduct that does not amount to fraud. For example, donor agencies have relied on sitting judges, prosecutors and public defenders from Latin American countries as key technical assistance consultants in their projects. This presents

---

[75] The telephone number in the United States and Canada is 1-800-831-0463. In other countries the free 800 number is accessible through the AT&T operator. They can be found on the World Bank's home page. http://www.worldbank.org/publicsector/anticorrupt/fraud.htm.

[76] 'Ethical Guide for Bank Staff Handling Procurement Matters in Bank-Financed Projects', 23 April 1988, http://www.worldbank.org/publicsector/anticorrupt/ethicalguide.htm.

[77] 'World Bank Listing of Ineligible Firms', http://www.worldbank.org/html/opr/procure/debarr.html.

[78] USAID states that: 'The purpose of the OIG Hotline is to receive complaints of Fraud, Waste or Abuse in USAID programmes and operations, including mismanagement or violations of law, rules or regulations by USAID employees or programme participants. Complaints may be received directly from USAID employees, participants in USAID programmes, or the general public. The IG Act and other pertinent laws provide the protection of persons making Hotline complaints. You have the option of submitting your complaint(s) via Internet electronic mail, telephone, or US mail. However, if you elect to submit your complaint(s) via Internet email you must waive confidentiality due to the non-secure nature of Internet electronic mail systems.' http://www.info.usaid.gov/oig/hotline/hotline.htm

the unusual situation of having a sitting Supreme Court judge, for example, from one country being paid a fee, which often is much more than his/her public salary, to further the Rule of Law goals of another country. In some instances, extensive utilisation of these public officials has resulted in questionable practices within their own countries in regards of leaves of absence and double dipping in per diem or other benefits. Unfortunately, donor agencies have not addressed this and other grey ethical areas.

3) Anti-corruption projects

As well as preventing corruption in the award and administration of their own projects, international development agencies have made combating public sector corruption a primary goal of their overall development strategy. Donors are to be commended for undertaking anti-corruption programmes, but many initiatives are curbed by the lack of donor resolve to compel recipient countries to undertake fundamental political reforms to remove the causes of corruption, as this might jeopardise the relationship with host governments. This can even lead donor countries to bypass local governments with weak and/or corrupt regulatory agencies in order to implement projects.

For example, USAID chose to award all its Hurricane George relief funds to NGOs rather than to the Government of the Dominican Republic. The World Bank and IDB, however, issued a contract to an international procurement firm to handle all hurricane-related relief, and a separate auditing contract to an international accounting firm to conduct pre- and post-audits of their funds, rather than rely on government institutions. By doing so these agencies avoided corruption, yet failed to take advantage of an opportunity to exact commitment to a fundamental change of government oversight practices and, instead, further weakened local regulatory institutions.

In other instances, in their desire to fund projects or to reward local partners for compliance with other goals of the international development institution, agencies have been too quick to overlook corrupt practices of recipient institutions. In the case of Venezuela, for example, the World Bank issued a multimillion-dollar loan to the Government of Carlos Andrés Pérez to reform the judiciary at a time when he was being investigated for corruption and following two attempted military coups. Some argued that the loan was a reward for Pérez's acceptance of extremely unpopular financial reforms imposed by IMF and the Bank. The loan was further complicated by the decision to award implementation to the Judicial Council, which was reputedly a highly politicised judicial body. Similar results were obtained when awarding another World Bank loan to the Bolivian judiciary.

b) Intra- and Inter-agency coordination

Implementation of Rule of Law programmes requires a great deal of inter-agency coordination at both donor and national level. Latin American countries have little experience in inter- or intra-agency coordination and this historical pattern can become a substantial barrier to the success of Rule of Law initiatives. Cooperation among donors is a critical aspect of any justice reform strategy, especially given the proliferation of reform programmes. Coordination mechanisms are most developed when the donor's interest is linked to national security or domestic concerns, for example narcotics and organised crime.[79] In these areas, donors have adopted international standards, established coordination mechanisms, supported the creation of regional bodies and entered into bilateral and multinational agreements. [80]

In traditional Rule of Law programmes, however, cooperation among donors has been the exception not the rule.[81] In Nicaragua, for example, more than eleven donors are involved in Rule of Law reform (See figure 2.1).[82] Although many of these reform programmes overlap with other existing initiatives, there has been little effort to coordinate activities. This led, for example, the Supreme Court to require an inventory of training programmes and the development of a training plan that included all donors.

Possibly the most significant result of a lack of interagency coordination is the ignorance, conscious or not, of the experiences of other international agencies. Seldom, for example, do project planners take into account assessments conducted by other donors in their own project design. This is due to a

---

[79] US Secretary of State Madeleine Albright referred to this when she said: 'Many threats to US interests are truly international in nature, whether from smuggling across our borders and shores, from distant safe havens around the globe, or via the borderless, technological web that harnesses the world's communications and financial systems. To respond to these threats, we must not only act in an efficient and effective way at home, but in bilateral and multilateral venues as well. Without effective law enforcement throughout the international community, criminals will continue to threaten US interests simply by conducting their activities from and through those jurisdictions where law enforcement is weak.' Statement of Madeleine K. Albright, 7 Jan. 1998.

[80] In the area of criminal justice reform, the United Nations has been a leader, especially through the UN Crime Commission, a functional commission of the UN Economic and Social Council, and the related Centre for International Crime Prevention (UNCICP). UNCICP will move from a criminology centre engaged in research projects to providing technical assistance and institution building programmes addressing high priority criminal activities, such as organised crime and corruption. Another major coordinating body is the UN Drug Control Programme (UNDCP) and the related Commission on Narcotic Drugs (CND) to advance the goals of the 1988 UN Drug Convention.

[81] The World Bank has admitted that 'in many countries legal technical assistance is provided from a variety of sources and often without proper coordination. This may lead to inconsistent legislation being drafted or inconsistent institutions being promoted.' World Bank Legal Department (1995) p. 9, cited in The Lawyers Committee for Human Rights and The Venezuelan Programme for Human Rights Education and Action (1995).

[82] Some of the major ones are: USAID, IDB, the World Bank, UNDP, Spanish Cooperation Agency, European Union, Sweden, Nordic Countries, and others. The Supreme Court of Nicaragua has named an international assistance coordinator and assigned space to many of these agencies in what looks like a miniature United Nations.

lack of communication among international agencies, consultants who want to prove their worth and receive their honoraria, or inter-institutional jealousies. Most often, however, it is simply due to ignorance of the actions of other donors. It is surprising that donors stress the need to establish sophisticated information systems and databases for recipient judiciaries but fail to do so themselves. Inter-institutional databases and information systems would not only provide basic information to agency users but also to the public at large.

Figure 2.1: Rule of Law Assistance Projects in Nicaragua

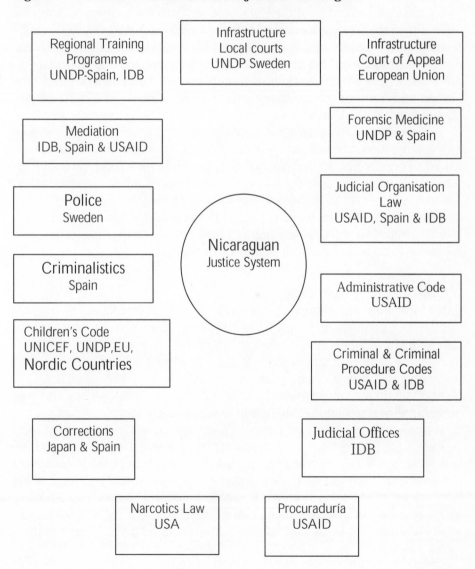

In other instances, different agencies of the same government, or different units of the same donor, have pursued different and sometimes conflicting Rule of Law reform strategies. For example, ICITAP has pursued the goal of removing police agencies from military control while narcotics' policies of other US agencies have militarised police units involved in the war against narcotics trafficking. Likewise, some US agencies have forcefully pushed for the enactment of white collar crime or narcotics legislation that establish special procedures, mostly inquisitorial and often violate fundamental rights, for the prosecution of these cases while other US agencies are seeking a more transparent and expedient procedural system. The most egregious example occurs when the foreign donor pushes for law reforms that would be unconstitutional in the country of origin. The most blatant example of this practice is the criminalisation of 'illicit enrichment', which compels the defendant to prove the source of his/her assets, thereby inverting the burden of proof. The US is a lead government encouraging this reform, which would be clearly unconstitutional in the United States.

Donors have often relied upon a division of legal areas among themselves as a coordination mechanism. For example, USAID is the primary donor involved in criminal justice reform in the region while the World Bank and the IDB have focused on commercial law, infrastructure and court organisation. These divisions have often failed to work due to the impact that any reform in one area can have upon another. Finally, in some instances too large or complex an inter-agency coordination group may impede programme progress as it introduces an additional layer of bureaucratic approvals.[83]

c) Conditionality

One of the most important components of any reform project is a determination of the conditions that must be met by the recipient government prior to disbursement of funds. A first consideration is the ability of project managers to meet the donor's financial management, procurement and administration requirements. Since judiciaries have little experience in these areas, donors often create project implementation units within the recipient agency and hold up disbursement until minimum requirements are met.

A more difficult task is to determine critical fundamental changes that must be met by the local agency prior to disbursement. These may be in the form of laws that must be enacted, regulations that must be issued, budgetary commitments that must be made, or changes in institutional policies. Donors have tended to shy away from the imposition of such conditions for a variety or reasons. Project designers argue that achievement of some of these benchmarks is often outside the control of the implementing agency. For example,

---

[83] US General Accounting Office (1996).

legislative change is dependent on the legislative branch and may not be affected by any of the project components. Likewise, financial commitments must be approved by the executive and legislative branches and may be affected by other national needs more pressing than judicial reform.

Political benchmarks are the most difficult for the donor to establish or impose. They may, however, be the most important conditions for project success. Obliging national governments to meet agreed structural conditions may affect the relationship of the donor to the recipient government, and may affect other donor priorities, possibly viewed as more significant than justice reform. Thus, it is commonly seen that such conditions fail to be included in the initial agreement and, in those cases where they are set out, it is unusual for loans or grants to be terminated as a consequence of failure to meet them.

d) Targets of reform

In order to overcome some of the problems inherent in structural reforms, donors have sometimes focused on the personnel who administer the judicial system rather than the institution itself. This has been partially justified on the basis that a key component of any reform strategy is the judicial culture, shaped and maintained by lower level justice officials and not necessarily by their superiors.

Projects driven by this philosophy will target project resources on shaping a core group of judges who will 'theoretically serve as the beginning point for the long-term transformation of the judicial culture from one subservient to political and economic influence to one in which the integrity and autonomy of the judicial branch is vigorously defended, regardless of the presence or absence of constitutional or legislative reforms "from above".'[84]

The strategy is first to develop a reform constituency within the judiciary. Thereafter, the donors and the new judicial change agents may advance legislative and other reforms. This participatory philosophy has often failed; first, because judicial superiors often fear that reform judges may assume an inordinate amount of power and may even engender the seeds of judicial unions. Secondly, judicial turnover is very high, especially in those countries in which judicial independence is most threatened. Thirdly, while the theory of changing judicial culture through internal change agents sounds plausible, it has seldom been thoroughly tested, especially in Third World settings.

Even when donors are successful in obtaining commitments from national governments, these agreements may evaporate when conditions change or leaders are replaced. In the El Salvador IDB-funded justice reform programme, for example, the priorities of the government changed to public

---

[84] The Lawyers Committee for Human Rights and The Venezuelan Programme for Human Rights Education and Action (1995) p. 98.

safety reform due to public demands to combat crime and a shift in the Executive leadership. A new Supreme Court in Honduras was reluctant, at first, to agree to implement a project that had been designed by the predecessor court. The World Bank's multimillion-dollar loan to the Venezuelan government was delayed and jeopardised when President Pérez was removed from office for corruption and the incoming administration had serious misgivings about accepting the previously negotiated loan.

All of these, as well as many other examples, point to the need to reach out beyond the judiciary and the government. Too great a reliance on the commitment of government or judicial officials may not prove to be enough. Projects that have no popular base of support may find themselves tied to the coat tails of temporary political leaders.

Conclusions

All of the aforementioned justice reform efforts have much in common. Their goals were lofty in seeking to encourage the establishment of uniformly applied norms by a cadre of legal functionaries committed to compliance with the law. Today, however, after more than a decade of aid and millions of dollars later, the justice systems of Latin America are facing their gravest crisis.

Today people are genuinely afraid for their safety, but this time the cause is crime rather than civil war. Opinion polls in Latin America reveal that public safety and corruption are ranked among the top four social problems facing the countries. Surveys also reveal growing distrust in the capacity of the justice system to combat crime and even raise questions as to its complicity in criminality. The public's fear is not unfounded. Latin America leads the world in violent crime. El Salvador, for example, has the most homicides per capita in the world and has been characterised as the most violent country in the world, overtaking even Colombia.

Concurrent with rising levels of violence and the increase in the public's level of fear is the public's lack of confidence in the ability of the justice system to provide an adequate response. One of the primary causes of the low regard in which the justice system is held is a widespread perception of corruption in the justice system as well as throughout the entire public sector. The inefficiency of the justice system, combined with perceived corruption, has led many to express growing distrust in justice system institutions.[85]

---

[85] In Central America, the United Nations Development Programme undertook national household surveys on the public's trust in the justice system. Over 50% of the persons surveyed reported little trust in the police or judiciary. In Panama, 60.3% had no confidence in the Judiciary; distrust reached 50.6% in Guatemala; 50.5% in Nicaragua; 50% in Honduras; 31% in El Salvador; and 26.9% in Costa Rica. Public distrust in the police was similar with 59.5% of the persons surveyed in Guatemala reporting no confidence in the police; 48.6% in Honduras; 45.9% in Nicaragua; 41.8% in Panama; 37.3% in Costa Rica; and 33% in El Salvador. Laura Chinchilla (1998) p. 3

Progress toward the goal of judicial independence has been slow and set-backs common. In many countries judges are still appointed on the basis of political affiliation rather than merit and judicial decisions are still influenced by non-legal factors. Bar associations fail to support judicial reform and lawyers are often the primary opponents of modernisation of legal systems.

Legal education is at an all-time low. The number of law schools has grown out of control and the profession has failed to take any steps to regulate the quality of the education being offered by law faculties. More and more lawyers, with less and less education, are entering already saturated labour markets. Judicial schools have commonly become remedial legal education centres striving to fill the educational vacuum left by the law school education.

Even though modern legislation is being adopted, especially in criminal procedure, jails are still overpopulated and the amount of pre-trial detainees continues to grow as governments turn to more repressive measures to counteract the rise in criminality.

In the face of this crisis, international agencies make apparently significant pronouncements about the importance of the Rule of Law linking it to democratic development and the achievement of capitalist markets. At the same time that they impose draconian economic measures as a condition of aid, they have failed to require fundamental change from recipient governments in their Rule of Law projects.

One of the most difficult tasks for government donors as well as international agencies is the determination of when to award assistance and when it is time to withdraw it. Philip B. Heymann, a Harvard law professor who directed Harvard's Guatemala's Criminal Justice Project, in justifying Harvard's withdrawal from that project, stated that:

> (i)t is not a useful expenditure of United States money to provide training or advice to the police, prosecutors or judges of any country whose political and military leaders are unwilling to support law enforcement efforts against every form of political violence, including that initiated by security forces or political/economic groups to which the government leaders may be sympathetic ... In any country where the President, the Minister of Defence and the Minister of the Interior are unwilling to create the conditions for a vigorous investigation of terrorist crimes, the United States should not be providing support for improvement in the more politically harmless areas of criminal justice. It will not work, for the people of the country...will come to hold the criminal justice system in contempt, leaving it deprived of the most valuable resource of any criminal justice system, citizen cooperation. And even if it did work, it would create a stunted, morally corrupted system of social control, not the rule of law.[86]

Professor Heymann argued that the test for commencement or termination of

---

[86] Philip B. Heymann (1990).

a project is the level of and type of positive impact that it will have on critical problems facing the criminal justice system. This can only be determined by evaluating the level of political will to implement the reforms and to hold the recipient accountable for meeting fundamental conditions critical for long-term reform. The fact that many of these conditions have political implications, both for the international agency and the recipient government, forces both to make extremely difficult decisions. A determination that democratisation benchmarks are not being met has long-term consequences for both and it is often easier to avoid this determination, either by not placing these conditions in the funding document or by excusing a failure to achieve them on technical factors.

Conditionality is a two-way street and many of the recipients of the law and development, administration of justice and Rule of Law projects have often failed to question the motives of donors and have primarily focused on the amount to be received and less on the strings that were attached. The little criticism that was voiced often came not from governments but from civil society, which complained about the 'imperialist' nature of some projects. For example, some observers have commented on the possibility that the notion of setting 'democratic' or 'rule of law' benchmarks that precondition economic assistance or international recognition could continue previous patterns of 'humiliating intervention by States bent on "civilising missions".'[87] This is of particular concern given the prior experience of these two preceding initiatives and the apparent recurring belief among some US academics in the exportability of the US political and legal system.

Developing countries may find themselves unable to resist the demands placed on them by foreign funding agencies and may adopt legal reforms implanted by developed countries with little public discussion or analysis. A troublesome characteristic of previous reform efforts was the lack of public participation in the design and implementation of projects. Unfortunately, this is being repeated once again. The World Bank was heavily criticised for the manner in which it developed a multi-million judicial reform effort in Venezuela.[88] As a result, donors and 21 human rights organisations attended a meeting with the World Bank, the IDB and the Venezuelan government to

---

[87] Thomas M. Franck (1992) p. 80.

[88] '… participation was not a recognised Bank policy in 1990, when discussions concerning the Venezuelan project began. Not surprisingly, many major actors in the judicial system – the Ministry of Justice and the Public Prosecutor most prominently – had very little input, and almost no actors in civil society – academia, bar associations, law faculties, NGOs – were contacted. More surprising is that only a handful of judges were consulted and the vast majority knew little of the contents of the Project other than that which they had read in newspapers as late as May 1995. In spite of the expressed willingness of Bank officials and the Judicial Council to begin to reach out to civil society, the Project is only slowly emerging from the cloak of secrecy which has covered it since its inception.' The Lawyers Committee for Human Rights and The Venezuelan Programme for Human Rights Education and Action (1995) p. 9.

ensure broader future participation. A key finding of the initial review and the conference was the need for 'greater involvement of the non-governmental community in the judicial reform project development process. In particular, national and local non-governmental organisations (NGOs) with practical experience working with national legal systems and institutions have a contribution to make not only to the substance of the reform efforts but also to building a broad-based consensus for reform that is necessary for its success.'[89]

While a great deal of lip service has been paid to the incorporation of civil society in the design and implementation of justice projects, the bulk of projects continue to be designed by foreign experts during brief visits, primarily consulting with government agencies and with little publicity. The projects are then awarded based on fairly closed bidding procedures with primary implementation responsibilities being awarded largely to foreign multinational consulting companies.

Although all ROL experts agree on the need for long-term reforms, many projects continue to be judged on the achievement of short-term indicators. Projects that have demonstrable short-term results are favoured over programmes whose success may only be revealed years later. For example, an area in which fundamental change is needed is in the improvement of the quality of new lawyers entering the legal profession. Law and development reformers were correct in assuming that the legal education of those who were to be the primary actors in the system should be a primary focus of any reform effort. Administration of justice and rule of law programmes overestimated the difficulties of such ventures by focusing on the political cost and cultural barriers of previous initiatives. On the other hand, they focused their initiatives on improving the operational efficiency of those actors that have the greatest impact on the application of the law; judges. A middle ground should be found. The experience of judiciaries throughout the region demonstrates that judicial schools can do little to create knowledgeable and efficient judges if the law graduates have serious basic deficiencies in their legal training. Thus, one finds that many judicial schools are primarily engaged in emergency basic legal training, trying to fill the educational vacuum that should have been filled by the law schools.

While the entry of new funding agencies into the justice reform field is commendable it presents new problems or aggravates existing ones. Local governments are often finding themselves recipients of competing or conflicting projects funded by different international agencies that seldom coordinate among themselves. The need for coordination of development programmes is not a new issue and has been a persistent problem.

International agencies long ago decided that significant legal problems in underdeveloped countries that affected the interests of developed ones could

---

[89] *Ibid*, p. i.

only be addressed through integrated policies that included all of the significant actors. Thus, transnational crime and narcotics trafficking have been addressed collaboratively and based on an agreed-upon strategy. On the civil law side, for example, intellectual property concerns have been dealt with by the establishment of an international body that sets standards and supports modernisation of norms and registries. Yet Rule of Law projects remain characterised by a lack of coordination among international agencies, an absence of common strategies and insufficient quality controls. Often the easiest development path is taken and hard choices avoided. While international agencies call for transparency in government operations, little is known about their Rule of Law projects or results. Procurement practices tend to favour multinational consulting agencies often staffed by former members of the funding agency. Despite growing calls for civil society participation in the design and implementation of reform projects, this is still limited and NGOs are often relegated to observer, rather than participant, status.

Lack of coordination is not limited to international collaboration and may also be found in programmes within the same international agency. For example, both the law and development and the AOJ programmes were primarily stand-alone initiatives with little linkage to other democratisation goals and initiatives. Programmes to improve the quality of journalists, to modernise legislatures, to promote elections or to improve the efficiency of legislatures had very little relationship to justice system reform projects. This pattern appears to continue under the current Rule of Law programmes and is not limited to USAID alone. For example, the Spanish Cooperation Agency is funding police training carried out by Spanish national police agencies while the Spanish Judiciary (Consejo General del Poder Judicial) is coordinating judicial assistance. In the case of the former, there appears to be encouragement towards a militarised model of policing while the latter attempts to bring about an opposite result. There does not seem to be coordination between these two agencies with disparate objectives and methodologies.

The inability of international agencies to take advantage of the current local conditions in the region is disturbing. Public opinion polls reveal a groundswell of support for justice reform among Latin Americans. Legal reform has now entered the political agenda of parties and is an electoral issue. Unfortunately, however, authoritarian forces have taken up the banner of legal reform and have called for 'renovation' of the judiciary. Concerns over crime have been addressed by increasing the size and power of police forces, militaries now patrol streets of Latin cities, criminal codes have become more repressive and due process rights are being curbed as reforms of criminal procedure are criticised as being too soft on crime. Although Rule of Law assistance cannot, in and of itself, turn the tide, a rethinking of the goals and practices of donors can at least furnish support to those who seek achievement of so lofty a goal as the Rule of Law.

CHAPTER 3

USAID's Support of Justice Reform in Latin America

Margaret J. Sarles[*]

Introduction

The US Agency for International Development (USAID) has for over twenty years supported comprehensive reforms in Latin America and the Caribbean aimed at strengthening justice systems and guaranteeing human rights. By the end of 1999 USAID, and allied programmes in the Departments of State and Justice, had provided about $300 million in grants to Latin America for work in justice and police reform, through regional and bilateral assistance programmes in 19 countries.[1]

Equality before the law is a defining characteristic of democracy. Therefore, justice reform and the support for human rights are embedded into a larger USAID strategy of democratic development. USAID has supported the return to civilian rule and the consolidation of democratic practices through electoral programmes, decentralisation and local government programmes, anti-corruption, and programmes to increase citizen participation and strengthen civil society. In the context of democratic development, USAID therefore views reforms to develop a fair and effective system of justice as being just as critical to the consolidation of democracy as free and fair systems of elections and representation.

Against a larger picture of declining resources for foreign assistance in the post-Cold War period, USAID in Latin America and the Caribbean (LAC) has been steadfast in its efforts to help consolidate democracy. While overall, approximately eight per cent of USAID's budget is allocated to democracy building, in the Latin American region, that proportion is 13 per cent. Within the democracy portfolio, justice accounts for over half of LAC's assistance,[2] with total grants in fiscal year 1999 of about $50 million.[3]

[*] Margaret Sarles is head of Democracy and Human Rights for the Bureau of Latin America and the Caribbean, Agency for International Development. This chapter represents her own views, not necessarily those of USAID. She thanks Erin Krasik and Abigail Horn for their assistance on this paper.
[1] See Appendix 1 for an inventory of justice activities, and Appendix 2 for brief summaries of individual country programmes.
[2] In fiscal year 1998, once police training funds are excluded, about 43 per cent of funding was allocated to justice and human rights; about 20 per cent to strengthening civil society; 12 per cent to elections and political party development; 15 per cent to accountability and anti-corruption; and nine per cent to democratic local government.
[3] This figure includes all funding sources and Deptartment of Justice police as well as prosecutorial training programmes.

USAID can point to significant accomplishments in the area of justice support in Latin America, as well as to failures.[4] As the first donor to work significantly in this sector, the agency's early programmes in the 1980s have provided a rich mine of assessments and hard lessons that have had an impact on other donors' programmes.[5] Perhaps USAID's most important achievement, in fact, has been to bring justice reform 'to the table' as an essential part of a comprehensive development programme. Partly as a result of the success of USAID's Latin American programmes, the context of justice development assistance is now very different from fifteen years ago. The creation of new models of justice is now a focus of national policy-makers and thinkers throughout the region.

With the end of military rule and commitment from national leaders to more democratic government, justice reform took on new importance. Major constitutional and legal changes began to revise the basic structures and culture of justice. Court systems are now slowly moving from inquisitorial to more accusatorial forms, with open trials, new rules of evidence, public defenders for the indigent and, of course, new roles for judges, prosecutors, investigators, police and others involved in the justice system. Governments are increasing their investments in career professionalisation and administrative modernisation. In addition to institutional reform, there is improved legal protection and access to justice for families, women and children through a host of new institutions and the enforcement of new criminal violence laws against women and children. Countries are modifying outmoded and less democratic penal and criminal procedures codes and reforming police institutions to underpin demilitarisation and professionalisation. As a further measure of citizen protection against possible state human rights abuses, 15 countries have established offices of human rights ombudsmen. Altogether, there is an overwhelming agenda towards developing a legal and institutional framework capable of providing greater justice.

At the same time, where USAID's financial support and technical assistance once provided the only source of outside justice assistance to Latin American countries, today there are multiple sources of support and knowl-

---

4 See, for example, US General Accounting Office, 'Foreign Assistance: US Rule of Law Assistance to Five Latin American Countries,' August 1999, a positive evaluation that concluded that 'US rule of law assistance has helped [Colombia, El Salvador, Guatemala, Honduras, Panama] undertake legal and institutional judicial reforms, improve the capabilities of the police and other law enforcement institutions, and increase citizen access to the justice system.' (p. 2) Some have concluded that USAID support led to reforms in El Salvador, Guatemala, Honduras, Costa Rica, Venezuela, Bolivia, Chile, Paraguay, Haiti, Ecuador, and in some provinces in Argentina. Other studies have pointed to failures, including the chapter by Luis Salas in this volume, or have criticised specific aspects of human rights or justice programmes (e.g., some of the papers prepared for the Washington Office on Latin America.).
5 Two very useful syntheses include Harry Blair and Gary Hansen (1994) and Madeleine Crohn and William E. Davis (eds.) (1996).

edge. The donor institutions are entering this field rapidly, with vastly more resources than can be provided by the US government. Expertise has developed not only within the donor banks; there is an explosion of expertise within the hemisphere as justice reforms are developed and implemented in country after country. At this point in time there is a wider comparative experience to draw on and experts in numerous countries capable of sharing expertise and experiences with each other.

The commitment to justice reform has arrived none too soon. Popular opinion in Latin America has already hardened on the ineffectiveness and corruption of judicial systems. In most countries, they have virtually no credibility.[6] While citizens do generally believe that their governments no longer tolerate human rights abuses as government policy, and support the new offices of human rights ombudsmen, they do not make a link between governments' improvement in human rights protection and improvement in the justice system generally. They are, rather, disillusioned with the justice system's apparent incapacity to address escalating common crime and the seemingly pervasive culture of official corruption. For most people, these two issues are now the dominant complaints about the new democracies, and both are closely linked to failures of state justice. In a recent poll in Guatemala, for example, citizens identified crime rates as the single worst problem confronting the country, even more serious than unemployment. An assessment of democracy financed by USAID in El Salvador in 1999 revealed that 22.1 per cent of citizens had been the victim of a crime during that year and that over half the citizens — 55 per cent — believed it was reason enough to return to military government.[7] Similarly, throughout the continent, anger over corruption in government remains intense. The impunity of public officials elected through democratic institutions is undermining faith in democracy as a system, has led to the impeachment and downfall of several governments, and to the implosion of political parties linked to corrupt practices. A new generation of political leaders seems to be emerging who openly disdain democratic institutions as inherently corrupt. Once in power, they undermine reforms to provide judicial independence.

In summary, the context of USAID assistance to justice reform in Latin America at the turn of the century is immensely different from fifteen years ago. There is now an overwhelming agenda in the hemisphere for reform; other donors are entering this arena of assistance; overall US assistance to Latin America is less than it was in the past; and citizens are now looking critically at weak justice systems that seem to permit impunity and corruption.

---

[6] Charles T. Call (2000) notes that in four of six Central American countries, more than half the respondents had 'no confidence' in the judicial system. USAID surveys in Haiti and South America reveal much the same pattern.

[7] Mitchell Seligson, Jose Miguel Cruz and Ricardo Cordova Macias (2000).

This is an opportune moment to examine the approaches USAID has taken in the past as well as its current programming to assess where best to allocate justice resources in the future.

1. Supporting and Nurturing a Justice Reform Process

USAID in Latin America entered the justice field early, when military and authoritarian governments were still the rule rather than the exception, and transparent, fair justice systems were not yet even considered goals of opposition democratic movements. Not surprisingly under these conditions, this timing meant pushing forward a reform agenda, rather than implementing ongoing reforms. USAID's initial efforts in justice reform began in the 1960s and early 1970s with what has been labelled the 'Law and Development Movement'. The weaknesses of its assumptions and its inability to develop strong national justice institutions are dealt with elsewhere in this book (see the chapter by Luis Salas). While institutional achievements were weak, however, it is fair to say that a number of the lawyers who spearheaded later reforms were trained under the programme and that the later successes in supporting reforms were in part based on lessons learned from this mixed experience.

A second area of justice reform began to focus specifically on protecting human rights, under guidelines in effect from 1978 to 1982. The first large-scale human rights programme developed out of this in 1984 in El Salvador aimed at investigating and prosecuting military personnel involved in the murder of four US churchwomen. This rapidly expanded into supporting more comprehensive programmes to replace emergency decrees and the outmoded code of criminal procedures.[8] That same year, the report of the Kissinger Commission on Central America recommended that USAID develop programmes to support justice reform in Central America as a way of strengthening nascent democracies. [9] It is interesting to note that this human rights thrust, which continues to the present, took root during the Cold War and under both Republican and Democratic administrations.

In virtually every Latin American country in which it has supported reform, USAID has entered the justice field early, seeking out reformers in civil society and the government. This approach has frequently had positive results in the long term, but often mixed and discouraging results for the first five to ten years. In El Salvador in the 1980s, for example, reformers made little headway. The political ground was too shaky, the commitment among high government officials insufficient. The frustrations led to long internal discussions on the need for 'political will'. The conclusion that a country 'lacked political will' is often heard in USAID as an explanation for reform failure,

---

8 Development Associates, Inc. (1988).
9 National Bipartisan Commission on Central America (1984).

particularly in justice. The phrase is a nebulous concept without much inherent explanatory value — a simple acknowledgement that stakeholders who opposed the reforms were stronger than those who favoured it at that particular point. In fact, only recently has the Congress in El Salvador passed significant justice reforms, after many years of USAID support. Similarly, USAID's programme in Honduras worked with reformers for a number of years to revise criminal procedures codes, modernise the justice system and give basic rights to citizens. Only in 2000, however, was a new criminal procedures code finally passed by the Congress, along with other major reforms to make the judicial system more transparent and independent.

USAID's experience in early intervention in justice offers several insights. One is that intervention under non-democratic or semi-authoritarian rule needs to consider not only institutional reform but also direct support for human rights work. A second is that we must be prepared to remain for the long run, and face considerable failure before seeing success stories. Third, a strong component of support must be to help strengthen indigenous reformers and constituencies for reform who in the long run have much to gain by justice modernisation. These are the people who will create and sustain public will for continuous reform over the long term.

This 'niche' of early intervention in the justice reform process is based on USAID's comparative advantage and is likely to continue. USAID's grants can be given either to a government or to non-governmental organisations as deemed appropriate. They can also be disbursed more quickly than assistance by the large donor banks, and are hence useful for directing assistance rapidly in a changing environment. USAID's long history in the region has also given it experience in identifying potential reform situations, and tools for responding to them. Even as 'first generation' reforms are implemented, the need for further reforms is obvious; this is an arena of action that will continue to be centre-stage for the foreseeable future. Justice reform is an on-going process.

2. Institutional strengthening to implement new reforms[10]

Typically, major reform legislation includes a critical period of one or two years for the judicial branch and other government institutions to develop the expertise, institutions and procedures needed for successful implementation. More than any other donor, USAID has devoted its energies to assisting countries to develop institutions and training during this early phase.

One emphasis has been on improving administration of justice through activities such as reducing case backlogs, decreasing detention time and improving court efficiency. Many programmes have supported new case track-

---

[10] For a comprehensive discussion of this topic in USAID/Latin American justice programmes, see Linn Hammergren (1998) and (1998a).

ing systems, often computerised. On the institutional side, programmes have provided the assistance to move management responsibilities from the judge to clerks of the court and similar reforms.

Comprehensive reforms often redefine the basic duties of judges, prosecutors, investigators, court personnel and justice personnel. All need considerable training and practice to prepare them for their new roles, in such areas as the use of new courtroom management mechanisms, investigative procedures and the handling of evidence. Over time the agency has also increasingly emphasised the cross-sector training of defenders, prosecutors, judges and police on case preparation, investigation and courtroom proceedings to ensure an integrated, coherent implementation of new legal codes and processes. The agency has also taken the lead in improving standards of professionalisation and preparing the first generation of public defenders.

USAID has led the development or restructuring of judicial academies and formal training programmes in law schools or universities in 14 countries, to help develop a permanent capacity to educate justice personnel. Judicial schools provide comprehensive training in courtroom management, investigative procedures, oral adversarial proceedings and the basic division of statutory responsibilities within an accusatorial system. In addition, they offer refresher courses and continuing legal education programmes that bring members of the justice sector up to date in new legal trends.

For example, with USAID support, the national law school in Guatemala has reformed curricula in criminal procedure and trial advocacy and set up a graduate programme in indigenous, customary law; and the Bar Association has institutionalised an academic unit for continuing legal education. In Honduras, the Court reorganised its Judicial School to rely on committees of judges and public defenders who plan their own training, increasing the relevance and coordination of justice sector training. In Haiti, a pilot programme provided intensive on-the-job training and mentoring for judges. In 1998, through the Department of Justice, the programme graduated 60 judges ready to be seated in Haiti's courts. Another 500 members of the judiciary have received some type of basic training.

Administration and training have been brought together through pilot programmes to revamp the court system. In the Dominican Republic, El Salvador, Guatemala and Haiti, for example, model courts bring personnel from all relevant institutions to put into practice the case and trial management taught in training programmes. The courts become a vehicle for further training and for replication throughout the country. The consequences can be impressive. In Guyana, for example, programmes to improve court infrastructure and legal libraries, train court reporters and modernise reporting, computerise case retrieval systems, train court clerks and improve docket management have helped reduce criminal case backlogs by 57 per cent in two years.

USAID's experience in implementing reforms has brought to light several potential problems. Two key ones relate to internal institutional bottlenecks and donor coordination.

In terms of bottlenecks, USAID experience has shown that emphasising reform of only one institution can create an imbalance, essentially moving the problem from one institution to another, rather than solving the problem. In Haiti, for example, while the programmes focusing on police reform and training were well done in themselves, justice modernisation continued to be stymied because successful programmes could not be developed in the court system. The lesson here is that a successful strategy of justice reform needs to consider the entire panoply of relevant institutions. During the first decade of the 2000s, the lack of attention to penitentiaries and punishment in general is likely to create a similar gridlock. Penitentiaries already represent a terrible human rights problem, with the great majority of detainees never having been brought to trial, and living in abysmally overcrowded conditions. If modernised justice systems significantly decrease impunity, leading to higher conviction and incarceration rates, the prison system will soon be even more overwhelmed. This suggests that countries and donors should already be analysing innovative pre- and post-trial arrangements that either do not exist in most Latin American countries or are very weak, including bail, plea bargaining (now beginning in Bolivia), prison rehabilitation, parole and alternative sentencing possibilities, for example. In training, too, a lack of balance can have disastrous results, with bottlenecks simply moving from one institution to another, or, not infrequently, resulting in training that does not include information on how other institutions must also function under a new reform.

A second concern is donor coordination. Justice investment flows from many sources. The World Bank, the Inter-American Development Bank, USAID, the United Nations, the Organisation of American States, the European Union and a host of other bilateral donors are all collaborating with Latin American countries in justice reform. Inevitably, these institutions have their own perspectives, which can easily lead to duplication and conflict over competing programmes if not attended to. Therefore, where justice reform is high on the donor agenda, donor coordination groups have become crucial in planning and implementation. Guatemala offers one example, as donors assist in the implementation of the Peace Accords. Ecuador provides a second, where donor coordination works well in the justice arena. USAID's Bolivia justice programme has offered lessons both of the advantages of collaboration and the costs of donor competition. This is the only country in which USAID and another donor (the German Deutsche Gesellschaft fur Technische Zusammenarbeit, or GTZ) have developed a common work plan and use the same contractor to implement the programme, ensuring programme complementarity. On the other hand, Bolivia offers a warning lesson as well. USAID has supported development of a new integrated case tracking and management system, used by police, prosecutors and the court system. The World Bank also supports a new system, grounded on experience in civil law, that is incompatible with this model. While the institutions are working to resolve the impasse, it has slowed implementation of the new reforms. As justice reform is now on the agenda of every major donor in Colombia, coordination will also assume great importance there in the near future.

Because reform is a continuous rather than one-off process, USAID will continue to support reform implementation. Formal donor coordination is increasingly a feature of justice programming, and should become even more important. The agency is currently planning a joint assessment in Jamaica related to violence, and this kind of early collaboration is likely to expand. Furthermore, the sequencing of assistance, with early grant support provided by USAID and later loan support from the larger donors, may become a feasible way to consider large-scale reform implementation support.

3. Supporting an Independent Judiciary

In every Latin American country, the judiciary is constitutionally an independent branch of government. Historically, however, presidents and legislatures have often controlled justice outcomes by controlling the appointment and promotion of judges and even intervening in particular cases. In the 1990s constitutional and legal reforms tended to de-link the judiciary from the executive branch, so that decisions can be made relatively free of partisan politics and presidential power, and the judiciary can develop an ethic based on norms of justice and rule of law. To further this objective USAID programmes have supported a variety of reforms. Examples include changing tenure rules so that judges' terms of office no longer coincide with those of the President, changes in appointment processes to put more weight on merit and transparency; support for judicial schools which give judges the expertise they need; support for internal review and accountability mechanisms to supervise judicial behaviour; an independent budget process; and support for civil society oversight and involvement in issues of judicial independence.

Two specific USAID interventions in Latin America illustrate a successful programme and one whose long-term outcome is not as certain. In the late 1990s, USAID and other donors in the Dominican Republic supported a strong coalition of reformers — including major players in the business community — intent on de-politicising judicial nominees, seen as critical to improving the country's reputation with potential international investors. USAID provided grants to the coalition, which successfully pushed the government to create a new National Judicial Council, charged with selecting judges through merit rather than through traditional political means. To ensure that the Council would adhere to this principle, USAID and the IDB both funded unprecedented activism by civil society organisations and the media to convince the Council to solicit nominations for the new Supreme Court publicly, publish the list of nominees and televise public hearings with the final candidates. This transparent process created strong public support for the justice system within the Dominican Republic, and resulted in the appointment of impressive Supreme Court justices. These justices in turn, with continued civil society support, developed their own process of selecting lower court judges, using high performance standards and public hearings in the process. At the end, two-thirds of the lower court judges were replaced. The success of this effort required governmental commitment to an independent judiciary along with the activism and leadership of strong civil society groups. In addition to having more qualified and independent judges, one direct consequence of this process was the education of citizens and their involvement in the process. As a result, the Dominican Republic is one of the few countries in Latin America in which citizens have a positive view of the judiciary, and the gains made are more likely to be sustainable.

Peru offers a more cautionary view of efforts to depoliticise the judiciary. In 1986, USAID invested in a broad-based programme of reform in conjunction with the Supreme Court, the Public Ministry and legal assistance groups. Among other activities, it helped establish a Judicial School and a merit-based system of recruitment, important steps in creating greater legitimacy for the justice system, as they were in the Dominican Republic. After 1992, however, President Alberto Fujimori began to interfere in the new system of judicial selection, bypassing the merit system and appointing 'provisional' judges among his own supporters. The Judicial School became increasingly irrelevant, and judicial independence suffered a severe setback. USAID responded by shifting its resources completely out of the public sector, with the exception of the Human Rights Ombudsman's office. In the recent aftermath of President Fujimori's resignation, the demand for revival of judicial independence has again emerged as one of the top priorities of the democracy agenda. The Peruvian case illustrates the need for continual vigilance: institutions less than a decade old were gutted by a determined President, and must be recreated. This time, however, civil society and government reformers are more knowledgeable and sophisticated as they develop new safeguards for judicial independence.

It seems clear that judicial independence will blossom as a focus of judicial reform during the next decade. In June 2000, USAID held a conference in Guatemala bringing together NGOs from 16 countries that are actively advocating greater independence. USAID or other donors support many of their efforts. The conference illustrated the great variety of experiences, successes and failures, in the hemisphere, and also the determination to continue working in this field.[11] Judicial independence will also be on the Presidents' agenda, most immediately at the Summit of the Americas in the spring of 2001. USAID will continue, and possibly expand, its interest in this arena.

4. Supporting reform of police forces

USAID in Latin America adheres to the belief that police systems are integral parts of justice systems, and that no donor serious about justice can ignore the role of the police. Police reform remains a critical requirement for democratic consolidation for at least three reasons. First, police have replaced the military as the source of many human rights complaints. [12] In Nicaragua, Charles Call noted that 54 per cent of the complaints received by the non-governmental organisation Centro Nicaragüense de Derechos Humanos (CENIDH) in 1997 were attributed to the national police. In 1998, the Human Rights Ombudswoman in El Salvador reported that the National Civilian Police (PNC) were charged with 45 per cent of the country's human rights violations, followed by other justice institutions with 19 per cent. From a strictly human rights point of view, therefore, retraining and restructuring of police is needed. Furthermore, like other justice personnel, police have a new role in a reformed justice system and have had insufficient training and preparation for assuming it. Third, and particularly critical at this time, police have been ineffective at combating crime and providing for the security of the citizens whom they are supposed to protect. The consequences have been dire: citizens taking the law into their own hands and pressuring their governments to bring in military forces to maintain internal order, and voting for candidates who put 'law and order' at the top of the political agenda, ahead of democracy.

The United States has invested heavily in strengthening the criminal investigative capacity of police in the post-authoritarian period, but not directly through USAID.[13] The US State Department and USAID transfer funds to the Justice Department's International Criminal Investigative Training Assistance Programme (ICITAP), which was established in the 1980s to

---

[11] Margaret Popkin, 'Efforts to Enhance Judicial Independence in Latin America: A Comparative Perspective,' paper presented at a USAID conference in October 2000. This is based on a series of country papers commissioned for a June 2000 conference, and will be published as part of a guide to working on judicial independence for USAID practitioners, prepared by the International Foundation for Electoral Systems.

[12] Charles Call (2000). The numbers presented in the next two paragraphs are from this work. Call's monograph on police systems in Latin America, and Rachel Neild (1998) are outstanding sources of information and analysis on Latin America police systems.

[13] For more than 25 years, USAID has been prohibited from directly supporting police, after providing assistance to Offices of Public Safety under authoritarian governments which often attacked their own citizens. With this legacy, USAID withdrew from providing direct assistance to the police.

provide police training and institution building.[14] In an effort to change the traditional culture of violence and militarism from which police forces were developed, the US government has supported the creation of national academies in Central America to select, train and professionalise the police, and much of the current ICITAP programme is oriented towards training and professionalisation at these academies. Other police reforms are also underway. New laws have created careers for police, increased their salaries, their budgets (in El Salvador the government budget for public security has more than doubled in the last decade)[15] and the size of the police forces. Within Central America, there are now about 193 police per 100,000 inhabitants, about two thirds the number per inhabitant found in the US and Western European countries. While there are still few indigenous people and women in police forces, the numbers are rising.

The current situation provides both opportunities and risks for USAID. One issue for the agency is whether it should re-engage directly with the police, since, even under the best of circumstances, some level of human rights abuses is likely to persist. One approach USAID could take in the future is to focus on the relationship between police and citizens. Citizens deeply mistrust the police, even when they desperately need police assistance. The legacy of military rule, coupled with the still poor human rights records and ineffectiveness of many police systems has led to a situation in which people will often not call the police when a crime is committed or underway. Policing only works when there is a basic sense of trust between citizens and the government forces armed to protect them. The NGO community, once stern critics of US government support for police, is radically shifting its position as it sees criminal impunity undermining citizen support for democracy. The Washington Office on Latin America has taken a strong leadership position in this field, developing welcome guidance in how to strengthen police effectiveness in the context of ensuring protection of citizens from police abuse. Latin American NGOs are going through a similar transformation process. Like the NGO community, USAID supports the great need to develop a professional police force, while recognising that police abuse will also remain a problem, and could undermine such assistance.

A second issue for USAID relates to the competing agendas of US government organisations involved in police activities overseas: drug agencies, the FBI and other parts of the Department of Justice, and so forth. While every agency supports the overarching foreign policy goal of democracy building, the fundamental interests of other agencies in the justice area are often more specific and time-bound than is USAID's long term development perspective. This can lead to disagreements over the relative importance of short-term

---

[14] In its early years the programme operated only in Latin America, but it is now worldwide.
[15] Charles Call (2000) p. 20.

training versus long-term building of training capacity; the relative weight of approaches focusing on international crime relative to domestic crime rates; and questions of 'leadership' in the justice sector overseas. Some of these disagreements are inherent in every government. In general, the answer to this issue seems to be developing good communication and an explicit sense of shared purpose — continual process of sharing information in a collaborative effort. Not surprisingly for a development agency, USAID's perspective is very long term, and based on engaging the real and perceived interests of national constituencies in Latin America who undertake and sustain police reform.

A third issue is the relationship of policing and security to local government. During military rule, local leaders often used police as personal militia to maintain order. One early democratic reform was therefore to overhaul police recruitment procedures and create National Academies that de-linked the police from local politics, and helped create an ethic of professionalism and national service, critical to democratic governance. However, at the end of the day most crime is local, and the solution to crime prevention lies at the community level. Some governments are now beginning to move in this direction. For example, in 1999 the Mexican congress gave new police powers to many municipalities. USAID and ICITAP are also seriously looking at community policing. [16] In this light, local officials are beginning to see security as simply another government service that must be provided, like education, infrastructure or water systems, with the same kind of political accountability. It is likely that USAID interest in local level policing will increase.

There is a great need for innovative thinking and pilot programmes in the area of citizen security. USAID is slowly losing its well-founded historical reluctance to enter this sector, but there are clearly risks in doing so. No country is completely free of police abuse, and the reform process in Latin America is very new. No one wants to be associated with the human rights problems that are still an issue for many Latin American police forces. Nonetheless, the risks of doing nothing are even higher, including increasing crime rates, citizen fear and the undermining of democratic institutions. Gradual incorporation of the police as an element of governance at the local level, particularly through community policing, offers one way to approach this problem. Multilateral donors, who seem increasingly interested in this issue, may offer another.

5. Access to Justice

The lack of rule of law hurts those in every social class, but the poor feel it more. Justice is fundamentally an issue of equity. Contemporary justice sys-

---

[16] Community policing was one of the principle themes discussed at the LAC Democracy Officers' conference in 1998. One remarkable success in local policing is in El Salvador, where the ICITAP programme has developed a 'street police' programme that is bringing down crime rates and leading adjacent local governments to emulate the programme themselves.

tems reach a small percentage of the population in most Latin American countries. Governments can often not guarantee even the minimum legal protections for the poor, address their grievances, or protect them from abuse. Rich and poor alike may suffer from violence and criminality; a multinational partner in an oil contract may be as adversely affected by justice corruption as the small landowner with a title claim. But the poor do not have access to private security systems or well-qualified lawyers. In many countries, traditionally marginalised groups (such as ethnic and indigenous groups, women and children) have had virtually no protection from violence and abuse through the court system. Local issues involving land and property disputes, family violence and petty crime often go unheard in judicial systems that are backlogged and inaccessible to those who lack representation. Without reforms to provide legal aid and public defence, institute alternative dispute resolution and improve basic efficiency in and access to the courts there can be no hope of equality before the law.

Nowhere is the issue of judicial fairness and equity more important than in the right to defend oneself when accused of a crime. This is a basic civil and human right. In support of this principle, USAID has supported the creation or strengthening of public defenders' programmes in seven countries, with similar programmes being planned in two more. Public defence programmes are a large, recurring expense for governments, and they are not necessarily the most popular programmes for a citizenry fed up with crime. Nonetheless, several governments have already taken on the costs of these programmes, including El Salvador, Honduras and the Dominican Republic. In 1997, more than 8000 individuals received free legal counsel in El Salvador, double the number served in 1995

In addition to public defenders' programmes, USAID supports access to justice in many other ways. In Haiti, for example, USAID supported a programme in seven model jurisdictions to ensure that poor detainees see a judge who determines whether their arrests were legal, and then works with private sector attorneys through the Bar Association and NGOs to provide legal representation to those who cannot afford counsel. Support at this early stage of incarceration is critical, given the high levels of pre-trial detention. Guatemala's programme is quite different, linked to the implementation of the final 1996 Peace Accords, which set out specific rights for indigenous populations. USAID has supported the training of 90 indigenous language interpreters in model courts to ensure that non-Spanish speakers have the same legal rights as Spanish speakers.

Among the most innovative forms of increasing access to justice is the rise of 'one stop shopping' — retail justice, offered through community-based programmes, often focusing on women and marginalised groups. Colombia, Ecuador and Peru are among the countries in which USAID supports such programmes. In Ecuador, Women and Family *Comisarías* are government-supported legal offices to support victims of domestic violence, using alternative dispute resolution (ADR) to help women bring cases against their abusers and find resolution by involving both parties. The *comisarías* function like lower level courts and handle first instances of domestic violence crimes ranked as 'minor offences'. Some receive 75 or more cases a day. The centres also help clients receive psychological counselling and social services through local NGOs. During financial year 1997, more than 28,000 women had their cases heard. In Colombia, the Ministry of Justice, with USAID support, is expanding the number of *Çasas de Justicia* to municipalities around the country to increase access to the justice system, relieve the formal court system, and provide links to local social services. In financial year 1997, after five new centres were created, the number of users grew from 18,000 to 64,000. The Ministry of Justice has received requests for 30 new centres in municipalities. Finally, in Peru, a network of conciliation centres and legal clinics are helping to manage the basic legal issues of Lima's poorest populations. Several centres have continued to operate after US government support ended. During 1998 the centres supported by the Ministry of Justice managed 31,000 consultations alone. With the passage of legislation that will make conciliation mandatory in a variety of civil cases beginning in January 2000, these centres will continue to play a critical role in serving justice.

USAID also provides strong support to the Inter-American Institute of Human Rights, the premier human rights education institution in the hemisphere. IIDH places a high priority on improving access to justice through its educational programmes and technical assistance provided throughout the region, an area USAID will continue to support.

Access to justice, defined broadly, is probably the fastest growing area of the USAID/Latin America portfolio, as it improves the inclusiveness and fairness of justice systems, is often cost efficient, and can be developed with both governmental and non-governmental organisations.

6. Human Rights Ombudsmen

Despite an overall decline in the number of human rights violations, figures remain unacceptably high. Extra-judicial killings still occur in more than half the countries in the region, cases of torture are reported in 22 of 33 countries, and extensive pre-trial detention without conviction remains a tremendous problem, with rates as high as 65-90 per cent.[17] Furthermore, the trend is not promising; the 1999 US State Department Human Rights report placed six countries in Latin America and the Caribbean in the worst category of human

---

[17] US State Department Human Rights Report, 1999.

rights abusers, up from only one the year before.[18]

Human Rights Ombudsman offices emerged in the 1990s primarily as a response to this problem, often with support from the European Community. Fifteen countries have now established such offices, under various titles.[19] While their initial role was primarily to provide a safe way for citizens to report human rights violations, to investigate charges of abuse, denounce violations and educate the public about human rights, their mandates are rapidly changing. Many now have a much broader accountability agenda to defend citizen interests, often cooperating closely with civil society organisations to insist on government accountability across a broad range of state activities. In Honduras, the Human Rights Ombudsman's office released an important report on transparency and corruption in government in 2000. Other offices have pursued environmental abuses by the state. Some countries have also delegated authority to them to monitor and scrutinise the administration of public services and functions, and many now receive claims by individual citizens of administrative problems regarding state-provided services and obligations. The ombudsman in Peru adopted a leading role in defending and restoring democracy during and after President Fujimori's tenure. USAID has provided support for the passage of legislation creating the office of Ombudsman in Bolivia, Ecuador and Nicaragua, and has also supported the offices in Guatemala. In Peru, support for the ombudsman forms a major portion of the USAID rule of law programme and has helped the *Defensor* provide public education, access to public services at a community level and, most significantly, the release of hundreds of persons in prison wrongly accused of terrorism.

In addition to providing bilateral aid, USAID has provided some assistance to the regional association formed by the ombudsmen, the Ibero-American Federation of Ombudsmen, whose executive secretariat is the Inter-American Institute of Human Rights. While the ombudsmen could be seen primarily as means of increasing 'access to justice', their variable roles and proactive positions seem to transcend this one category, and their potential as an independent force for improved social justice seems to merit a separate discussion. However, while the office of ombudsman generally enjoys high legitimacy and respect, there are concerns about the future of these offices.

---

[18] In addition to Cuba, this included Venezuela and Colombia.

[19] Argentina (enabling legislation introduced in 1993), Bolivia (1994), Brazil, Colombia (1992), Costa Rica (1992), Ecuador (1997), El Salvador (1992), Guatemala (1986), Honduras (1995), Mexico (1992), Nicaragua (1996, with first official named in 1999), Panama (1996), Paraguay (1995), Peru (1993) and Venezuela. In Argentina and Mexico, the office exists at both the national and subnational level. Ombudsmen officers also exist in six Caribbean countries, including Barbados, Guyana (1967), Haiti, Jamaica, St Luica and Trinidad and Tobago (1977), although they are not affiliated with the regional ombudsmen association and may not handle human rights cases.

Partly as a result of their success, the positions are becoming prized political appointments, and may increasingly be seen as stepping-stones to higher office. Office-seekers may become more interested in the position for personal advancement rather than as committed voices of citizens. Furthermore, the danger of politicisation is real and has already occurred in several countries. Budgets are insufficient and staffs badly need training in both substance and management. Perhaps most important, the HROs are trying to fill a large vacuum to provide government accountability across a huge range of issues. While the work is important, the offices will have to set very firm priorities and stick to them — not easy when both NGOs and the international community see them as capable institutions. These indigenous institutions are still in the process of defining their roles, with high expectations and credibility but in danger of politicisation and with serious financial and training needs. The international community's assistance in helping institutionalise these offices would be timely and appropriate.

7. Supporting civil society reformers

What differentiates USAID justice reform efforts from those of other large donors is reliance on non-governmental organisations: to advocate for reform, to implement reforms (usually with government institutions), and to monitor and provide oversight of government. The USAID 'lessons learned' literature on justice reform strongly recommends that civil society be a central component of reform. In fact, throughout its history in Latin America, USAID has provided much more direct funding to non-governmental than to governmental institutions. Supporting civil society is a crosscutting approach to problem solving, evident throughout this analysis.

'Civil society' clearly includes a vast array of institutions, from law schools, to business groups, to women and minority groups, human rights groups, professional associations and many other reform groups in every country supported by USAID. The earlier discussion of judicial independence in the Dominican Republic, for example, noted the agency's support for FINJUS, a broad coalition of business and reform groups, which took the lead in the passing and monitoring of reform legislation. In Peru the USAID mission has supported human rights NGOs which defend those unjustly jailed for terrorism, increase citizen access to justice and strengthen legal services to the poor. As an example, it provides funding for IPEDEHP, the Peruvian Institute for Education in Human Rights and Peace.[20] IPEDEHP was founded in 1985, as a member of the National Coordinator for Human rights, a coalition of over 50 NGOs that aimed to fight violence and support the rights of Peruvians. For

---

[20] For an evaluation and a comprehensive case study analysis, see Marcia Bernbaum (1999); also available from USAID.

its first ten years, it focused on training teachers in human rights and democracy; in 1996, USAID supported its expansion to the training of community leaders. The Dominican Republic and Peru examples illustrate different kinds of civil society support; every USAID mission has an important civil society component in its justice programme.

For both philosophic and practical reasons, USAID's concentration on civil society will remain at the heart of our programming. It is possible that there will be some shifting in the kind of civil society organisations most supported. As human rights becomes less of a problem, and justice reforms such as judicial independence, commercial code reform and defendant rights become more important, the spectrum of groups supported are more likely to include universities, business groups to a greater degree and professional associations such as lawyers' associations. Moreover, media training in justice areas has not generally been part of USAID programming, but with continued major reforms underway, the need for civic education and media sophistication on this topic is likely to become more important.

8. Anti-Corruption

The rise of democratic governance has brought an increase in reports of corruption leading to the perception that new democracies are more corrupt than the authoritarian governments that proceeded them. While this increase in reports may be attributed to a more open society with free press and improved access to information, there is no doubt that corruption is rampant in many Latin American countries. Corruption in the judicial system is particularly troublesome. Until citizens can be assured that the system is based upon an even playing field, where those with political or economic pull do not get preferential treatment in court, no new law or reform package can ensure a fair and equitable system. Establishing a corrupt-free judicial system is also important for economic development as investors and businesses realise the benefits of a reliable, predictable system free of individuals whim and the added costs of bribes.

USAID's extensive work in many Latin American countries to help develop and implement new penal laws and criminal procedures laws combats corruption by creating a more efficient justice system with reduced chances for corruption and appropriate sanctions for corrupt behaviour. In addition, USAID is supporting many other initiatives with explicit anti-corruption goals. In Ecuador and Honduras, special Anti-Corruption Units within the Prosecutor General/Public Ministry receive technical assistance to improve their ability to investigate and prosecute corruption cases. This includes the creation of anti-corruption strike forces that coordinate the efforts of judicial police, the office of the Controller General and public prosecutors.

In Guatemala, USAID supported the creation of the first Clerk of Courts office ever in a Latin American capital city. This office removes individual discretion by keeping a computerised inventory of its caseload, with a transparent distribution system. Previously, corrupt officials could be persuaded to 'lose' case files. (From 1 October 1996 to 31 August 1997, the Court system 'lost' 1,061 cases in Guatemala City alone). Under the new system, from 1 October 1998 to 31 August 1999, only five have been 'lost'. In addition, litigants can no longer 'shop' their cases to a favourite judge as they are automatically assigned and time limits are respected. The Clerk of Courts generates reliable statistics and reports on court actions, leading to a more transparent and accountable system.

Supporting special offices and units such as these is proving successful in the fight against corruption; however, no system is infallible. While justice systems can be reformed to reduce opportunities for corruption and to increase the likelihood of being caught and punished, loopholes in the system persist through which crooked officials can operate. Political will at the highest level must be fostered and maintained to fight corruption in the long term. Reforms must be permanent and sanctions enforced. This political commitment can best be achieved by an active and vigilant civil society that understands the benefits of a fair and effective judicial system and will not tolerate impunity.

Modern justice systems introduce mechanisms that ensure transparency and accountability. USAID and other donors will continue to support these reforms and special units, while also supporting checks and balances to guarantee that the mechanisms are indeed functioning. Such checks and balances include investigative journalism with a good knowledge of how the justice systems works, watchdog groups that oversee the courts and track the progress of important cases, and regular diagnostics of access to justice, its effectiveness and its equity.

9. Common justice approaches in democracy and economic development

Over the past two years, support within the agency for justice reform programmes has begun to expand well beyond its original constituency of those working in democratisation and human rights protection. The development community has begun to understand that the lack of a well-functioning justice system is an impediment to economic growth and investment, and that foreign and domestic businessmen consider corruption and the lack of transparent, stable rule of law as major disincentives to investment and employment. Trade and globalisation require a stable and transparent legal environment.

Investors and the development community have, of course, been aware that many governments do not have the capacity to fairly adjudicate claims, protect intellectual and physical property, or enforce contracts. What is new is the belief that something could actually be done about it. Now that governments are in fact reforming their systems, they are increasing investor demand for even more reform. At this point, developmental economists have become among the most fervent advocates of rule of law programmes, seeing them as an essential 'enabling condition' of sustained development in Latin America.[21]

The potential for joint effort among those focusing on democracy and those focusing on economic growth is great. Joint endeavours marrying their diverse expertise and approaches should foster better outcomes on both fronts, but will involve an integrated approach that has not yet developed. Some of the specific programming recommended by economists is already underway to some degree through democracy programmes. This includes legal analysis and research, legislative assistance in policy drafting, institutional support for organisations such as local law schools and bar associations and training programmes, alternative dispute resolution for commercial disputes and development of public administration and institutional development.

It is likely that the tightening of democracy and economic growth objectives will lead in the medium term to a significant shift in programming, particularly towards civil law and regulatory frameworks, which affect economic development directly, and to greater emphasis on legal processes related to property ownership. Equally significant, the US government distinction between support of criminal justice reform and civil reform will be rethought. The historical origins of this distinction are easy to understand, given USAID's support for human rights, and later US government interest in the drug war and corruption. The World Bank and IDB adopted the opposite approach, focusing on civil law. In fact, the World Bank has had a specific injunction against working in criminal justice.

At this point, USAID justice reform — and also reform by the banks — should encompass both, for a number of reasons. First, the same basic justice system is ultimately used for both civil and criminal law. The same courtrooms, the same judges and court personnel, the same administrative procedures are used for all cases. Reform in one area means reform of the whole system, and the reform is likely to be better if it considers the consequences for both criminal and civil justice. Justice schools and training also need an integrated approach. In addition, the balance between civil and criminal reform should be in equilibrium, which does not happen at present, since the larger donors are not working much in the criminal area. Finally, the two distinct approaches that exist today can lead to misunderstanding, donor competition and ultimately hurt the overall development of the justice system.

It is probable that USAID will move tentatively into some aspects of civil law, largely by identifying niches, such as property or trade, that seem impor-

---

[21] Leading proponents of this view are in USAID's Economic Growth Centre/Emerging Markets office, which has jointly sponsored conferences with the Democracy Centre on rule of law and synergies between the two sectors.

tant to both economic and democratic objectives, and will coordinate more closely with the large donor banks. This will require a much closer relationship than has been the case traditionally among the donors, however.

10. Regional Justice Institutions

The Latin American and Caribbean region is unique in the strength and number of regional institutions focusing on human rights and justice, and for more than twenty years USAID has had a transnational programme to provide some assistance to them. Similarities in political history, democratic transition and justice system reform in the 1980s and 1990s throughout Latin America make a transnational approach to justice feasible and cost-effective.

The Inter-American Commission on Human Rights (founded in 1970) and the Inter-American Court of Human Rights (founded in 1980), both established through the Organisation of American States, have protected individual human rights for several decades. USAID has not provided direct funding to these organisations, with a few exceptions, but they do receive US government funding through the OAS. In the late 1990s, in response to a Summit of the Americas mandate, USAID funded for two years the creation of a Special Reporter for Freedom of Expression, under the Inter-American Commission. (The US government continues to support this office through the US/OAS office). The Reporter's function is to promote freedom of expression and help protect journalists in the hemisphere who have become the target of violence.

Since its establishment over twenty years ago, USAID has supported the Inter-American Institute of Human Rights, whose basic purpose is to educate and conduct research in the area of human rights, broadly defined. This assistance has helped the institute assist countries in the consolidation of democracy through electoral assistance, courses, publications and seminars focusing on human rights, civil society strengthening and public institution reform. Its current emphasis on access to justice and inclusion of women and minorities into full citizen participation and rights continues to receive USAID financing. USAID has also provided early financing to ILANUD, the Latin American Institute for the Prevention of Crime and Treatment of the Offender, in Costa Rica, which provided invaluable assistance in the first stages of justice reform in Central America.

In response to the current wave of justice reform, and a mandate through the Summit of the Americas, in the year 2000 USAID allocated one million dollars to the establishment of a new regional organisation, the Justice Centre of the Americas, located in Santiago, Chile. The purpose of the centre is to help countries strengthen their national justice system, taking advantage of the knowledge of reform processes now being created throughout the hemisphere. It aims to serve as a clearinghouse for sources of information on justice reform; to strengthen the capacity to train justice personnel in the region; to promote interdisciplinary and comparative research, particularly in human rights, public security and economic and social development; and help improve national justice policies. The General Assembly of the OAS approved the statute for the Centre on 15 November 1999.

In addition to regional institutions, USAID is supporting less formal 'virtual' organisations and networks linking reformers across the hemisphere. In fact, even the new Justice Centre is envisioned primarily as a facilitator for sharing expertise and training, rather than as a central place where such expertise is located. IIDH has also become the secretariat for a number of networks, including the Federation of Ombudsmen, again reflecting the explosion of knowledge in the hemisphere in the area of human rights, justice reform and democratic consolidation. This networking magnifies the effect of national reforms, and helps foster and sustains national reform movements by putting reformers in touch with one another. No one organisation can hope to capture all the expertise in the region, and as the Internet and global information exchange further lower transaction costs and make communication easier, this 'expert facilitator' role is likely to become more and more important. Organisations such as IIDH capitalise on 'horizontal' or 'south-south' cooperation, fostering the sharing and development of expertise in the region in a way those bilateral programmes alone cannot.

Furthermore, the number of transnational non-governmental organisations and associations in areas related to justice and security is increasing rapidly; these become both consumers and participants in networks. For example, in Central America, the Central American Association of Chiefs of Police was founded in 1992 and the Central American Security Commission was renewed in 1994. In 1995, a Framework Agreement on Democratic Security was agreed upon. Hemispheric-wide associations of lawyers and human rights groups are also being established. Networking and association building is a growth industry at the transnational level.

Such efforts are further strengthened at hemispheric summit meetings. In the 1998 Santiago Summit of the Americas, the 34 heads of state committed themselves to the 'strengthening of justice systems and judiciaries' in the hemisphere. This was to include greater access to justice, criminal justice systems founded on judicial independence, effective prosecutors, defenders and oral proceedings, support for family courts, and the establishment of a Justice Studies Center of the Americas to support national reform programmes through assistance in training judicial personnel, information exchanges and technical cooperation. The human rights portions of the Plan of Action — which includes specific agreements to provide equality under the law for women and all citizens, release prisoners never brought to trial but who have been in prisons longer than if they had been found guilty, and other provisions — should have a direct impact not only on protecting human rights, but on the entire administration of justice system. At the time of writing, the next summit was scheduled for the spring of 2001 and continues to push for national and transnational justice reform. USAID has been fully engaged in the policy discussions leading to the summit, and in translating summit mandates into new hemisphere-wide programmes.

Conclusions

In Latin America and the Caribbean, the US Agency for International Development has supported justice reform in Latin America and the Caribbean for several decades through a wide variety of programmes, and participated in the 'take off' of this sector of democratic development. In some countries, it has provided long term, consistent institutional assistance; in others, shorter-term technical assistance and networking assistance. Given the importance of this sector to democratic consolidation, and USAID's vast experience with it, the agency is likely to continue to play an important role in justice reform.

Justice reform is a dynamic sector for countries in the hemisphere, and USAID needs to continually rethink its strategy, both in terms of arenas of action and in terms of approach. It seems clear, for example, that much more attention needs to be given to justice reforms that affect trade, investment and globalisation. This probably means more emphasis on transparency and accountability, judicial independence, civil and property law and harmonisation of legal systems. In addition, citizen outrage at high crime rates, criminal impunity and high levels of violence may lead us to expand programmes such as the Ecuador project focusing on domestic violence and women's issues. More significantly, UUSAID needs to rethink, with other US government agencies, the thrust of its police reform efforts. Support for police modernisation needs to concentrate not only on professionalisation, but also on developing the community linkages essential to lowering crime rates. In addition to these two critical areas, USAID's emphasis on access to justice, including the rights of prisoners and defendants, as well as traditionally marginalised populations, may need to be strengthened.

USAID's approach, and that of other US government agencies in justice, must take better account of changes in the donor community. The growing involvement of the Inter-American Development Bank in this sector is an example. Recently, for example, the IDB gave its first loan in Argentina for a large community-oriented police modernisation programme. The new directions IDB may take, as well as its increasing financial support, will have an impact on USAID's choices. It is already leading to much greater collaboration, through both donor coordination groups at the national level and high-level policy discussions in Washington. As the World Bank also increases its interest in this sector, donor coordination becomes even more critical. USAID's grant financing, usually to non-government organisations, can provide a useful counterpart to the governmental loans provided by these donors.

Long term trends outside the justice sector will also have a strong impact on future USAID justice programming. Renewed interest in regional integration within Central America, for example, has important implications for justice system harmonisation and transparency. The increasing sophistication and broad-based nature of justice reform coalitions gives USAID opportunities to have a greater, more sustained impact on reforms than in the past. New technologies and communications capacities may lead to a greater emphasis on supporting networks and regional training. In another vein, if there is a rise of leaders elected in part on a strong 'law and order' platform, with less commitment to democratic institutions and a fair justice system, USAID programming must be able to adapt its programmes accordingly. So far, USAID justice programming in the region has been flexible enough to deal with such challenges as they emerge.

USAID will continue to have a strong commitment to justice reform in the hemisphere. The US government has a strong national interest in justice reform for objectives such as expanded international trade and investment, international criminal justice and drug-fighting efforts. Most important, however, supporting democracy in the region remains a critical US foreign policy goal, and justice reform critical to democracy. Until democratic governments in the hemisphere are able to make their justice systems work effectively and fairly, they cannot regain the promise, lustre and legitimacy they held when first brought into office to end military rule. In short, unless democratic governments focus more attention and resources on justice sector reform, the promise of democratic consolidation will remain unfulfilled.

Appendix 3.1

Inventory of USAID Assistance in
Justice and Human Rights Programming by Area

Italics indicate a programme previously supported by USAID
Note: This inventory is not exhaustive and is for representative purposes only

Revision of Legal Framework, Code Reform[22]	Judicial Independence Professionalisation, Judicial Councils	Judiciary Training[23]
Bolivia	*Bolivia*	*Argentina*
Colombia	*Colombia*	Bolivia
Dominican Republic	Dominican Republic	*Brazil*
Eastern Caribbean	Ecuador	*Chile*
Ecuador	*El Salvador*	Colombia
El Salvador	Guatemala	*Costa Rica*
Guatemala	*Haiti*	Dominican Republic
Guyana	Honduras	Eastern Caribbean
Haiti	Mexico	Ecuador
Honduras	Peru	El Salvador
Nicaragua		Guatemala
Panama		Guyana
Paraguay		Haiti
Peru		Honduras
		Mexico
		Nicaragua
		Panama
		Paraguay

---

[22] Constitutional reform, new Criminal Procedures Codes reform and reform of organic laws. Numerous other countries in the region have undertaken legislative reforms, independent of USAID programming: Argentina, Chile, Costa Rica, Mexico, Uruguay and Venezuela.
[23] Includes, but is not limited to, training of judges, prosecutors and defenders. Training varies by country.

National Judicial Schools	Establishing/ Strengthening the Public Ministry	NGO Strengthening (for justice reform)
Argentina	*Bolivia*	Dominican Republic
Bolivia	Colombia	Ecuador
Chile	Dominican Republic	*El Salvador*
Colombia	Ecuador	Guatemala
Costa Rica	El Salvador	Guyana
Dominican Republic	Guatemala	*Haiti*
El Salvador	*Haiti*	Honduras
Guatemala	Honduras	*Mexico*
Haiti	Nicaragua	Panama
Honduras	Paraguay	Peru
Mexico		
Nicaragua		
Panama		
Peru		

Model Courts for Oral Trial Procedures	Legal Assistance, Access to Justice	Creating/Assisting Ombudsmen
Colombia	*Argentina*	*Bolivia*
Dominican Republic	Colombia	El Salvador
El Salvador	Dominican Republic	Guatemala
Guatemala	*Ecuador*	Nicaragua
Guyana	Guatemala	Peru
Haiti	*Guyana*	
Honduras	Haiti	
	Nicaragua	
	Peru	

Court Administration, Case Tracking	Alternative Dispute Resolution	Law Schools, Universities
Argentina	*Argentina*	*Bolivia*
Bolivia	*Bolivia*	Ecuador
Chile	Colombia	El Salvador
Colombia	*Costa Rica*	Guatemala
Dominican Republic	Eastern Caribbean	Mexico
Eastern Caribbean	Ecuador	Peru
El Salvador	El Salvador	
Guatemala	Guatemala	
Guyana	Guyana	
Haiti	Mexico	
Honduras	*Nicaragua*	
Nicaragua	*Panama*	
	Paraguay	
	Peru	

Police Assistance	Creating/Strengthening Public Defence
Bolivia	*Bolivia*
Brazil	Colombia
Colombia	Dominican Republic
Dominican Republic	El Salvador
El Salvador	Guatemala
Guatemala	*Honduras*
Haiti	Nicaragua
Honduras	
Nicaragua	
Panama	

Appendix 3.2

Outline of USAID Administration of Justice Programmes — Latin America and the Caribbean*

Central America

El Salvador

In El Salvador, USAID has helped to catalyse support for the drafting and passage of important criminal justice system reforms. Starting in financial year 2000 funding will be provided to operationalise the newly passed criminal procedures code by strengthening the relationship between police, prosecutors, and other actors in the system. The objective is to help all justice system personnel to better understand their roles under the new code. The curriculum of the judicial school will be revised to reflect the training needs of the new code. Likewise, law school curricula will be reformed at selected law schools. Capacity of local institutions (NGOs) and the media will be established or strengthened to monitor progress in key cases of impunity involving influential Salvadoreans. Four legal clinics will be established in four rural municipalities to improve access to justice to poor populations. Lastly, greater public confidence in the justice system to implement the new criminal procedures code and provide fairer, more transparent justice will be promoted and measured.

FY 2000 Funding: $3 million
Life of Project Funding (since 1997): $6.2 million

Guatemala

USAID justice activities in Guatemala have promoted greater access to justice, particularly in marginalised regions, and increased efficiency and transparency in justice administration. The USAID-inspired local 'justice centre' concept serves to coordinate police, prosecutors and judges in selected municipalities and promote more efficient administration of justice through the use of alternative dispute resolution. Assistance to the judiciary has succeeded in promoting an equitable and transparent case distribution system, reducing the potential for corruption, relieving congestion and permitting the generation of much needed judicial statistics. The Clerk of Courts office in Guatemala City — in its first year of operation — has reduced 'lost' cases from over 1,000 to just one. Nevertheless, the justice system still requires major reform including better coordination at the policy level among key institutions in order to address its inability to provide timely and effective justice.

FY 2000 Funding: $2.5 million
Life of Project Funding (since 1997): $11.4 million

---

* This appendix was written by Norma Parker, former Deputy Assistant for USAID/LAC

Honduras

The rule of law programme in Honduras supports the Public Ministry, justice sector reforms, strengthening of Supreme Court and lower courts and public participation in the justice system. USAID has helped advance the major reform of the Criminal Procedures Code that will modernise the judicial system through an oral advocacy process. Now passed by the Congress and signed into law, USAID will help provide the training and technical assistance to put the new code into practice and implement it effectively. The challenge will be to overcome the resistance of justice sector personnel who have become used to and benefited from the existing system; and to train key personnel in the functions they must fulfil to make the new system work. USAID also supports administrative reforms and case tracking systems to improve the speed and efficiency of judicial processes in both the Public Ministry and the courts.

FY 2000 Funding: $0.6 million
Life of Project Funding (since 1997): $2.0 million

Nicaragua

USAID facilitated achievement of a working consensus among the Court, the Assembly and the Attorney General on a high-level commission to review and recommend essential legislation for modernisation of the justice sector. The Organic Law for the Public Ministry is being passed as part of the constitutional reforms, creating an independent Prosecutor's Office and allowing for modern criminal procedural reform. A new Criminal Code is pending congressional approval, and a law (Administrative Litigation) to remove de-facto immunity from Executive Branch agencies was drafted and is under discussion. A Public Defender's office was inaugurated and is functioning in Managua. The Human Rights Ombudsman was appointed. USAID will finance development of new codes such as administrative litigation, penal, criminal procedure, and the creation of an independent prosecutor's office (Public Ministry), plus training programmes to assure proper implementation. It will continue to strengthen the public defender's office, the attorney general's office, the Public Ministry once formed, and support court administration.

FY 2000 Funding: $3.6
Life of Project Funding (since 1997): $ 7.7 million

Panama

Since Panama's return to democracy in 1990, efforts have been undertaken to re-establish independent Panamanian judicial institutions, strengthen judicial operations and modernise laws. Prospects for making an impact have improved with the entry into the justice sector of substantial donor assistance from the IDB and Spain. Complementing IDB and Spanish assistance, USAID is focusing in particular on completing the programme to strengthen the relationship between police and prosecutors and initiating new activities in the area of civil and commercial law.

FY 2000 Funding: $1.0 million
Life of Project Funding (since 1997): $3.1 million

Mexico

USAID's rule of law activities support Mexican initiatives to make the administration of justice more efficient, effective and accessible. USAID is supporting a detailed diagnostic of the Mexican court system that will provide recommendations for improved court administration and prosecution of cases. USAID also supports improved judicial education and professionalisation of judges through a sub-grant to the National Autonomous University's (UNAM) Judicial Research Institute to develop a model curriculum for a Master's in Judicial Law. The grant also funds scholarships for 41 state judges from four states to study at the Iberoamericano University Law School in Leon, Guanajuato, exchanging experiences and building momentum for reform.

With USAID support, an NGO in Guadalajara, the Centre for Attention to Crime Victims (CENAVID) opened and staffed a centre for court-annexed mediation in the public defender's office of the state court of Jalisco. With on-going USAID support the centre provides mediation services for family and civil law cases. Ten other state courts have requested technical assistance from CENAVID for assistance to open their own court-annexed mediation centres.

FY 2000 Funding: $1.5 million
Life of Project Funding: $4.2 million

Peru

Since withdrawing direct support to the judiciary after a 1992 government *autogolpe* eliminated judicial independence, USAID has spent $1.6 million to support human rights NGOs working to defend those unjustly jailed for terrorism, to increase citizen access to justice. In addition, USAID has bolstered the Office of the Human Rights Ombudsman (OHRO) and has strengthened the Ministry of Justice's defender programme. Additionally, USAID-sponsored legal clinics provided free legal and conciliation services to the poor in more than 86,000 cases, and 32 of the 40 legal clinics and conciliation centres registered to date with the Ministry of Justice have been supported by USAID. Within the democracy strategy, USAID has emphasised broader citizen participation in democratic processes through greater access to justice and citizens better prepared to exercise their rights and responsibilities. A new democracy strategy is being prepared for implementation after the April 2001 presidential elections.

FY 2000 Funding: $0.8 million
Life of Project Funding (since 1997): $ 2.7 million

Ecuador

USAID's strategy in Ecuador assists public sector justice institutions and promotes the active participation of Civil Society Organisations to establish a more effective and fair criminal justice system that better fights corruption. With USAID assistance, the establishment by the Prosecutor General's Office of a 'Financial Crimes Task Force' played a key role in jailing one of the most powerful bankers for the fraudulent use of public finances. A new Criminal Procedures Code, which now includes important modifications proposed by the Presidency, will allow effective investigation of criminal cases. An agreement was signed between the Prosecutor General and the National Judicial Police to cooperate in crime investigations. NGO services and access to justice for women's and indigenous groups underwent a significant expansion and institutionalisation during 1999. A total of 32,432 victims of domestic violence accessed legal services; and 660 families used ADR and related legal services. After the recent change in government the mission is reviewing its democracy strategy.

FY 2000 Funding: $1.5 million
Life of Project Funding (since 1997): $4.1 million

Bolivia

In the last ten years the US government has helped Bolivia make significant strides in strengthening and modernising administration of justice through technical assistance provided to the Attorney General and the Public Defender's Office in case tracking, court administration and public access. Currently, USAID is focusing resources on four programme areas. First, the programme sought and succeeded in promoting the passage of codes key to justice reform. In March 1999, the Government of Bolivia adopted a new Criminal Procedures Code that will overhaul the criminal justice system and limit opportunities for corruption. USAID coordinated with other donors to facilitate legislative committee discussions on devising a two-year phase-in plan that will equip key judicial institutions to use the new procedures correctly and efficiently. Two years ago, with USAID assistance the Bolivian Congress approved two important judicial reform laws, the Ombudsman Law and the law that established the Judicial Council. The latter reform facilitated the Bolivian judiciary's move towards a more merit-based appointment process for judges, the second programme's focus area. The programme intends to increase public confidence in the justice system by professionalising judges and establishing a merit-based judicial career system. Third, the programme increases the legal security and predictability of the justice system by promoting the establishment of a Constitutional Court. Finally, the programme increases access to justice by expanding the Public Defenders system and the provision of alternative dispute resolution services. Two years ago, the number of cases handled by public defenders in nine judicial districts exceeded the target figure by 30 per cent for judicial cases and by 28 per cent for police cases.

FY 2000 Funding: $3.9 million
Life of Project Funding (since 1997): $8.4 million

Paraguay

Since emerging from a 34-year dictatorship in 1989, Paraguay has been steadily improving citizen access to justice. USAID has provided assistance to enact a new Penal Code, which went into effect in 1998, and a new Criminal Procedures Code, which went into effect in 1999. These are two of the four major legal reforms targeted by USAID that have modernised the judicial sector by moving toward a mixed system which will include oral trials.

FY 2000 Funding: $1.1 million
Life of Project Funding (since 1997): $ 3.2 million

Venezuela

In Venezuela USAID is considering a focused training programme to implement the new Venezuelan Criminal Procedures Code enacted in 1999. The new code replaces the inquisitorial system with a move toward a more adversarial system. Under the new system, judges cease to be investigators and become arbiters of the law, prosecutors and defence attorneys confront one another in open court, and, in the most serious cases, lay juries render verdicts. US-based training would target key actors vital in successfully implement the new code — judges, defenders and appropriate civil society organisations. This activity would complement prosecutor training being done under the International Narcotics and Law Enforcement (INL) funded Office of Professional Development and Training (OPDAT) programme.

Proposed funding: $0.5

Colombia

In support of the Government of Colombia's *Plan Colombia*, USAID will build upon and expand the existing $38 million programme to improve transparency and increase citizen access to the Colombian judicial system. To help improve the administration of justice, USAID will support the Superior Judiciary Council to expand the pilot oral courtrooms to a greater number of locations and will publish court procedures for the oral public courts, as well as training judges, prosecutors, defenders and lawyers in the new procedures. Training will be coordinated with the bench and the bar associations. Additionally, USAID will help the government of Colombia improve its capacity to have the results of forensic investigations recognised by courts and to improve the definition of standards of proof. The case tracking system put into place in 1993 with USAID and IDB assistance will be revived and expanded.

To improve access to the judicial system, USAID will help the Colombian government expand the capacity of the Public Defender's Office to represent poor defendants by increasing the number of public defenders to 3,000 from the present 1,300. To expand access to the justice system USAID will assist establishing 75 new *Casas de Justicia* in marginal communities. The intent is to bring adjudication of minor civil and criminal cases into the reach of persons who cannot afford to bring a case in formal court. The *Casas* are maintained through the municipal budget, supplemented by the national ministries whose staff work in the *Casa*.

Proposed FY 2000 Funding: $21.5 million; FY 2001 $16.0 million (Supplemental)
LOP Funding: $37.5 million (Supplemental)

Haiti

In Haiti, USAID's assistance focuses on broadening access to justice of the poorest segments of Haitian society and improving the administration and management of the justice system. Legal assistance and public education is provided to the poor through local NGOs, Bar Associations, and — in the future — through the Office of the Human Rights Ombudsman. Assistance to the Ministry of Justice is improving case management, reducing case backlogs and improving budgeting and administration within the judicial system. Specifically, OPDAT is developing a standardised case tracking system. Training, also an important part of US government assistance, is provided to judges and prosecutors in the model prosecutors' office in areas such as investigative techniques and case preparation. Additionally, USAID is encouraging a Haitian human rights monitoring and oversight capability through the UN to ensure that abuses of human rights are monitored, documented and publicised, and that greater deterrents to abuse are established.

FY 2000 Funding: $2.5 million
Life of Project Funding (since 1997): $ 20.0 million

Dominican Republic

Since USAID began supporting justice sector reforms and modernisation beginning in 1997, remarkable advances have been made in strengthening judicial organisations and rule of law. Modest USAID resources have successfully catalysed Dominican state and civil society funded initiatives to modernise the criminal justice system while deepening independence of the judiciary from special interests. Strong coordination between key Dominican government officials and an active and lively civil society has defended the justice sector reform agenda from anti-reform backlashes. The achievements of the past two years are unprecedented. Key achievements over the last year include: the enactment of a Judicial Career Law; the creation of an Inspector General of Tribunals; modernisation of the offices of the National District Public Ministry (National Prosecutors); the drafting of a Career Law for prosecutors based on best regional practices and presented to the Executive for approval; the creation of a state-funded Public Defence organisation; the drafting and presentation to congress of a Public Defence system bill; the drafting of a modern Criminal Code and Criminal Procedures Codes, based on the accusatorial system, in a joint venture between government and civil society; administrative improvements in 22 trial courts and all prosecutor offices in the National District; the reduction by half of time awaiting trial in the National District (this is projected to be reduced further with the introduction of a USAID-funded automated criminal case tracking system); and the design of a community-based conciliation and mediation centre established with programme assistance and Dominican government funding, which will be the model for a future national system. This and other alternative dispute mechanisms have reduced the inflow of criminal cases by more than half in the National District.

FY 2000 Funding: $3.0 million
Life of Project Funding (since 1997): $8.5 million

Jamaica

USAID recognises that in Jamaica, violent crime is one of the principal deterrents to economic growth and investment. Furthermore it directly reduces the quality of life for the citizens who must cope with a reduced sense of personal and proprietary security. With over 800 murders last year, Jamaica had the highest murder rate in the region, concentrated within 15 inner city neighbourhoods in the Kingston/St. Andrew metropolitan area. USAID is designing a project in FY2000 that will address this problem combining assistance in community policing and alternative dispute resolution with activities aimed at increasing employment and entrepreneurial opportunities with the inner city.

Proposed funding level: $1.5 million
Life of Project Funding: $3.0 million

Eastern Caribbean

USAID is launching a regional programme in the Eastern Caribbean to assist in the alleviation of large case backlogs in the justice systems of the Organisation of Eastern Caribbean States (OECS) countries through improved court efficiency and management, and the introduction of alternative dispute resolution (ADR) mechanisms. In addressing the problem of inefficient case management systems and weak administrative processes in court registries, USAID will provide alternative models of court reporting systems and re-engineer court administration procedures to rationalise functions and implement automated record keeping systems. The increased use of ADR will help to channel cases from the formal legal system to more informal settings where they can be amicably settled. At the policy level the lack of any real growth in budget allocations made by OECS governments to their justice systems will be pursued.

FY 2000 Funding: $ 2.0 million
Life of Project Funding: $4.0 million

CHAPTER 4

Legal and Judicial Reform: The Role of Civil Society in the Reform Process

Maria Dakolias

Legal and Judicial Reform

Many countries are today implementing legal and judicial reforms as part of their overall development programmes. There is a strong realisation that economic reform requires an updated legal framework and a well-functioning judiciary that can interpret and enforce laws in an equitable and efficient manner.[1] A well-functioning judiciary should provide predictability and impartiality and resolve cases in reasonable time. It should also be accessible to the public. Many developing countries find, however, that their judiciary is not consistent in its conflict resolution, and that it carries a large backlog of cases, causing the erosion of individual and property rights. Delays affect both the fairness and the efficiency of the system; they impede access to the courts by the public. To solve these problems, governments across the world are launching legal and judicial reforms. Their aim is to improve access to justice by increasing the quality, efficiency and transparency of dispute resolution. This is part of economic and social development to achieve a judicial system which is efficient and transparent, provides quality decisions and access to the public. In this way, the overall objective is to create trust in a judicial system that is both independent and accountable.

One way to improve access to justice is through participation of civil society in the reform process. This process of change formulates the legal and judicial reform programme for the long term. While many countries are responding to the calls for legal and judicial reform, modernisation cannot be completed in one five-year project. Reform requires both cultural change and a systematic change in the delivery of justice,[2] which, in turn, require countries to develop a programme of stages for the reform process. Another way to improve access to justice is civil society participation in formal legal and judicial reform programmes; that is, using law to promote social change through legal information and education, legal assistance and law reform. Finally, both the reform process and formal programmes can benefit from greater interconnection among groups within civil society, thus sharing

---

[1] For an examination of the hypothesis that effective judicial systems are requisite to optimal market functioning, see Robert M. Sherwood et al. (1994) p. 101. The authors estimate that a country that attempts economic liberalisation under a weak judicial system suffers 'at least a 15 percent penalty in their growth momentum', p. 113.

[2] See John Henry Merryman, David S. Clark and Lawrence M. Friedman (1979).

experiences and amplifying their voices.

'Civil society' is broadly understood here as all organisational activity that falls outside the orbits of the government or for-profit sectors.[3] Civil society is a highly diverse entity that is made up of civic associations with widely differing objectives, memberships, institutional forms and organisational cultures. Such diverse interests and actors require, in some cases, that hard choices be made by donor organisations. It is therefore difficult to generalise about civil society and the term should not be equated only with non-governmental organisations (NGOs). Some of the forms that civil society takes include NGOs, human rights organisations, trade unions, business associations, religious bodies, academic institutions, student organisations, professional organisations, ethnic lobbies and community groups.

Inclusion of Actors in the Process of Reform

Many different actors are involved in the reform process: the judiciary, the executive and legislative branches of government, the legal profession, bar associations, academia, the business community and civil society, among others. Each actor is important. Very often the assumption is that the judiciary is the main actor in the reform of justice. However, for complimentary legal reform, the legislature is crucial. In addition, the legislature can play an active role in supporting judicial reform.

In the same way, civil society is just as important to the process of reform as the judiciary itself. There is a need to enable different voices to be heard, especially from weaker groups. Diagnosis of the judicial sector by various actors allows a more open dialogue and helps to make government aware of voices of the weaker parts of society. Tension among the various actors may appear in various instances; indeed it is common either between civil society and the government or the executive and the judiciary. Balancing these actors is crucial and co-ordination among them is key to ensuring commitment and ownership in the programmes. Building co-ordination among the appropriate actors allows for greater participation in the reform process; it is this participation that is key to achieving consensus on reforms and provides greater probability of success.

Judicial reform is a long-term process that requires building support among stakeholders and taking into account vested interests. Any programme of reform often includes, among other things: court modernisation; legal reform; increasing alternative dispute resolution mechanisms; training for judges, court personnel, lawyers, students and civil society; and improving access to justice. Judges and lawyers, due to their traditional culture, are often not accustomed to change and seldom initiate reform themselves. The process of reform in-

---

3 World Bank (1998) p. 3.

cludes, therefore, different actors active in the push for judicial reform. Only together will the more difficult reforms take place.

In addition to respect for governance structures, coordination is important during any reform process, and particularly when the actors include international and bilateral development organisations that are financing part of the reform process. With the increased emphasis on governance and accountability, there is greater importance on governance structures. If such structures are weak, institution building is also necessary to ensure sustainability. If such structures are also known for a lack of independence, there is often considerably greater concern that reforms will not be on solid ground.[4]

Citizens are the users of the legal and judicial system, and they rely on the system to enforce their property and individual rights. It is therefore imperative that civil society be one of the main actors in judicial reform, as it can act as a voice for the concerns of the public. A well-developed civil society can potentially influence the government in two ways: 1) by enhancing political responsiveness by gathering and expressing the public's wishes through non-governmental forms of association, and 2) by safeguarding public freedom by limiting the government's ability to impose arbitrary rule.[5] Civil society action can increase government accountability and contribute to good governance. Government institutions which have a mandate to serve or distribute entitlements to citizens can be held accountable for discriminatory or arbitrary distribution.

While there is a growing sense of identity among civil society organisations which transcends international boundaries, specific country circumstances can mean considerable differences in the prominence and roles that civil society plays.[6] Therefore relationships between the different sectors of civil society and the government become all the more important.[7] Such relationships should be taken into account during a reform process in order to determine the type of role that civil society can play. In some cases, it will be merely to educate society in general, while in others it could be a more active role.

Legal and Judicial Reform Plan — Ownership and Commitment from the Judiciary and Civil Society

Ownership and commitment is not only needed from the government but also from civil society in order to make the judicial reform process legitimate. Vested interests will often prevent structural reforms from happening. If the

---

[4] One example is Peru. See Lawyers Committee for Human Rights (2000).
[5] Clark et al. (1998) p. 2.
[6] World Bank (1998) p. 3. For instance, some countries still have relative little NGO activity and other sectors of civil society are more prominent, such as community groups, labour movements, or religious organisations. In other places, NGOs are more prominent.
[7] *Ibid.*

judiciary is left to its own devices it might limit reforms to infrastructure and information systems which only provide temporary solutions, especially when corruption is prevalent. Civil society and other actors can help to press for difficult structural reforms, though they may not speak with one voice about what reforms are necessary.

Developmental reform requires long-term planning to ensure that a holistic approach is followed. This should lead to greater co-ordination among stakeholders as well as donors, particularly as there are many different actors/stakeholders and in some cases as many donors in the field. Such co-ordination allows governments to better organise reform programmes and allows donors to be up front about where they can help. In addition, co-ordination is crucial to avoid duplication of efforts since resources are scarce. The process of building co-ordination and involving the appropriate actors should also ensure commitment and ownership of reforms. More and more governments are realising that broader participation is key to achieving consensus on reforms and that such consensus provides greater ownership and a higher probability of success. In addition, participation by civil society in the reform process, especially in the development of an overall plan, may improve both law and justice within society and ensure that the poor are specifically taken into account.

Participation in the planning process is needed not only from the government but also from a vibrant civil society; ownership and commitment are required from both in order to make the process legitimate. Although such inclusion may require lengthy preparation time in order to reach an effective level of cooperation, in the long run such a process may prevent reversals of the reforms in the future. In some countries, government reforms occur on the basis of Presidential Decree, and though this may be speedier and more effective in the short term, in the long term it may have higher social costs and may mean that the voices of the citizens, especially the poor, are not taken into account. In many countries public trust in the judiciary is weak, but civil society's ties to a range of communities can help to strengthen the public's confidence. Civil society groups have also given voice to different perspectives and experiences and often help to bring to the surface the more difficult issues. Civil society can make governments listen and can help secure greater sustainability in the reform process by promoting more participatory approaches. Successful partnerships demand effective communication — legal and judicial reform is a long-term undertaking which requires a consistent and constructive exchange of ideas. Systematic dialogue has also contributed to overcoming communities' deep-rooted mistrust of both NGOs and government agencies in some projects. Addressing questions and issues as they are raised, as well as having direct access to middle and senior-level managers, contributes to effective working relationships and problem-solving.

Another pressing issue is that many aspects of judicial reform are contentious and need pressure from actors outside the governmental realm. Many judicial reforms attempt to make legal procedures more efficient and transparent, partly by redistributing responsibilities. They also seek to improve access, efficiency and quality of the delivery of justice. Where there is an entrenched network of corruption, many actors will clearly oppose such reforms: judges or staff members may resent losing control over procedures that are a source of illicit income.[8] They could slow reform by openly opposing it, or by covet interferance. As a result, civil society has been assigned an ever-increasing role in ensuring accountability and transparency in information and practices.

Corruption scholars have further argued that corruption slows reform by providing sticking plaster solutions, thus detracting from the urgency of fixing the underlying structural problems.[9] If companies are effectively able to bribe their way through certain procedures, they will have less incentive to lobby for change. Moreover, corruption also hurts the poor to a far greater degree.

Legal and judicial reform activities have benefited from the assets of civil society. For example, World Bank Judicial Sector Assessments are often conducted by a combination of academics, researchers, government officials and NGO staff in borrowing countries when there is interest in judicial reform. These assessments permit greater dialogue with the government on the issues involved and may bring up matters that had not previously been considered. In one such case with the World Bank's Ecuador Sector Assessment, the issue of domestic violence was raised by women's organisations, resulting in the inclusion of a special activity in the project to provide legal aid for poor women. The strong grassroots links and language skills that such organisations often have make them valuable partners in this work.

In addition, the World Bank's efforts to develop National Judicial Reform Action Plans also benefit from NGO involvement. These plans set the stage, as discussed previously, in describing the long-term goals of legal and judicial reform with respect to priorities as well as donor involvement. Here, NGO participation ranges from consultation in identifying problem areas, obstacles and strategies, to actually preparing the entire plans themselves, as mentioned in the case of Ecuador.

Building Civil Society Participation in the Process[10]

NGOs can play an important role in the judicial reform process, and one region where they have been particularly active is Latin America. Until the mid-1960s NGO activities in Latin America were largely limited to charitable welfare, with the intention of helping to relieve suffering until the development

---

8 See Edgardo Buscaglia (1997) pp. 42–3
9 Robin Theobald (1990).
10 David C. Korten (1991) pp. 26–9.

efforts of official agencies could improve conditions. In the 1970s NGO activity became highly politicised and NGOs became committed to strengthening civil society, styling themselves as a bulwark against the political and economic oppression perpetrated by the state. In the 1980s the growing democratisation process led to more community-based organisations and social movements promoting the interests of ethnic minority groups, women and ecology, broadening the scope of participation and issue-consciousness. Although there has tended to be some tension in the relationships between NGOs and the government which has been overcome only gradually, cooperative initiatives have become relatively common. Furthermore, Latin American NGOs demonstrate a growing interest in forming national and international networks through which they can co-ordinate their efforts in support of social transformation. This collective commitment of NGOs to pluralism and the strengthening of civil society is an important theme, which can contribute to improved governance.

One area where NGO participation has increased in recent years is in the administration of justice. With greater democratisation in Latin America, NGOs have been created to participate in the reform process and push for the more difficult reforms. This effort has broadened both the scope of participation in the region as well as the scope of the reforms themselves. Citizens, especially the poor, have less access to information and collective action can be difficult, although through NGOs such voices and concerns can be heard more effectively. Individually, and sometimes collectively, citizens may fear reprisals from voicing their concerns, particularly about issues of law and justice if the concerns are related to judges, lawyers and the police. Although these important issues go to the very heart of their individual and property rights, harassment by the police can be a reality.

NGOs have emerged in Latin America focusing on the area of legal and judicial reform. Their activities centre on such issues as improving access to justice and legal aid programmes, strengthening alternative dispute resolution and mediation facilities, enhancing professional development and training, increasing the awareness of legal and judicial reform issues, improving technical and management assistance and conducting research on the issues and practices in the field. It is probably most common for organisations to span a number of different issues, for instance, both training people to know their rights and understand the judicial system, as well as providing legal aid services and mediation mechanisms.

One of the key objectives of legal and judicial reform is improving access to justice. That is, to use law to improve conditions and promote equality. One way to do this is using law to promote social change through legal information and education, legal assistance and law reform. Legal aid can take many forms including private attorneys providing pro bono services, a system of 'judicare' which entitles eligible people, based on income, to use private lawyers, legal insurance or prepaid legal services for eligible parties, staff attorneys who specialise in public interest law, law school clinics and non-governmental public interest organisations to protect the legal rights of groups or causes. Public interest organisations work to use law to change public opinion, to advocate law reform and litigate cases. Public interest litigation is an integral part of holistic social change that also includes community mobilisation, leadership, media outreach, policy analysis and empirical research. This approach has been used in many countries through assistance from the United States Agency for International Development (USAID), as well as the Ford Foundation since the 1960s.

The World Bank is a relatively new participant in legal and judicial reform. It began its activities in the early 1990s and during the decade its strategy evolved with a broad spectrum of activities in different countries. In the beginning the Bank expressed its strategy as being focused on commercial law and judicial reform aimed at resolving commercial disputes. However, by the mid-1990s a project in Ecuador was prepared to address some issues related to access to justice. This project is still under implementation, however, the early results are positive and may serve as a basis of discussion as to how future programmes will be developed. At the very least the legal aid activities financed under the Ecuador judicial reform project indicate the need to work in parallel with the judiciary and civil society.

The projects have evolved over time and the Bank is learning how to better include the many different actors in legal and judicial reform. Several organisations representing civil society are involved in the process of reforming and modernising Ecuador's judicial sector. Those organisations have pushed forward many initiatives designed to facilitate access to justice for underprivileged social sectors. This came at a time when there was more NGO involvement in World Bank projects generally. Popular participation is increasingly recognised as an essential ingredient in achieving effective and sustainable development, and NGOs have played an important role in promoting participatory approaches in Bank-financed projects. The World Bank defines NGOs[11] as 'private organisations that pursue activities to relieve suffer-

---

[11] There are many different types of NGOs, varying in size, capabilities and focus, and the term generally applies to any organisation that is independent of any government and is not operated for profit. The World Bank makes further distinctions between national and international organisations and local grassroots or community-based organisations (CBOs), and also between advocacy and operational NGOs, though this distinction is more blurred. *International* organisations are usually based in a developed country and carry out operations in more than one developing country. *National* organisations operate in individual developing countries. These types of NGOs are usually formed to serve others, and are intermediary participants in the development process between the CBOs and institutions such as the World Bank or government. They would typically be contracted to design projects, deliver services, or conduct research. They often work in partnership with CBOs by either channelling resources to them or

ing, promote the interests of the poor, protect the environment, provide basic social services, or undertake community development'.[12] While there had been some involvement of NGOs in World Bank projects in the 1970s, official relations did not begin until 1981 when the Bank adopted its first 'Operational Policy note on NGOs' and the NGO-World Bank Committee was established to discuss ways that the Bank could increase NGO involvement in Bank-financed projects.[13] In the mid-1980s, advocacy NGOs concerned with poverty and the environment became vocally critical of the World Bank and many urged increased Bank collaboration with developing country NGOs in operational work. This led the World Bank to establish an institution-wide effort to expand its work with NGOs, and in 1989, Operational Directive 14.70 on collaboration with NGOs was introduced. Its purpose was to set out a framework for involving NGOs in World Bank-supported projects.[14] Since then, NGO participation in Bank-financed projects has increased steadily.[15]

Consistent with this, the Ecuador project finances a Law and Justice fundto promote and support initiatives aimed at assisting those Ecuadorian social

---

providing technical assistance or other services. *Community-based* organisations generally serve a specific population in a local area; i.e they are usually formed by individuals working together to further their own interests (women's groups, cooperatives, credit circles, youth clubs, etc.) CBOs are likely to be the beneficiaries of project goods and services, and may be consulted during the design phase of projects to ensure that beneficiaries' interests are being met, or may undertake community-level project implementation and become responsible for the ongoing operation and maintenance of such works. They also may be given funds to design and execute sub-projects. Technically a distinction is also made between advocacy and operational NGOs. *Advocacy NGOs* are those whose main purpose is to defend or promote a specific cause and who seek to influence the policies and practices of the World Bank. The primary purpose of operational NGOs is the design and implementation of development-related projects. However, more and more, that distinction is blurred, as many large operational NGOs have a growing advocacy component, and most international advocacy groups have partnerships with developing-country organisations which are at least partially operational.

[12] Operational Directive 14.70, Aug. 28, 1989, replaced by Good Practice (GP) 14.70, March 1997.

[13] Dialogue was pioneered by a group of industrial-country NGOs with operations in developing countries, that hoped that the World Bank would be a new source of funding. The NGO-World Bank Committee formalised the discussions, which were also pursued by a series of country-level 'trilateral' (government-NGO-World Bank) meetings. Developing country NGOs played a growing role in these discussions. Since 1983 an 'Annual Report on Co-operation between the World Bank and NGOs' has described the World Bank's evolving work with NGOs, and since 1986 these have been sent to the Board for information. See Paul, p. 5.

[14] Operational Directive 14.70 was replaced by Good Practice (GP) 14.70 in March 1997.

[15] Between 1973 and 1988, only six per cent of World Bank-financed projects involved NGOs. In 1993 over one third of all approved projects included some form of NGO involvement and in 1994 this percentage increased to one half. In 1997–98, 47% (112 of 241) of the projects approved by the Board had involved or would involve NGOs to some degree. In 1997–98, the 82% of the projects involving NGOs involved local NGOs, 79% included newly-created or existing CBOs, an increase from 66% in 1996–97. In an effort to expand participation, in 1997–98, 59% of projects with NGO involvement incorporated both CBOs and either national or international NGOs, up from 49% the previous year.

sectors that suffer obstacles and hindrances for access to justice.[16] To that end, NGOs, universities and foundations involved in legal aid from all around the country have participated. This demand-driven fund aims to allow innovation among civil society in the areas of access to justice, legal information and research. It has permitted greater geographic participation, more diversity, piloting of different ideas and has encouraged the grass roots level to design solutions to the problem of greater access to reliable and fair dispute resolution, whether in the formal judiciary or in community mediation.

The programmes have varied from mediation centres to legal aid for poor women and professional development for law professors. Where there are four public defenders in a city with a population of two million and the law requires that individuals be represented by a lawyer, there are serious impediments to access to justice. The legal services for poor women is a programme that was originally developed for Quito and Guayaquil and was then expanded to Cuenca and to the Province of Guayas, especially in the sectors of Duale and Santa Elena, which are remote and poor. NGOs co-ordinate their activities with governmental and non-governmental organisations. The general objective of the activity is to defend the rights of the underprivileged population through a service rendered with efficacy and efficiency.

The women's legal service centres in Quito and Guayaquil — Centros Ecuatorianos de Apoyo a la Mujer (CEPAM) — provide essential services of ensuring access to the judiciary and dispute resolution proceedings. They offer legal aid to women, especially women in crisis as well as psychological counselling and medical advice. The centres employ lawyers as well as psychologists and medical assistants to provide the lawyers with the support services needed to establish their clients' cases and to provide professional services to women resorting to the centre. During the last trimester of 1999 there were 344 consultations at the Quito centre which resulted in 100 new cases being handled. Since in several studies it has been stated that over 70% of partnerships involve domestic violence, it is not surprising that the majority of the cases involve violence within the family, as well as cases related to children and family issues more generally.[17] The centres assisted women in hearings before the judiciary, as well as convening mediation sessions. Some

---

[16] See World Bank (1996).

[17] Although it was not the objective of the centres to assist in prosecuting penal cases, the very functions vested in them require engaging in such prosecution in a variety of cases. In addition there is a need for legal assistance during the penal process in Ecuador, since victims are also required to be represented by lawyers. The limited experience in Ecuador thus far clearly demonstrates that attending to issues of family violence and the related adverse effects on both women and their children is an indispensable prerequisite for any efforts to enable these women to enter the work force, provide proper care for their children, and in general improve their economic status. It is also vital for both the mental and physical health of the children and for the provision of a stable environment enabling them to continue their education.

272 consultations with the psychologists and 408 with the medical assistant took place and all in all the Quito centre provided legal services to 641 women during this period.

In addition to the legal service centres for women funded in Quito and Guayaquil, two new women's centres have been opened by an NGO in two 'zonas urbanas' in Duale and Santa Elena. These provide legal services for poor women. Each centre includes two lawyers, two psychologists and two social workers plus fourteen available mediators shared between the centres. They provide services to an average of thirty women per day in populations of 80,000 and 100,000, respectively. The majority of the cases handled concern child support (since women rarely ask for support for themselves), child custody, domestic violence and sexual violence against children. In the past it was not unusual to find cases for child support that lasted sixteen years before the courts. These centres report that most child support cases are resolved within 20 days to two months and child custody cases within 48 hours. The centres also conduct mediation in cases of child support and separation of material goods as well as the dwelling. However, when a written agreement as a result of such mediation exists, some judges initially fail to give them full legal force, something that is inconsistent with the law of mediation.

The women attending these centres often come by word of mouth, at the insistence of a friend or family member or through knowledge from conferences or television. They come because they value the holistic service offered by the centre. Such services can perhaps improve knowledge and skills that can effect attitudinal change. The centres accompany the women through the legal process. They take cases that perhaps other lawyers could not. For instance, one woman's husband attempted to influence the judicial process. The centre was able to challenge this and provide the necessary support and independence. The centres also provide shelter and educate women about their legal rights, providing a service which women say is lacking in the courts. They also trust the centres and those that work in them. Some women come after having been frustrated with other lawyers working on their case.

As well as providing legal services, there is also a need to assist in changing the attitudes of judges and the sexual stereotypes they have. The centres also provide training in prevention of domestic violence and violence in general within the family to citizens, religious groups, students of all ages and those who use their services. They are also disseminating the law against family violence passed in 1995 which gives abused or otherwise wronged women the right to file a case against their husbands. In addition, other organisations promote 'una vida sin violencia' (life without violence) by helping to protect aggrieved women, promote affirmative action regarding gender violence and encourage women's participation in society.[18]

Several law schools offer legal orientation for economically underprivileged people in order to facilitate their access to justice, and their work includes legal aid centres where law students complete their training offering mediation services.[19] Other legal aid clinics include a mediation and legal aid service.[20] This provides students with more practical training. The main objective is to create a culture of conciliation in society by means of promoting the desirability of alternative dispute resolution (ADR) among students and the community at large. The methodology includes co-ordinating ADR with a legal-aid programme, training students and counselling the public. Legal aid clinics in law schools offer essential legal services to the poor, provide students with practical skills, expose them to the public service profession and perhaps encourage them to follow this professional path.[21] However, the main objective is to train students and prepare the next generation in public service.

Mediation is also being promoted in areas which are remote from any formal judicial system. The NGO Corporación de Educación y Promoción Popular (CAUSAI) offers mediation services in the Azuay province. The programme, in the Tarqui, Quingeo and Cumbre zones, trains mediators in areas where the population is mostly indigenous and female. The objective is to create a culture of dialogue and consensus building and it includes practical training for community mediators in diagnosis, co-ordination, evaluation, promotion and training of other mediators. Using mediation with women should be approached with caution, however. In some places, like Bangladesh, mediation — although adopted to address better the needs of women and the disadvantaged — rarely treats women equally. Despite an 80 per cent rate of dispute resolution, it remains tainted by gender bias and legal ignorance.[22] Evidently mediation and other legal services are not enough alone to advance women's issues.

Providing legal information is another form of legal aid. Often people do not have knowledge of the legal process nor trust and need to be better educated about the system. One example is legal training and assistance for prisoners' organisations and prisoners' relatives carried out by the Instituto Ecuatoriano de Antropología y Geografía. The objective of this training and assistance is to encourage prisoners' relatives to participate in resolving prisoners' legal conflicts, understand the judicial process and the process of

---

[18] Centro de Estudios e Investigaciones de la Mujer Ecuatoriana (CEIME), y Foro Nacional Permanente de la Mujer Ecuatoriana – Capítulo Bolivar.

[19] Facultad de Ciencias Jurídicas de la Universidad del Azuay and Universidad Católica de Santiago de Guayaquil.

[20] The Universidad Católica de Santiago de Guayaquil and Pontificia Universidad Católica del Ecuador – Sede Ibarra – y Centro Sobre Derecho y Sociedad – CIDES.

[21] Ford Foundation (2000) p. 13.

[22] *Ibid.*, pp. 136–9.

rehabilitation. Training is also provided for NGOs and public officials related to prisoners' problems, establishment of a prisoners' relatives association and a mechanism to involve judges and court personnel in prisons' problems. Public education is essential and together with educating the next generation of lawyers is important for social change. One example is education of groups at risk — indigenous population, poor, women — of their constitutional rights. At the same time, educational activities can provide information for practitioners, judges and NGOs of their role in constitutional protection. Another example is research by the Facultad Latinoamericana de Ciencias Sociales (FLACSO-Quito) about access to justice for indigenous sectors. This aims to facilitate understanding about indigenous customs and disseminate knowledge about indigenous ways of administering justice in the Quichua communities of Sierra and Amazonia and in the Shuar community of Amazonia. The aim is to disseminate such knowledge within the legal community and the legal education system. Training is also provided in applying traditional justice methods with ordinary justice through the Federación Nacional de Organizaciones Campesinas, Indígenas y Negras (FENOCIN).

Replication Possibilities

In many countries public interest litigation has been used to document injustice and expose inequities which has fostered the development of new jurisprudence. It is yet to be seen how jurisprudence will be affected by current efforts in Ecuador. It is one of the first experiences of this kind for the World Bank and there is a need for further research and time to study the real impact of legal aid under the project. Public interest litigation can be one means to educate the judiciary, and training seminars can raise awareness as a complement to other formal judicial training. The early signals are that there has been some positive effect, especially in women's legal cases. An impact study is in process to assist in the replication of legal services for women in other countries.[23] One important lesson from an evaluation carried out by the Ford Foundation is the need to select test cases that can inspire attention from the press and the public and provide access to vulnerable groups.[24] In Ecuador training has been given to journalists so that they may report more accurately on judicial reform issues and it is hoped that they will monitor these cases. This is an activity which has been more widely included in other legal and judicial reform projects financed by the World Bank.

The question of sustainability is always an issue for legal aid activities. Many NGO weaknesses stem from their typically low levels of financial resources and lack of financial independence. Large national NGOs tend to be

---

[23] See Marcela Rodriguez (2000).
[24] Ford Foundation (2000) p. 75.

dependent on foreign contributions, many of which are project-based.[25] In Bangladesh, the Ford Foundation found that multiple donor support was positive for legal services. As in Ecuador, each donor funded different aspects of the women's integrated legal services including health, education community mobilisation and other programmes.[26] The shared funding enabled the donors to share the risk when legal aid may have been controversial. Perhaps private sector support or sliding scale fees could also assist with financial sustainability. Since it is unrealistic to expect most public interest law groups to become self-supporting, such cooperation among donors is vital to continued existence of such legal aid. However, although these activities were financed in Ecuador, it does not mean that such activities are appropriate for other countries. Strategies can and should vary, depending on time, place and organisation. Other examples of legal aid could include support for the Ombudsmen's Office which can assist citizens to investigate, mediate and resolve complaints against public officials. Such an office is being supported in Peru by the World Bank through an Institutional Development Fund Grant. Whatever the model for legal aid, it should be effective, efficient, affordable, independent and trusted by the clients.

One of the most important benefits of civil society involvement in this area is that it can provide an essential complement to other legal aid activities in a country. Such involvement, in whatever form, can provide greater accountability, transparency and better information to the public, all of which are integral to the process of legal and judicial reform. While the most common World Bank-NGO operational collaboration is at the implementation stage, as in the case of the activities described above, many NGOs offer experience in participatory project design and possess skills in areas such as participatory research, community mobilisation, facilitation techniques and group dynamics.[27] Since NGOs come in such shapes and sizes, it is vital to research and thoroughly assess potential partner NGOs to find the ones most suitable.

National and international NGOs can also make long-term commitments to the communities they serve and be a source of stability and sustainability, particularly where governments are weak or prone to change. NGOs in Ecuador have also provided a mechanism to voice the issues related to the poor and their lack of access to effective and efficient resolution of disputes.

---

[25] Some of the large international NGOs do have well-established mechanisms through which they raise a significant amount of their funds from diverse sources. Most NGOs, however, are limited by the irregular project-based funding they receive and are not able to develop their administrative capabilities beyond basic levels as most of their finances are used for operations.

[26] Ford Foundation (2000) p. 134.

[27] The World Bank is often asked why it does not lend directly to NGOs. The Bank works directly with governments or with a guarantee from the government. As a result the entity receiving financing must be creditworthy of World Bank financing and able to repay the loan. Most NGOs do not qualify and thus member countries would not guarantee such financing.

NGOs and CBOs have proven to be effective, and sometimes provide the only institutional link to some of the poorest and most disadvantaged members of society who are very often the most difficult to reach. Often these groups live in remote or transient situations beyond the sphere of public service networks and the formal judiciary, but NGOs have played a key role in establishing contact with some of these high-risk groups. NGO and CBO networks are particularly effective in these situations when they are able to penetrate large numbers of dispersed communities.

NGOs can further help to give a more complete and balanced view of the issues at hand by offering another perspective from that of the government or private sector. In the case of Ecuador, they drew attention to the fact that the obstacles to an efficient and effective justice system were not solely related to the courts. They are particularly effective in drawing attention to issues or groups that may otherwise be overlooked or whose political voice is the weakest. Women, ethnic minorities and other groups who do not enjoy equitable representation in formal institutions often form NGOs in order to make their voices heard. Working through these groups in the case of Ecuador helped to ensure that important issues were not overlooked in the development process of legal and judicial reform.

NGOs can also provide learning and innovation experience in the design and implementation process. Because of their smaller size and greater flexibility, NGOs are better able to develop and experiment with new approaches and innovation in development. It is not unusual for World Bank-financed projects to incorporate or 'scale-up' successful NGO innovations, or for NGOs to be vehicles to test or pilot new strategies. In the Ecuador project NGOs designed the proposals which were subsequently financed.[28]

Notwithstanding the strengths and benefits of NGO participation, it is important to realise that NGOs have weaknesses that should also be considered. For instance, some do not have technical expertise, some are not legitimate among their peers, and in an advocacy role they may create tension with governments. For this reason it is beneficial that such groups have consistently been non-partisan. One should further be aware of where their funding comes from, particularly in cases where the financial backers are international groups with separate agendas. In addition, the following limitations may be present: financial, analytical and management expertise, institutional capacity, gaps between the stated mission and actual operational achievement, low levels of self-sustainability, lack of inter-organisational communication or coordination and limited expertise in broader economic, social or development issues.[29]

---

[28] Still only about half of World Bank-financed projects approved with NGO involvement have them participate at the project design stage.

[29] Lawrence F. Salman and A. Paige Eaves (1991).

Networks of NGOs

Even with these limitations, NGOs have a role to play. One such role is educating each other and forming broader networks. Although they are diverse and often have conflicting interests, NGOs need to be more united when it comes to advocating legal and judicial reform. Every Latin American country is now characterised by the presence of an ever-increasing web of grassroots organisations.[30] However, as these organisations begin to expand or multiply, they are often faced with obstacles that are beyond their control or capacity. In these cases, small grassroots organisations will often join forces, which may bring strengths in other areas, such as lobbying power and/or technical expertise. Each group brings its own resources, strengths or interests into the partnership, improving the outcome of the relationship and, in time, may also join with other groups to work together towards a common end, eventually creating an interlocked web of organisations.

In poorer countries, while community organisations do exist, the opportunities for 'linking up' with a network of groups are much more limited. One of the main limitations of functioning independently is the lack of information. The growth in technology has contributed to the expansion of networks, particularly through cross-boundary linkages. Internet user groups, bulletin boards and web-sites have created new forums for proposing and debating political and social issues, where experience working on these issues can be shared. Internet communication creates a community of informed individuals, unconstrained by hierarchy or territory, based on common values, interests and objectives.[31] As networks, groups have greater strength to lobby for change and increase their effectiveness. The increase in technology has allowed for the expansion of networks to promote change and keep a healthy watch on the reform activities being sponsored by both government and international organisations. This oversight can help to ensure that reforms are not transplants and that they are indeed owned by civil society.

An example of such a network in operation is the growth in women's organisations and their effort to make causes, such as violence against women, universal rather than country-specific issues. By creating a universal term for what may go by different names in different countries, they have given important issues global recognition. Working together under an international campaign rather than isolated national movements, lets their voices and influences be stronger and even more effective. One example of such a coalition is the many women's NGOs which have participated in the World Conferences on Women and in the United Nations process by providing their expertise in the area of concern, lobbying their governmental delegates and

---

[30] Sheldon Annis (1987) pp. 129–34.
[31] Julie Mertus (1999) p. 1335.

representing the citizen's voice. By joining in international conferences and coalitions, these organisations are making their voices heard on a global level in women's rights and gender equality, where their work ranges from advocating and monitoring legislation to providing social, emotional, financial, health and environmental support for the well-being and empowerment of women. It needs participation from all levels and types of organisation to sustain such a broad range of activities, much aided by coalitions and networks of organisations.

Transparency International is an international NGO dedicated to increasing government accountability and curbing both international and national corruption.[32] Through the formation of 'national chapters', Transparency International has brought together a coalition of people in civil society, business and government to be independent, supportive, yet critical partners in pursuing the implementation of laws, policies and anti-corruption programmes. The various national chapters participate by lobbying their governments, informing the media and bringing together people concerned about corruption. By forming a coalition of independent, yet supportive, international organisations, Transparency International is able to have a powerful role and voice in defining and implementing an international agenda against corruption. While individually these smaller groups may not have much chance of having their voice heard or having a significant effect, as a group they can draw on each others' experiences and work together as a strong, united front to really make a difference.

NGO involvement in policy making has particularly increased in the area of environmental law. While states have traditionally been the dominant actors in the creation and maintenance of conventional international law, recent changes have enabled NGOs to have greater opportunity for participation in international environmental law.[33] NGOs are now major actors in the formulation, implementation and enforcement of international environmental law. While there are as yet no formal guarantees of access across the board, NGO participation has been formally mandated or permitted in a number of recent international legal instruments, and NGOs have also played a major role in the negotiation of these conventions.

NGOs are further involved in the International Law of Development (ILD), a growing body of legal instruments created by the UN system.[34] NGOs have played a vital role in building the ILD and are a powerful force behind it, and the ILD legitimises their demands for more participation and has increased their role at the national and local levels. By mandating NGO participation at local, national and international levels, the ILD seems to also

---

[32] See the Transparency International Website at www.transparency.de/index.html.
[33] Kal Raustiala (1997).
[34] James C. N. Paul (1995).

mandate their more active role in the development of international law in all spheres related to development. The future of the ILD is linked to the future strength of NGO networks and to the increased activity of NGOs in development processes.

Legal and judicial reform programmes have been launched in a number of countries throughout Latin America. As part of this process, NGOs have filled the gap left by governments by providing necessary activities to foster legal aid, public education about the legal system, research, legislative drafting and court reforms. This increased involvement of NGOs has had the added benefit of providing a monitoring mechanism of judicial performance, an increased public awareness of the adverse effects of inefficiency, and a better understanding of the imperative for the judicial system's independence and integrity. In this way, the NGOs in Latin America working on judicial reform have been an integral part in the strengthening of rule of law in the region.

The Inter-American Judicial Reform Network was established to co-ordinate various organisations that are participating in judicial reform in Latin American countries. Because a well-functioning judiciary is an integral part of good governance, organisations seeking and engaging in reforms to strengthen the judicial process in their countries can gain much insight and support from similar organisations in their own as well as other countries. It is also important that there exists some structure that independently examines the reform process, disseminates information about it and organises active participation. NGOs involved in judicial reform serve as vehicles through which public participation, dissemination and review might take place. The relationship of NGOs during a process of court reform can influence the public's perception of the court system and can help the legislative and the executive as well as the judiciary place reform issues in a broader perspective.

An exchange of ideas, experiences and insights between and amongst these groups is invaluable in countries that are currently attempting to strengthen governance. Often well-reasoned approaches to a particular problem can be developed better by exchanging experiences with others. In this regard, these groups have experience at the local and national level in areas of access to justice, alternative dispute resolution mechanisms, court administration, judicial training, legal reform and others. Other NGOs in judicial reform as well as the World Bank can benefit from these important experiences.

Such networks can improve the information available and the co-ordination among both civil society, donor agencies and governments. They will improve access to knowledge and skills and allow donor agencies to develop effective partnerships with civil society. This means that these NGOs involved should have credibility (acceptability to relevant stakeholders, focus on development objectives); competence (relevant skills, experience and track record); local knowledge (proven high-level understanding of country context); repre-

W l import that NGO can add - they really represent the underrepresented?

sentativeness (community ties, accountability to members/beneficiaries, gender and minority group sensitivity); and institutional capacity (sufficient scale of operations, human resources and facilities).

Working in networks will allow for greater consultation with NGOs on draft reform agendas as well as providing a mechanism for greater disclosure. It will also allow the World Bank to understand funding needs and issues better so that NGOs can make valuable contributions within their means and capacity. Additionally, this would permit the NGOs to build their capacity by learning what others are doing, and spreading the responsibilities among a group of NGOs. This approach uses the multiple sources of energy available and promotes greater pluralism in society by encouraging networks of NGOs to create linkages and collaborative arrangements. There is also a need for an interlocking network of complementary institutions — lawyers, grassroots community activity and academic think-tanks. For example, there is much to gain from greater interaction among the organisations working on legal aid.[35]

As legal and judicial reforms advance in many countries, it is clear that there is a parallel need for attention to the poor and access to justice. It is not enough to train judges, create new case management tools and pass new laws if the poor cannot access dispute resolution mechanisms to enforce their rights. Different legal aid models can be tested and evaluated simultaneously during this reform process. Civil society can play an important role in advocating change in the legal framework and in the judiciary to promote greater access to justice. One of the mechanisms that we have seen is the development of local NGOs specialising in justice issues. As they grow in numbers and competence, they are likely to gain more respect and trust. In other words, they would have a more active role in initiation, design and implementation of projects so as to ensure a complimentary approach between the judiciary and civil society is being followed in legal and judicial reform.

Conclusions

One the of the key lessons of the World Bank's initial experience working with civil society in the area of legal and judicial reform is that it is important to develop a parallel strategy by working with governmental legal institutions while at the same time working with reform-minded groups and individuals in civil society. It is likely that some institutions that are part of the legal and judicial framework of a country will *not* be reform minded and, for this reason, legal and judicial reform must draw on as many sources of support as possible. Participatory or 'bottom-up' approaches have proved extremely successful in building consensus among disparate stakeholders when designing, implementing and promoting reforms in the legal sector. Incorporating key

---

[35] Ford Foundation (2000) pp. 118 and 133.

stakeholders in the decision-making process lends credibility to the reforms and often ensures more effective enforcement. Partnerships with the private bar, legal academia and other civil society organisations to share knowledge and experience can enhance legal and judicial reform programmes in developing countries. Although the World Bank has been working with various members of civil society, there is still more to be done, especially with such groups as the bar associations as they too are vital to the reform process.

CHAPTER 5

Justice Reform in Latin American and the Caribbean: the IDB Perspective*

Christina Biebesheimer

I. Why the IDB is Working on Justice Reform

As a regional development bank, the Inter-American Development Bank (the IDB) develops its priorities around those themes that the region defines as important. The IDB is working on justice reform in particular — and on modernisation of the state and strengthening civil society more generally — because the countries of the region identify these as important areas of action. Policy documents by the board of governors of the IDB — a group that directly represents member governments of the institution — indicate that member countries of the IDB understand that the success of economic reform hinges not only on better macro-economic policies, but also on the existence of a suitable institutional, regulatory and political climate. The sustainability of market-oriented economic reforms depends on a steady flow of private investment into productive sectors over the medium and long term, and this can only occur in a climate of lasting political and legal stability and security. This, in turn, is only possible in a system where the rule of law prevails.

A regional consensus has formed around the concept that democratic stability on the one hand, and economic and social development on the other, tend to reinforce one another,[1] and that democratic governments must confront the long-standing challenges of poverty, inequality, violence and political and institutional weakness if they are to survive and thrive. There is growing consensus that the justice system must become more effective in confronting rising violence, and that it must address citizens' demands for fairness, transparency and access if democracy is to become legitimated and consolidated.

There is broad regional consensus, then, as to the economic and social importance of a well-functioning justice system; there is also recognition that the current performance of justice institutions in the region is not ideal. Statistical and survey evidence about trends in justice in Latin America and the Caribbean indicates that the performance of the justice sector in much of Latin America and some of the Caribbean lags behind other regions of the world.[2]

* The opinions expressed in this chapter are those of the author and do not necessarily reflect those of the Inter-American Development Bank
[1] 'Declaration of Viña del Mar', Chile, Nov. 1996. VI Summit of Heads of State and Government.
[2] Among the sources which indicate deficiencies in the justice area are: the aggregate indicator of the 'Rule of Law' developed by Daniel Kaufman, Aart Kraay and Pablo Zoido-Lobaton

The countries of the region themselves recognise that justice is a priority development area.

Brief Overview of IDB Projects in Justice Reform, 1993–99

A. First steps and definition of principles of assistance in the justice sector

The IDB initiated its work in support of modernisation of justice systems in Latin America and the Caribbean by soliciting input from chief justices, ministers of justice, attorneys general and judges regarding needs in the justice sector and whether they perceived a role for the IDB in this area. The opinions of justice sector officials were solicited in a 1993 region-wide conference in Costa Rica titled 'Justice in Latin America and the Caribbean in the 1990s: Challenges and Opportunities'. This event served to communicate to the IDB that its borrowing countries were indeed interested in seeking Bank assistance with justice reform, and helped to coalesce interest on this topic among IDB borrowing counties.

The goal of modernisation and strengthening of the justice systems was incorporated into the document authorising the IDB's Eighth General Increase in Resources of 1994, which identifies modernisation of the state as a key area of IDB activity, and provides that the Bank 'can help governments that request assistance in supporting their efforts to promote strengthening and modernisation of the judicial system'.[3] The Eighth Replenishment document sets out broad parameters and goals for judicial modernisation, stating that the IDB should aim at 'ensuring that the judicial system is independent and effective, that it guarantees the rights of citizens, and that it contributes to effective and rapid settlement of disputes'.[4]

Elaborating on the Eighth Replenishment goals, the Strategic Planning and Operational Policy Department prepared a document entitled 'Frame of Reference for Bank Action in Programs for Modernization of the State and Strengthening of Civil Society'. This document establishes general principles and criteria for IDB action including, in the justice sector, a recommendation for work in areas such as law reform and promotion of citizen rights, administrative strengthening of the judiciary, alternative methods of conflict resolution, legal aid and civic education programmes, training, infrastructure and public safety.[5] The document also affirms that modernisation of the state 'entails a complementary and reciprocal process of strengthening civil society'.[6] This document, too, provides general guidance, and leaves room for

---

(1999); and the question on judicial predictability from the private sector survey carried out for the World Bank (1997a).

[3] IDB (1994) paragraph 2.37(h).

[4] *Ibid.*

[5] IDB (1996).

[6] *Ibid.*

the IDB to develop some field experience in a range of justice reform projects before formulating a detailed strategy for the sector.

The IDB's process of determining what areas to focus on within the justice sector, what limits to establish, and what processes of reform to employ has been, very intentionally, gradual and evolutionary. The IDB decided to begin with some general principles, gain some field experience through development of projects, and then formulate a more detailed strategy or policy based on that experience. The general principles are set out in the paragraphs above; the IDB is now in the process of formulating the more detailed justice sector strategy. Some of the issues being discussed in strategy formulation are set out in Section III, below.

B. Areas of assistance

Since the 1993 conference, 41 loans and technical cooperation operations to promote aspects of justice reform have been approved in 17 of the IDB's 26 member countries. These operations also include projects to fund conferences and research: the IDB has financed conferences on justice and development, a judicial roundtable in Williamsburg, Virginia, a workshop on access to justice in Rio de Janeiro, Brazil, seminars for judges on international human rights standards and national workshops to build consensus about justice reform in Costa Rica, Honduras, the Dominican Republic, Colombia, Guatemala and Venezuela. The IDB has also supervised research and publications on various issues of justice reform, including works on human rights issues and best practice research to identify experiences from outside the region that may be useful in guiding the process of reform of court administration and the judicial process in Latin America and the Caribbean. In addition, the IDB has sponsored regional conferences on violence prevention, and two violence prevention loans have been approved. The Annex to this chapter provides brief descriptions of IDB justice reform projects approved to date.

The IDB has financed a wide range of types of reform processes; it has also shown a willingness to focus project activities on a wide range of substantive areas of the law:

1. Types of reform processes funded

With respect to processes or types of justice reform activities, IDB funds have gone to institutional strengthening, law reform, consensus-building activities and research, as follows:

Institutional strengthening. This category comprises assistance designed to bring about organisational change; it does not include law reform. Thus, the category includes modernisation of managerial and administrative structures, procedures and processes; creation of the capacity for strategic planning, including creation of mechanisms to gather data and create data-bases; installation of information technology systems; training (encompassing not only training in administrative areas, but also substantive training for judges and other justice system personnel in areas such as how to apply inter-national human rights law in cases before national courts, courses in professional ethics, etc.) and infrastructure support. Most IDB justice projects contain some components of institutional strengthening; some IDB justice projects consist almost entirely of institutional strengthening. Institutional strengthening in IDB projects is aimed at modernising judiciaries as well as executive branch justice agencies.

Law reform. This category includes activities aimed at getting good laws drafted, passed and implemented. It thus comprises assistance in the revision or creation of legislation, technical assistance to legislatures to improve their law-drafting capacity and training for justice officials in the application of the new laws. Laws being written or revised in IDB projects include civil and criminal procedure codes, domestic violence law, commercial codes, adminis-trative codes, constitutional provisions and laws governing children and juveniles.

Consensus-building and preparing the way for justice reforms. This is a category of activities that, while relatively small in dollar terms, has been an important component of IDB action, in that it comprises activities to develop a consensus among officials of the justice sector, legislators and the general public as to the general importance of justice reform, and to define priorities for action within the sector. Often this process is required before real reform can be undertaken. Included in this category are regional operations that have permitted seminars and workshops to be held on specific topics of justice reform, as well as country-specific projects that have funded studies and workshops to define reform strategies.

Research. In addition to staff time spent on research, the IDB has also begun to approve projects aimed at increasing knowledge of justice reform so as to improve the quality of projects.

Some or all of these areas of assistance are probably common to most agen-cies working to strengthen rule of law and promote justice.

2. Substantive areas of the law addressed

IDB justice projects seek to improve those portions of the civil law system that are considered important for the operation of a market economy, often containing civil law reform efforts to aid efficient and equitable growth. However, IDB justice projects go beyond market-driven reforms, to encompass projects aimed at increasing access to justice by the disenfranchised, at building consensus about the need for greater judicial independence in a democratic system and at improving the justice system's ability to confront crime and violence.

Thus, IDB projects include both civil and criminal justice reform, working with the judiciary; with executive branch agencies such as ministries of justice, public defenders, police, prison officials and rehabilitation officers; with civil society organisations active in the justice sector; and with legislatures responsible for legislation affecting the justice sector. The IDB's violence prevention and public security projects, while not exclusively focused on justice sector institutions, often heavily involve those institutions.

In large part, the IDB's broad focus on many substantive areas of the law arises from the needs of the countries of the region itself: statistical and survey evidence from countries of Latin America and the Caribbean indicates that there is considerable variation in the functioning of justice systems from one country to another. Thus the IDB must be able to respond to widely differing needs if it is to act as a truly regional development bank and be responsive to each one of its member countries in the region. Nonetheless, some common trends are discernible: court delay and rising crime, for example, are major issues that justice systems throughout the region are grappling with.

Recent compilations of quantitative data regarding efficiency of the courts, using indicators such as the number of cases pending and the average delay encountered by litigants before their case is dealt with, show that, for the countries for which there is such data, there are an unusual number of cases pending and the average delay is extraordinarily long in the typical Latin American judicial system. It also appears that the problem worsened between the 1980s and 1990s. One study reports that the median delay in the disposition of cases and the number of pending cases increased in Argentina, Brazil, Chile, Colombia and Venezuela between 1983 and 1993. According to this study, the 1993 median times to disposition in the civil jurisdictions of Argentina, Ecuador and Venezuela are 2.5, 1.9 and 2.4 years, which represent an average increase of 76 per cent since 1987.[7] When particular areas of law are considered the situation looks grim. The expected duration of property cases in the Argentine courts was almost ten years, domestic relations cases twelve years and commercial cases three years. Ecuador told a similar story. Thus institutional reforms aimed at improving court administration will continue to be an area in which the IDB focuses its work in the region.

In a region of increasingly strong democracies, there is increasing interest and willingness to invest in a judicial system that will provide protection and access to all citizens, and that will contribute to the balance of power in a democracy. IDB justice projects focusing on access by disenfranchised citizens — women, children, minorities and the poor — have been supported with enthu-

---

[7] Edgardo Buscaglia and Maria Dakolias (1996).

siasm by the IDB's management and board of directors. Because the IDB has traditionally focused on social sectors and poverty alleviation, access to justice seems a natural outgrowth of its traditional work along these lines.

IDB justice projects that work on improving the criminal justice sector, on dealing with juvenile offenders and on violence prevention, also arise primarily from demand from countries in the region, where crime and violence statistics are in many countries alarming and worsening. The homicide rate for all of Latin America has followed an almost exponential pattern of growth between the early 1970s and the early 1990s. From 10 per 100,000 people in 1970-74 the rate has climbed to over 20 per 100,000 in 1990-94. The homicide rate is considerably higher in Latin America than in either the high-income countries or the rest of the developing countries. El Salvador, Colombia, the Bahamas and Jamaica not only are countries with homicide rates that are among the highest in the region, they also are the countries in which the increase has been most marked. Guatemala also had a particularly high murder rate in the early 1990s but we lack data from the early 1970s. By contrast, in Chile, Argentina, Uruguay, Trinidad and Tobago and Costa Rica the murder rate is comparatively low and has experienced only a slight increase or has fallen.[8]

Victimisation surveys indicate that Latin America leads other global regions not only in terms of homicides but also in violent crimes and crime in general.[9] In addition, in every country the majority of survey respondents believe that crime has increased a lot in the past year and in several countries the proportion believing this exceeds 90%. Such surveys also indicate that relative to other regions Latin American victims of contact crimes and burglaries are least satisfied with the handling of their cases by the police.

Entry by the IDB into criminal justice reform has been somewhat polemical within the institution, and it is clear that this is an area in which some limits must be set. The IDB is now grappling with what limits may be needed in areas such as police and prison reform. However, staff, management and the board of directors have shown a willingness to deal with regional realities in crafting justice projects: public security and safety, provided in a way that protects human and civil rights, is one of the basic deliverables expected from the justice system and one of its tasks that is most important to citizens in the region. Much academic literature indicates that crime and violence has a direct — and negative — impact on economic development, and countries concerned with the tourism market are particularly sensitive to the relationship between crime and growth. Juvenile justice and crime prevention projects seem to provide a natural follow-on to IDB work to aid street children and youth in especially difficult circumstances; again, this work seems to be a natural outgrowth of the IDB's focus on the social aspects of development.

---

[8] United Nations (1993).
[9] United Nations (1999).

III. Conceptual Framework: How the IDB Is Thinking about the Justice Sector.

At the IDB, overall priorities are established through policy and strategy documents, as well as through the precedent of approved projects. As stated earlier, the IDB has begun to acquire some experience and precedent through the development of projects, and has formulated a very general policy in the justice sector. It is in the process of developing a more detailed conceptual framework and strategy for work in the justice sector.

The analytical framework for justice reform in the IDB is evolving, informed by work in the field. It is progressing with an understanding that justice reform projects are not ordinary projects for the IDB: thinking about them must take into account the peculiarities of the work. Projects intended to reform the delivery of justice are highly political in nature, in that they involve the balance of national institutional power among the executive, legislative and judicial branches of government, and in that they may potentially alter the balance of power among groups in society (for example, lower levels of partiality in the rendering of justice may reduce favouritism toward a particular socio-economic group).

Like government reform projects generally, rule of law or justice reform projects require a consensus for change and may therefore be feasible only within relatively narrow windows of opportunity. Most justice reform projects require institution-building, which is almost always a long-term enterprise, outlasting any one project cycle (the IDB projects are ordinarily designed to be implemented over a period of two to four years, although extensions in the execution period are permitted). Institutional complexity characterises many justice reform projects, often entailing the work of agencies from both the judicial and executive branches of government, and sometimes also the legislature. Many of the projects are cross-disciplinary in nature. As this is a new area of IDB work, entering into it requires staff to learn new expertise, and raises questions as to what types of limits, if any, should be placed on IDB activity in the sector.

The remainder of this section of the paper sets out some of the issues that the IDB's justice reform strategy will need to address.

A. Entry strategies

Should the IDB condition assistance to a country's justice sector on, for example, a showing of independence and accountability of the judiciary? Or on political consensus for reform?

Reform is not a short-term or easy task, and broad-based consensus is often required to achieve it. The IDB is sometimes asked to work on justice reform projects in countries or institutions in which consensus for reform is partial or nearly non-existent. It is also sometimes argued that as judicial independence is a sine qua non of effective justice administration, entities such as the IDB should not undertake reform projects in the absence of such independence. This is sometimes used to suggest that the IDB set judicial independence as a condition for approval of justice reform projects in a country.

IDB projects approved to date indicate that the IDB is working both in countries where there is broad-based support for reform and admirable judicial independence, and in countries or contexts in which only partial independence and consensus for reform exist. When consensus is not broad-based, the IDB has funded consensus-building activities. When independence does not exist, the IDB has developed projects that address some of the obstacles to independence.

It does seem to be the case that the IDB should be engaged in working to develop the policy environment that will enable judicial reform to take place. It might very well be counter-productive for the IDB to refuse to do any justice reform work in those countries that do not meet IDB-established standards for judicial independence or for consensus for reform. Instead, the IDB should work to bring about greater consensus for reform and greater judicial independence, especially where they are most lacking.

It is clear, at any rate, that both judicial independence, as well as consensus or political will, should be carefully assessed in the diagnostic stage of project preparation, and projects should be designed to build, realistically, on the base that is present. Since profound reforms have a better chance of being successful in institutions that demonstrate a great interest for change, the IDB should try to respond with agility when consensus for change and thus possibilities of reform appear in countries of the region. The IDB's policy on justice reform will probably need to deal with entry strategies generally, and with some potential strategies for developing judicial independence and the consensus for reform, in particular.

B. The process of project design and implementation: standards for diagnostic studies and sector planning

Ideally any long-term reform effort first should start with an idea of what a more effective justice system would look like, a specification of what the primary shortcomings are in respect to that vision, and the definition of a strategy for moving the functioning of the system toward its improved state. Any practical strategy for reform must be developed considering the costs and benefits of the reform for the nation as a whole as well as for particular social groups, court officers, politicians and other stakeholders. If such a long term and complex process is to lead to real improvements then reform efforts must be planned in a sequence of stages in which short- and long-term needs, as well as political obstacles to reform, are considered.

Early IDB justice projects tended to be based on rather general diagnostics of the justice sector; later projects developed more sophisticated diagnostics. Now the IDB is conducting in-depth sectoral studies of the public sector in some countries in recognition of the need to improve diagnostic tools and sector studies in this area, and to permit the definition of medium- to long-term strategies for reform in public sector management. This sort of diagnostic exercise and the establishment of a long-term strategy is important because the sorts of problems faced by justice institutions cannot be solved in one project cycle alone and because more than one source of international aid is likely to be involved. Thus, a long-term strategy, to be implemented over several project cycles, is key to establishing an organising idea for the projects developed in the sector, and to help assure co-ordination among the many actors working to better the administration of justice.

A detailed IDB policy on justice reform might well establish suggested tools for diagnostic analysis and strategy formulation. It would be useful, for example, to develop a checklist of questions that a diagnostic of the justice sector should address, at a minimum, together with some methods for measuring a country's performance under each question on the list. This would facilitate staff work in supervising the execution of sector diagnostics, and would provide some continuity in IDB work from country to country. If it were possible to formulate an indicator for each major attribute of a well-functioning justice system, this might help identify central problem areas and plan more appropriate reform steps. The existence of indicators might also help justice systems to develop better data collection systems, not only so as to determine how they are doing and what their priorities for reform might be, but also to allow for better strategic planning and improved management of the court system. Though it is clear that development and use of indicators will not in itself be a panacea, measures of justice system performance and related outcomes are needed to inform the setting of reform priorities, to enhance the rigour and relevance of sector studies at the basis of the design of IDB-sponsored reform projects, and to permit evaluation of project impact.

Another area in which the diagnostic process is critical is the analysis of existing institutional capacity, including the capacity for transformation, so as to permit design of an intelligent strategy to effect reform. This would need to include an analysis of political will, within and outside the institution, and of how to influence it.

C. Standards for stakeholder (including NGO) participation

Many IDB justice projects tend to be quite participatory, either in design or execution. Not all IDB justice projects, however, are bringing input from the ultimate users into the design and execution of projects, and there is no one model for participation in these projects. An IDB policy on justice reform will need to set forth standards for participation in development, execution and monitoring. It will probably be based on *The IDB Resource Book on Participation*,[10] which provides a very useful guide to methodologies and techniques for inclusion of stakeholders in project design, execution and evaluation, and includes some examples of justice projects.

There are important ramifications of civil society presence in operations: citizen participation makes the projects more accountable to the users of the justice system, but it also may increase the design time when the project team allows for a ground-up definition of priorities. Clear objectives and full participation by stakeholders in a project helps to generate consensus for reform, a critical element discussed in the prior section. Without stakeholder participation in project design it is very difficult to analyse the demand for justice — that is, the needs of the users of the justice system; and it makes it nearly impossible to design a project that aims at expanding access to justice, since to do so requires consulting those who do not have access to determine how they define the obstacles to access.

D. Benchmarking, monitoring and evaluation

Most IDB justice projects define quite specific quantitative goals and indicators for components and activities (specifying that, for example, ten laws should be passed or 500 people trained), such that it should be possible to measure accurately, over time, whether the components have been executed as designed. Not all projects, however, define final impact indicators — that is, indicators designed to measure whether and how the project has really made a difference in reforming the justice sector. It is also notable, in reviewing the means of verification or indicators in justice projects, that not many of them include public accountability or public service — this may be an area in which the IDB could improve project indicators and means of verification.

An interesting feature of a number of IDB justice projects is that they depart from more traditional projects in that they define outputs for only the first year of project execution and then for final overall execution. Outputs for the years between the first and last years of project implementation are established through a meeting between the IDB and the executing agency to go over a review of the past year's execution and establish a work plan for the next year. This design structure permits a good deal of flexibility during execution, since it calls for on-going monitoring, feedback and planning of project activities. This feedback and on-going adjustment may be especially appropriate for projects designed to bring about institutional reform: it is difficult to foresee, when the project is designed, the collateral impact that the reform process may have and new demands and challenges that may arise during project

---

[10] *IDB* (1996a).

execution. Institutional reform, in other words, is a dynamic process and institutional reform projects must thus be designed to deal with this dynamism.

This process of continuous feedback and adjustment, in addition to increasing possibilities of project success, could also provide a great deal of data from which to formulate lessons about the reform process. As the IDB's justice projects are executed in the field, the IDB may want to consider monitoring activities in order to identify best practices within work areas — best practices in case-flow management, for example, or in civic education to promote the rule of law. Other organisations, and the IDB itself, are developing lessons learned as to how to make projects most effective in these areas. This sort of feedback process, however, calls for greater participation of IDB staff during the stage of project execution (thus adding to the costs of project administration for the IDB), and requires executing units to have the ability to monitor and propose adjustments to project activities during execution.

Need to add evaluation to the justice reform agenda

The development and implementation of justice reform projects will come at a cost to the countries carrying them out (in that many take on loans to carry out the projects); and at a cost to the IDB itself (in that the projects require high commitment of staff time and longer preparation time, and often do not represent large disbursements). They will be worth their cost if they have real development impact. Not many IDB projects are far enough along to measure development impact. Developing expertise to measure whether projects are making progress toward longer-term development objectives, and toward making necessary adjustments during implementation, must be on the IDB's justice reform agenda. Because experience from around the globe indicates that not all justice reform efforts have been wholly successful, it is clear that learning quickly from the past will be critical to success in the future.

E. Substantive areas of work: should the IDB do a bit of everything or develop special expertise in certain areas?

Objectives and activities in IDB justice projects approved to date are wide-ranging, which raises the question as to whether the IDB ought to be doing a little of everything in the justice arena — that is, essentially adopting a strategy of meeting needs as they arise — or whether it should seek to develop cutting-edge excellence in several areas. There is strength in variety, in that projects can be designed to meet the specific needs of country in which they will be carried out (rather than based on an immutable model or selected from a short menu of potential activities). It would also be possible, however, for the IDB's strategy to recommend that the institution seek to develop cutting-edge expertise in areas likely to represent growing needs in the region, in which the

IDB may have unique strengths, and in which other donor agencies may not be working.

Along these lines of thought, an argument might be made for developing serious expertise in the areas of:

judicial independence
civic education and consensus-building
institutional management
access to justice
juvenile justice reform, and
violence prevention.

In deciding whether to pursue special expertise in certain areas, the IDB would need to ask what the demand for justice system projects is likely to be in the future, what the IDB's strengths are, as well as what expertise is already being provided by other donors.

Judicial independence is becoming a topic increasingly mentioned in the context of discussions about the need to consolidate democratic systems and assure transparency and accountability in the public sector. Since some degree of judicial independence, like some degree of consensus for reform, constitute foundations upon which wider justice reforms can be built, the IDB will need expertise in analysing and supporting judicial independence and consensus for reform. Civic education programmes may be one method for supporting independence and consensus for reform.

The need to reduce judicial delay, and the more general need to strengthen the managerial capacity of institutions involved in justice administration, including civil society institutions, will undoubtedly be an area of continued and increasing demand. The IDB could build on its existing expertise, bringing its experience in public sector management and civil service reform to bear on justice sector institutions.

Requests for assistance with juvenile justice programmes is also likely to grow, given that Latin America and the Caribbean have very young populations. Countries in the region are asking the IDB to work not only with youth already in trouble with the justice system, but also to work on violence prevention among youth. Demand for violence prevention projects, too, is likely to grow in the next few years given rising violence in some IDB member countries, especially if the projects recently initiated prove effective.

In addition to indicating areas of emphasis, a detailed IDB strategy on justice reform may also need to set some limits to work, particularly in the area of criminal law reform, with particular attention to the areas of police and prison reform. A detailed policy on justice reform would offer guidance on what areas to include in IDB projects and what activities to leave to more specialised agencies.

IV. Some Closing Thoughts

This volume begins by looking at what is new and what is old in the rule of law agenda. That the IDB can talk about the role of NGOs in development and include strengthening civil society in its policy goals; that countries of the region have made it explicit that they are willing to let the light of international scrutiny fall on the internal working of justice institutions — these things are truly new. Only a decade ago this was not thinkable. The consensus in the region regarding what development is has changed. This presents a window of opportunity, a moment for new actors to take on new roles in development of justice; it has been an important force in bringing multilateral development banks into justice reform.

Establishing a good agenda for work in the area of justice reform is critical, of course. This seems to be a moment when citizens and governments in Latin America want to discuss ways to reform civil service, prevent violence, resolve conflicts, put more power into the hands of local governments and confront corruption. It is a moment when multilateral development banks are willing to provide assistance toward those ends. In setting an agenda, we need to ask whether we are correct in thinking that these aims are critical for achieving social and economic development in the region. We need to ask whether and how multilateral development banks and NGOs can help countries achieve those ends, and what is the best role for each.

This chapter has indicated some of the areas the IDB has learned that it must address in the process of establishing a good agenda — or policy — regarding justice reform. The IDB's evolving agenda recognises that justice reform projects often require political and popular consensus for change. The IDB must thus be able to assess — and help create — consensus, and be able to act quickly in response to changing conditions in member countries. But the IDB must also have a long-term perspective, since institutional change and institution-building are long-term processes. The ability to be flexible and fast, within a long term vision or strategy, requires very good country and sector diagnostics. It also requires working with member countries to encourage formulation of medium- to long-term strategies. IDB projects themselves are likely to be specific to one institution or one problem, and each project in itself is short-term; but the more that a project is part of a coherent and larger plan, the more likely it is to have a beneficial impact on the justice sector. Longer term and integrated strategies also help a country to encourage donor coordination, to avoid overlap or even conflict among different projects in the sector.

The IDB has learned the importance of involving participation of a broad range of stakeholders and users and concerned citizens in the design as well as the implementation and oversight of justice projects. The IDB has also learned that we need to be creative regarding monitoring and evaluating. The vast

majority of IDB-financed justice projects to date are still in the process of implementation, so lessons learned are those gleaned from analysis of the process
of project design and start-up. It is critical to learn as we go, using benchmarking and monitoring mechanisms in order to be able to make changes in
existing projects as needed, and to bring lessons learned to the design of new
projects. Because experience from around the globe shows that attempts at
justice reform have not always met with unmitigated success, learning from
experience as it happens, and translating that learning quickly into better
projects and policies, is key to providing truly valuable assistance to countries
seeking to improve delivery of justice to their citizens.

The IDB's process of determining what areas to focus on, what limits to establish, and what processes of reform to employ, has been gradual and based
upon the experience the IDB is gaining in the development of projects. The
IDB has learned, over the last six years, that its ability to have a broad focus
on many substantive areas of justice reform has been useful in responding to
the needs of Latin America and the Caribbean. Since not all multilateral development banks and other agencies working in justice reform are able to act
in all areas of justice reform, the IDB has sometimes been able to provide assistance where others do not. This is reflected in the projects in areas such as
access to justice, juvenile justice reform, criminal law reform, domestic violence, human rights and violence prevention — in addition to more traditional
projects in commercial law reform, court administration and case management. The IDB is now examining whether to develop areas of particular
expertise and emphasis, although it seems unlikely to abandon its potential
breadth of action.

In the opinion of this writer, establishing the agenda for justice reform in
Latin America, though an important and delicate task, will be easy in com-
parison with the task of implementing that agenda. The need for increasing
the quality and efficiency of court functioning, for example, is not very polemical as an agenda item. Achieving that end, however, may take much time
and great effort, because it will involve more than one public institution and
because the process of bringing about institutional change is often difficult and
rarely entirely predictable wherever it is attempted. But also because change of
this nature changes the ability of parties to influence the court process and
may therefore challenge entrenched interests.

The true challenge will be whether we can carry out the agenda we set.
Will citizens and governments see that, as a result of reform efforts, judiciaries
are serving citizens, serving the economy, serving justice? Will they see that reform efforts bring about access for all? Will they perceive greater respect for
human rights, lesser incidence of corruption, more equitable court decisions?
Will they see utility in changing the balance of political power to give greater
voice to the legislative and judicial branches of the government? In short, will

justice projects have real impact, such as to make it worthwhile for countries to incur debt to carry them out? Will the reforms be sustainable over time?

Part of our agenda must be to work in a collaborative manner to make it possible to learn quickly enough from experience gained to make it likely that justice reform projects will be successful. NGOs, governments, universities, policy institutions and multilateral development banks will need to collaborate in thinking about improved methodologies for design, execution and oversight of justice projects. We need to make this sort of collaboration part of the agenda, too.

Appendix 5.1

Inter-American Development Bank:
Approved Projects in the Areas of Justice Reform and Citizen Safety*

JUSTICE REFORM
I. Loan Operations

1994 URUGUAY
Programme To Strengthen Social Areas

Borrower: Eastern Republic of Uruguay
Executing agency: The Planning and Budget Office, Office of the Presidency of the Republic as general coordinator; the Supreme Court of Justice as one of the co-executing agencies.
Total Amount: US$ 42.5m   **IDB contribution**: US$ 30.0m
Cofinancing: Local counterpart funding US$ 12.5m
Financial terms: Loan with a 25 years amortisation period, and a 4 years grace period, disbursed over 4 years.
Objectives: The programme intends a comprehensive approach towards facilitating actions in the areas of health care, education, labour and justice, accompanied by nutrition programmes. The objective in the field of justice is to lay the groundwork for a comprehensive reform of the sector. In order to do so, the project contemplates a small component with the following objectives (i) to identify existing problems and propose alternative solutions; (ii) to establish a data bank that will allow for efficient planing and follow-up on the administration of the justice systems; and (iii) to prepare detailed plans for the implementation of measures to improve the quality of justice and increase access to and coverage of the system.
Components: The judicial component includes: (i) law reform, which includes a) an analysis of current socio-economic legislation and its application, streamlining procedures to increase participation by marginal social groups and b) steps to make legislation compatible for better regional integration: (ii) introduction and improvement of alternative dispute resolution mechanisms. (iii) detect measures that will improve access to justice; and (iv) institutional strengthening of the Judiciary, which includes: training to improve administration and management of the resources and personnel of the courts, establishment of parameters to measure the system's internal efficiency, training of judges and legal assistants, the design of a programme for civic education and education on the functions of the country's judicial branch, through the strengthening of the Supreme Court office of public relations to enhance communications with the community and keep it informed about the institution.

1995 COLOMBIA
Programme to Modernise the Administration of Justice

Borrower: Republic of Colombia

---

* This document was prepared by Bárbara Zegers, State and Civil Society Division, Sustainable Development Department, Inter-American Development Bank, March 2000.

Executing Agency: Fiscalía General de la Nación (Office of the Attorney General)
Total amount: US$ 15.7m   **IDB contribution**: US$ 9.4m
Cofinancing: local counterpart funding US$ 6.3m
Financing conditions: reimbursable Technical Cooperation with a 20 years amortisation period, and a 4 years grace period, disbursed over 4 years.
Objectives: To modernise the Attorney General's Office through: (a) upgrading the technical and strategic planning capacity of its personnel and introducing computerisation and statistical systems for efficient assessment and management, (b) formulating the Office's input into national criminal justice policy, and (c) establishing selection and resource allocation criteria for infrastructure investment.
Components: To achieve these objectives, the programme comprises four components. First, to strengthen the court system, it will focus on human resource management, information systems, mechanisms for handling case investigations, and a system to assess administrative management. The second component will provide training to public attorneys, investigators and administrative personnel in planning and administrative techniques. The two additional components relate to developing a criminal justice policy and preparing an investment plan for physical infrastructure.

1995 COSTA RICA
Programme to Modernise the Administration of Justice

Borrower: Republic of Costa Rica
Executing agency: Supreme Court of Justice.
Total amount: US$ 16.0m   **IDB contribution**: US$ 11.2m
Cofinancing: local counterpart funding US$ 4.8m
Financial terms: loan with 25 years amortisation period, and a 5 years grace period, disbursed over 5 years.
Objectives: To help Costa Rica create a more equitable, accessible and dependable judiciary, enabling authorities to reduce the backlog of cases and relieve congestion in the court system.
Components: The project involves strengthening the administration of justice through an analysis and redesign of administrative procedures and administration training courses for the Supreme Judiciary Council. It also includes introduction of a new organisational structure, computer networks and word processors, a case flow management system and training in new functions and systems. Assistance to law faculties in enhancing the effectiveness of legal training is an important feature of the project, as is the development of a strategy to set up a computerised centre for legal documents.

1996 EL SALVADOR
Programme to Support the Reform of the Judicial System

Borrower: The Republic of El Salvador.
Executing Agency: Coordinating and co-executing agency: Technical Executing Unit/Coordinating Commission for the Justice Sector (UTE/CCSJ) Co-executing agencies: the Judicial Branch, the Ministry of Justice, the Attorney General's office, the Solicitor General's Office, The National Council of the Judiciary, and the

Salvadorean Institute for the Protection of Minors.
Total amount: US$ 27.3m   **IDB contribution**: US$ 22.2m
Cofinancing: local counterpart funding: US$ 5.1m
Financial terms: loan, with 25 years amortisation period, and a 4 years grace period, disbursed over 4 years.
Objectives: To facilitate modernisation and strengthening of the justice system by enhancing legal and public security and making the system's institutions more efficient.
Components: Three components have been designed to meet these objectives. The first will help carry forward the criminal law reform work already underway, launch a study of administrative laws and introduce legislation on alternative dispute settlement. The second component seeks to reform the juvenile justice system through the building of infrastructure such as youth detention centres, a special fund to promote juvenile justice initiatives by civil society organisations and an administrative training programme. The final component aims to strengthen enforcement agencies by upgrading their planning units, developing a comprehensive criminal justice policy, creating an integrated justice centre, and improving and unifying information systems.

1996 HONDURAS
Programme to modernise the Administration of Justice.

Borrower: Republic of Honduras
Executing Agency: Supreme Court of Justice
Total amount: US$ 8.0m **IDB contribution**: US$ 7.2m
Cofinancing: local counterpart funding US$ 0.8m
Financial terms: loan, with a 40 years amortisation period, and a 10 years grace period, disbursed over 4 years.
Objectives: The overall objective is to support the government in its efforts to modernise the administration of justice and create an efficient and reliable system that will enhance access to justice and bolster the investment climate.
Components: The project aims at institutional strengthening through measures to enhance the efficiency of administration and planning, also to train and improve capacity building for agencies involved. The programme also promotes access to justice by upgrading public defenders; encouraging resort to alternative dispute settlement methods; implementing public oral court hearings and strengthening justices of the peace. A non-reimbursable technical cooperation was given to the Honduran government to draft and enact new legislation on organisation and attributions of courts, constitutional jurisdiction, Civil Procedures, domestic violence, rights of children, and investment promotion.

1996 PARAGUAY
State Modernisation Programme

Borrower: Republic of Paraguay
Executing agency: Supreme Court of Justice, Office of the Attorney General, and the Ministry of Justice and Labour.
Total amount: US$ 33.9m   **IDB contribution**: US$ 12m
Cofinancing: Spain US$ 7.0m; local counterpart funding US$ 4.9m

Financial terms: loan, with a 25 years amortisation period, and a 5 years grace period, disbursed over 5 years.

Objectives: To strengthen the judicial system and the climate of legal certainty and predictability to allow economic and social development and reinforce the rule of law.

Components: The project will have two sub-programmes: (1) strengthening of the judiciary through a management organisation system, an information system and a pilot project for court office infrastructure to provide the capacity for the judiciary to properly evaluate performance and to plan and formulate policies; and (2) modernising the civil registry, development of a records management system and a financial and administrative management system, modernisation of the legal framework, provision of infrastructure, and efforts to increase registration rates.

1997 ARGENTINA
Judicial System Reform

Borrower: The Nation of Argentina

Executing Agency: The Ministry of Justice and Justice system agencies, the National Treasury Prosecutor's Office, the Public Prosecutor's Office, the Public Defender's Office and The Federal Board of Provincial Courts.

Total amount: US$ 21.0m. **IDB contribution**: US$ 10.5m

Cofinancing: local counterpart financing US$ 10.5m

Financing terms: loan with a 20 years amortisation period, and a 4 years grace period, disbursed over 4 years.

Objectives: To support judicial reform by financing replicable pilot projects for changing and modernising the judicial sector

Components: The project includes a legal protection sub-programme to strengthen the National Treasury Prosecutor's Office by modernising case management and training administrative and legal staff. It will also strengthen the Public Prosecutor's Office by supporting administrative, financial and human resource management, developing internal regulations, introducing information systems and training prosecutors. The project also supports the design and implementation of crime prevention programmes and access to justice, promoting mediation as an alternative dispute settlement method, technical upgrading and training for staff of the Public Defender's Office to promote access to justice for underprivileged sectors of society; development of information systems and technical reinforcement of the National Department of Criminal Policy for use in formulating crime prevention policies; and computerising the penitentiary system to facilitate access to justice and to monitor the rights of prisoners and the status of their sentences. The programme will also support establishment of a new Institute for the Enhancement of Provincial Justice and development of a compendium of existing national legislation.

1997 BRAZIL
Programme to Modernise the Executive Branch of the federal Government

Borrower: Federal Republic of Brazil

Executing Agency: Ministério de Administração Federal e Reforma do Estado (MARE)

Total Amount: First phase: US$ 114.0mSecond phase: US$ 66.0m
IDB Contribution: First phase: US$ 57.0m Second phase: US$ 33.0m
Cofinancing: Local counterpart funding: 1st phase: US$ 57.0m; 2nd phase: US$ 33.0m
Financial Terms: Loan with a 20 year amortisation period, and a 3 year grace period, disbursed over 3 years.
Objectives: to improve performance within Brazil's federal civil service, seeking increased efficiency and cost effectiveness in public servants' execution of their tasks.
Components: To strengthen the technical capacity of human resources the programme is divided in four sub-programmes: institutional reform, management and human resource development, management and information technology and citizen support services. Of those sub-programmes two incorporate measures to improve the justice system. The first one, the sub-programme for management and human resources development, contemplates, among other measures, the design and implementation of a new basic curriculum for law enforcement officials at the state and federal level, as well as the pertinent teaching materials and training programmes for instructors. The new curriculum will emphasise courses on human rights and community policing, among other topics. The second one, the management and information technology, finances the computerisation of the federal public administration through 10 projects. One of those projects will create a single national computer information system for criminal and penitentiary records. The programme will provide resources to hire consultants and purchase equipment for the computerisation of state databanks; creation of a national index by name and serial number of weapons registered or seized by the police; design and installation of a network of information systems and compilation of a listing of authorised users to maintain the confidentiality and security of the system.

1997 DOMINICAN REPUBLIC
Programme to Modernise Real Property Adjudication and Registration System

Borrower: The Dominican Republic
Executing Agency: The Supreme Court of Justice
Total Amount: US$ 40.0m   **IDB contribution**: US$ 32.0m
Cofinancing: local counterpart funding US$ 8.0m
Financial terms: loan with a 25 years amortisation period, and a 4 years grace period, disbursed over 4 years.
Objectives: To achieve a Real Property Adjudication and Registration System within the Judicial Branch that performs its adjudication and arbitration functions efficiently and transparently.
Components: The project includes components relating to legal and institutional issues, reform of the Land Registry Law and related legislation, the organisational decentralisation of jurisdiction and measures to regularise deeding and ownership procedures; infrastructure upgrading and headquarters renovation for the Superior Land Tribunal and creation of new tribunals and regional offices; technical updating and new information systems; training programme for staff of the Superior Land Tribunal.

1997 PERU
Improving Access to Justice System.

Borrower: Republic of Peru
Executing Agency: Peruvian Judicial Branch, through the Executive Committee of the Judiciary, which in turn will act through its Project Management Office.
Total amount: US$ 28.6m   **IDB contribution**: US$ 20.0m
Cofinancing: local counterpart financing US$ 8.6m
Financial terms: loan, with a 25 years amortisation period, and a grace period of 3 years, disbursed over 3 years.
Objectives: To support the Peruvian justice system's efforts to broaden access to justice and enhance its quality. In particular, the project seeks to strengthen the grassroots levels of justice administration in low-income areas where the problem of court backlogs is greatest.
Components: Three components have been designed to achieve these goals. The first will create approximately 83 basic justice modules (MBJ), and involves the building of 83 centres to house the MBJs; purchase and installation of furnishings and equipment for their operation; design of an IT system; design of a training programme for MBJ staff; technical assistance in the preparation of documents, plans, etc. The second component seeks to enhance the protection of women's and children's rights, and involves training for judges in gender and youth issues, enlisting the help of NGOs that are equipped to mediate between these groups and the justice system; and recommendations for nation-wide access programmes. The final component consists of developing and disseminating information, using the mass media to reach the communities concerned; an education programme on basic rights and fundamental liberties; and holding 332 seminars to generate political and social support among communities affected by the programme.

1998 GUATEMALA
Programme in Support of Judicial Reform

Borrower: Republic of Guatemala
Executing Agency: Secretaría Ejecutiva de la Instancia Coordinadora de la Modernización del Sector Justicia [Executive Secretariat of the Coordinating Authority for Modernisation of the Justice Sector] (ICMSJ). Co-executing agencies: The Judicial Branch, The Public Prosecutor's Office, the Public Defender's Office, and The Ministry of the Interior.
Total amount: US$ 31.0m   **IDB contribution**: US$ 25m
Cofinancing: local counterpart funding US$ 6.0m
Financial terms: loan, with a 30 years amortisation period, and a 4 years grace period.
Objectives: To strengthen the democratic and multicultural rule of law by providing support to the institutions of the justice system, at the individual institutional level as well as in terms of coordination between institutions, in order to improve access to justice and the quality of judicial services.
Components: The programme is divided in two sub-programmes: (a) Access to justice: improving coverage of the judicial system in deprived communities, facilitating physical, linguistic, and cultural access to justice through the construction and

placement of 8 Justice Administration Centres (Centros de Administración de Justicia) (CAJs), 47 juzgados de paz (justice of the peace offices), and 10 district prosecutor's offices, as well as the implementation of special activities designed for the indigenous communities. (b) Institutional Strengthening: in an initial phase, provide support to institutions in the sector seeking to strengthen their managerial, technical, and administrative capacities, and in a second phase, establish the mechanisms for inter-institutional coordination, allowing for greater recourse to deliberation and joint action in addressing common problems within the sector.

1998 PANAMA
Improvements in the Administration of Justice stage one

Borrower: Republic of Panama
Executing Agency: Judicial Branch, Procuraduría General de la Nación (PGN) [Office of the National Public Prosecutor] and Procuraduría de la Administración (PA) [Office of the Government Solicitor].
Total amount: US$ 27.0m   **IDB contribution**: US$ 18.9m
Cofin**ancing** local counterpart funding US$ 8.1m
Financial terms: loan with a 25 years amortisation period, and a 3.5 years grace period, disbursed over 3.5 years.
Objectives: To improve the quality of the country's legal and judicial services to strengthen the rule of law.
Components: The operation is stage one and involves some activities that can be implemented at the national level in the short-term. The activities will be executed through two models for judicial management and reorganisation, one in an urban judicial district and one in the countryside for a second stage. It is divided in two sub-programmes: (a) clearing of court backlog, strategic management and planning, training and judicial career path, reorganisation and management of judicial services, strengthening of the investigative capacity of the PGN, procedural reform and access to justice and citizen participation; and (b) institutional restructuring of the PA, plan to expand the coverage of services, staff training, automation of management process, reform of administrative regulations and legal training for public servants.

1999 BOLIVIA
Programme for Civil Society and Access to Justice

Borrower: Republic of Bolivia
Executing Agency: Ministry of Justice and Human Rights
Total Amount: US$ 3.0m **IDB Contribution**: US$ 2.7m
Cofinancing: local counterpart financing US$ 0.3m
Financial terms: reimbursable Technical Cooperation with a 40 years amortisation period, and a 10 years grace period, disbursed over 4 years.
Objectives: To help the most vulnerable segments of the population gain access to justice and awareness of their rights by strengthening the mechanisms for participation of civil society in the sector.
Components: The programme has two components: (a) channelling resources to projects by civil society organisations whose objectives are to strengthen and expand the services they provide in the area of access to justice, and train and educate the

most vulnerable sectors of the population in their rights; and (b) technical assistance to conduct training and dissemination activities designed to strengthen project design and management skills; conduct periodic evaluations to assess the accomplishment of the programme objectives and its impact and design an information, statistics and control systems for the management of the programme and its projects.

II

Non- Reimbursable Technical Cooperation

Alternative Dispute Resolution for the Commercial Sector

1994 PERU
Development of Alternative Dispute Settlement Systems

Total amount: US$ 1.47m   **IDB contribution**: US$1.47m
Non-reimbursable technical cooperation
Applicant: Ministry of Justice
Executor: Asociación Peruana de Negociación, Arbitraje y Conciliación in coordination with the Ministry of Justice
Objectives: To develop and disseminate alternative mechanisms for settling disputes, training for public and private sector personnel in the use of such mechanisms, and supporting arbitration and conciliation centres in Lima and in the provinces.
Components: The programme contains five components to meet these goals. The first involves setting up an executing agency to promote arbitration, negotiation and conciliation. The second component consists of familiarisation conferences and workshops on the use of alternative dispute settlement mechanisms, for the public sector (the judicial branch), the private sector (producers and trade associations), law societies, schools and the general public. The third component seeks to strengthen the Arbitration and Conciliation Centre of the Lima Chamber of Commerce, and to set up similar centres in the provinces. The fourth component will set up pilot projects to track the outcome of arbitration and conciliation under different scenarios. The final component will develop proposed legislative changes to make alternative dispute settlement mechanisms operationally more effective.

1995 COLOMBIA
Promotion of Alternative Methods of Commercial Dispute Settlement

Total amount: US$ 1.808m   **IDB contribution**: US$ 1.22m
Non-reimbursable technical cooperation
Applicant: Arbitration and Conciliation Centres
Executor: Cámara de Comercio de Bogotá
Objectives: (a) to build institutional capacities for arbitration and conciliation centres; (b) training for arbitrators, conciliators, and administrative personnel at the centres; (c) strengthening capacities of the Justice Ministry to support arbitration and conciliation centres; (d) disseminating information on the advantages of arbitration and conciliation as commercial dispute settlement methods.
Components: Three components have been designed to meet these objectives. First, strengthening the centres involves taking steps to improve their administration, such as providing procedural manuals and administrative software. The second component, personnel training, involves introducing mediation techniques, special training for arbitrators, mediators and administrators, and institutional capacity building for regional chambers of commerce. The final component will set up workshops and discussion forums for promoting alternative dispute settlement methods among business people and entrepreneurs

1995 COSTA RICA
Establishing Alternative Systems for Settling Commercial Disputes

Total amount: US$ 1.36m   **IDB contribution**: US$ 1.13m
Non-reimbursable technical cooperation
Applicant: Fundación para el Mejoramiento de la Administración de Justicia
Executor: Fundación para el Mejoramiento de la Administración de Justicia
Objectives: To support the establishment of alternative mechanisms of dispute settlement that will reduce the cost of conflict resolution.
Components: To achieve this goal, the programme has three main components. The first seeks to encourage private sector resort to alternative dispute settlement methods. It includes designing information packages and disseminating them by radio, TV and the press, and holding seminars and workshops. The second component is aimed at establishing a legal framework and an Alternative Dispute Settlement Programme (PRAC). This component involves training judicial personnel in coordinating arbitration and regular court functions, and creating a legal framework conducive to alternative dispute settlement methods. The third component will develop a training plan to upgrade technical and administrative skills needed for making use of mediation and arbitration services. The training will be targeted at lawyers, mediators, secretaries and other administrative personnel. The final component is establishment of an arbitration and mediation centre, to be located within the Costa Rica Chamber of Commerce.

1995 URUGUAY
Support Programme for the Conciliation and Arbitration Centre.

Total amount: US$ 1.68m   **IDB contribution**: US$ 0.835m
Non-reimbursable technical cooperation
Applicant: Centre for Conciliation and Arbitration of the Bolsa de Comercio de Montevideo S.A.
Executor: Centre for Conciliation and Arbitration of the Bolsa de Comercio de Montevideo S.A. **Components**: The programme contains four components to achieve this objective. The conceptual development component will analyse the legal framework as it affects the use of alternative dispute settlement methods. The organisation and operations component will strengthen the Centre's capacities. The training component offers training in arbitration and conciliation techniques, directly and through the instruction and qualification of training personnel. The fourth component, promotion and dissemination, sponsor conferences and workshops to familiarise the private sector in how to make use of the centre.

1996 EL SALVADOR
Modernising Commercial Legislation and Developing Alternative Methods of Commercial Dispute Settlement

Total amount: US$ 1.024m   **IDB contribution**: US$ 0.662m
Non-reimbursable technical cooperation
Applicant: Unidad Técnica Ejecutiva Sector Justicia para la Modernización de la Legislación Comercial [Technical Executing Unit of the Justice Sector] and Chamber

of Commerce and Industry of El Salvador
Executor: Unidad Técnica Ejecutiva Sector Justicia and Chamber of Commerce and Industry of El Salvador
Objectives: To reform commercial legislation, including development of inexpensive and swift alternative methods for settling disputes.
Components: The programme involves the updating of commercial laws, including the study, analysis and revision of existing legislation and training in the enforcement of new regulations. It will also develop alternative mechanisms for settling commercial disputes, including the revision of legislation governing conciliation and mediation, and establishment of an arbitration and conciliation centre for the Chamber of Commerce of San Salvador.

1996 HONDURAS
Promoting Alternative Methods of Commercial Dispute Settlement

Total amount: US$ 0.774m **IDB contribution**: US$ 0.497m
Non-reimbursable technical cooperation
Applicant: Cámara de Comercio e Industrias de Cortés y Cámara de Comercio e Industrias de Tegucigalpa.
Executor: Cámara de Comercio e Industrias de Cortés y Cámara de Comercio e Industrias de Tegucigalpa.
Objectives: To facilitate the settlement of commercial disputes by developing out-of-court resolution methods and providing the private sector with an effective, swift and inexpensive instrument for settling commercial disputes.
Components: These include updating the legal framework and designing an arbitration law; strengthening the Conciliation and Arbitration Centre of the Cortés Chamber of Commerce and establishing and supporting a conciliation and arbitration centre for the Tegucigalpa Chamber of Commerce, and disseminating information to encourage out-of-court settlement of commercial disputes.

1996 PANAMA
Promoting Alternative Methods of Settling Commercial Disputes

Total amount: US$ 0.470m **IDB contribution**: US$ 0.270m
Non-reimbursable technical cooperation
Applicant: Cámara de Comercio, Industrias y Agricultura de Panama.
Executor: Cámara de Comercio, Industrias y Agricultura de Panama.
Objectives: To speed up settlement of commercial disputes in Panama through out-of-court procedures that offer efficient and specialised services to the private sector.
Components: There are five components to the programme. The first seeks to review the legal and regulatory framework governing conciliation and arbitration to identify needed reforms. The second component will provide institutional and technical capacity building for the Panama Centre of Conciliation and Arbitration. The third component sets out a plan for mediators, arbitrators and administrative personnel. The fourth component will promote the use of conciliation and arbitration services through business workshops and the design of information materials. The final component is aimed at helping the various chambers of commerce already using alternative dispute settlement methods to share experiences and lessons learned.

1997 ECUADOR
Programme to Establish Centres for Training and Dissemination of Commercial Dispute Resolution Alternatives

Total amount: US$ 1,047,618m **IDB contribution**: US$ 0.720m
Non-reimbursable technical cooperation
Applicant: The Chambers of Commerce of Quito and Guayaquil
Executor: The Chambers of Commerce of Quito and Guayaquil
Objectives: To establish a coordinated and properly structured commercial dispute resolution system in Ecuador, that will gradually introduce swift and cost-effective commercial dispute resolution alternatives.
Components: The programme has three components: (a) establishment of the training and dissemination centres at the Quito and Guayaquil chambers of commerce, where each will train some 200 participants. A plan for disseminating commercial dispute resolution alternatives will be devised and put into practice, part of which will be a marketing strategy using workshops, seminars, audiovisuals, and the preparation of material; (b) support for the regulatory framework, to assist the two chambers of commerce in their efforts to modernise current legislation on commercial arbitration and mediation; and (c) strategic development, which includes a midterm evaluation (at month 16) to use the findings in the design of a medium-range development plan for the rest of the programme term. It will include a programme to strengthen the administrative and technical capacity of the centres and a plan to continue the activities for at least another three years after the programme is completed.

1998 GUATEMALA
Programme to Strengthen Alternative Methods for Commercial Dispute Resolution

Total amount: US$ 0.650m   **IDB contribution**: US$ 0.450m
Non-reimbursable technical cooperation
Applicant: Chamber of Commerce of Guatemala (CCG)
Executor: Chamber of Commerce of Guatemala
Objectives: To strengthen and consolidate Guatemala's alternative methods for commercial dispute resolution.
Components: The programme has three components: (a) consolidation of the institutional and administrative framework to provide adequate and reliable alternative dispute resolution services; (b) preparation of a development and dissemination strategy for ADR services that will lead to the consolidation of a market for those services; and (c) improving the technical capacity of the ADR system, through the operators, support staff, users and their representatives, and member of the judicial system.

1999 BRAZIL
Programme to Strengthen Labour Dispute Negotiation and Mediation Processes

Total amount: US$ 1.561m   **IDB contribution**: US$ 0.841m

Non-reimbursable technical cooperation
Applicant: Brazilian Government
Executor: Federal Republic of Brazil through the Ministry of Labour (MTE) through the Department of Labour Relations
Objectives: To help with the transformation of culture of labour relations by introducing new ways to resolve disputes based on free collective bargaining, independent mediation, and self-determination of employers and workers.
Components: A highly participatory process involving stakeholders associated with the country's labour relations will be followed during all the phases of design and implementation. It will finance technical assistance for the development of methodologies, work seminars, technical visits to countries with relevant experience in collective bargaining and/or mediation; design of a public domain information system; publications; training courses to upgrade the professional profile of negotiators; and awareness and communication. Three components will be executed: (a) methodology and design development, (b) awareness and dissemination, and (c) training courses.

1999 BRAZIL
Strengthening Alternative Dispute Resolution Methods

Total Amount: US$ 3,340,360m **IDB contribution**: US$ 1,599,400m
Non-reimbursable technical cooperation
Applicant: Brazilian Federation of Trade Associations (CACB)
Executor: Brazilian Federation of Trade Associations (CACB)
Objectives: To strengthen and consolidate Brazil's alternative methods for commercial dispute resolution at both the national and regional levels, thereby improving the efficiency of Brazil's dispute resolution mechanisms and reducing the backlog in the court system.
Components: The project will: (a) strengthen participating Arbitration and Mediation Centres (CAMs) by consolidating their technical and institutional organisation so that they are able to provide their services with greater efficiency and effectiveness, (b) train arbitrators, mediators and operation personnel of participating CAMs, providing them with the technical and administrative skills required by their institutions, and (c) publicise the importance and benefits of ADR methods in order to ensure the gradual adoption of these mechanisms by the private sector.

1999 CHILE
Expansion and Improvement of Commercial Arbitration and Mediation Services

Total amount: US$ 1.313m **IDB contribution**: US$ 0.650m
Non-reimbursable technical cooperation
Applicant: Cámara de Comercio de Santiago A.G.
Executor: Cámara de Comercio de Santiago A.G.
Objectives: To contribute to the development of a culture of commercial dispute resolution by extra-judicial methods, thus helping to alleviate the burden of cases in the regular justice system and to establish a favourable environment for private investment.

Components: The programme involves (a) strengthening of the Santiago Centres for Arbitration and Mediation (CAM) and establishing a CAM in Valparaiso; and (b) instructing arbitrators, mediators and clerks involved in arbitration for the two CAMs on the techniques and practices of general and technical arbitration and mediation and promote the use of ADR methods in the business, judicial and legal communities of Santiago and Valparaiso.

1999 PARAGUAY
Programme to Strengthen Alternatives for Dispute Resolution in Commercial Conflicts

Total amount: US$ 0.830 **IDB contribution**: US$ 0.503
Non-reimbursable technical cooperation
Applicant: Asunción Chamber of Commerce and Commodity Exchange
Executor: Asunción Chamber of Commerce and Commodity Exchange (CBCA)
Objectives: To provide technical assistance to the Paraguayan Centre for Arbitration and Conciliation.
Components: The programme will (a) strengthen the legal, institutional, and administrative framework for alternative for dispute resolution mechanisms (ADR) in order to adapt it into and ADR system for use in Paraguay and disputes with other countries, particularly in the context of MERCOSUR; (b) enhance the technical capacity of the operators, support staff, users and their representatives, and members of the judicial system in order to obtain a quality supply of ADR services and adequate and reliable demand for such services; and (c) prepare and implement a strategy for development and dissemination of ADR services, in an effort to consolidate their use and make them financially self-sustaining.

1999 VENEZUELA
Institutional Strengthening of a Commercial Mediation and Arbitration Centre

Total Amount: US$ 1.5m **IDB contribution**: US$ 0.729,170m
Non-reimbursable technical cooperation
Applicant: Caracas Chamber of Commerce (CCC)
Executor: Caracas Chamber of Commerce
Objectives: To provide institutional strengthening for the Arbitration Centre of the CCC and increase the demands for its services.
Components: The project is divided into four components: (a) review of laws and regulations, including an examination of the applicable legal framework governing alternative dispute resolution mechanisms and submission to Congress on proposals for expanding its use; (b) institutional strengthening of the CCC, seeking to consolidate its operating capacity and provide logistical support, enabling the centre to provide high- quality ADR services; (c) training programmes for the preparation of arbitrators, mediators, clerks of arbitration boards and multipliers; and(d) promotional campaign and public awareness activities to create an effective level of demand over the short and medium terms within the business community and among academic, government and judicial authorities involved, as well as the community at large

1999 DOMINICAN REPUBLIC
Support for the Establishment and Strengthening of a Centre for the Study, Prevention and Resolution of Social Conflicts

Total Amount: US$ 0.500m　**IDB contribution**: US$ 0.340m
Non-reimbursable technical cooperation
Applicant: Pontificia Universidad Católica Madre y Maestra [Madre y Maestra Pontifical University] Dominican Republic.
Executor: Centre for the Study, Prevention and Resolution of Social Conflicts.
Objectives: To help institutionalise forums for dialogue and the spread of democratic participation and consensus-building processes as a mechanisms for social, economic and political inclusion.
Components: The project is intended to support the University in establishing and strengthening a centre for the study, prevention and resolution of social conflicts as an institutional basis for training, research, use and dissemination of mechanisms to prevent and settle social disputes. The programme will finance (i) technical advisory services to design and introduce programmes on conflict resolution; (ii) institutional development; (iii) a seminar on consensus-building and conflict management ; and (iv) training workshops.

2000 TRINIDAD AND TOBAGO
Strengthening of the Alternative Dispute Resolution System

Total Amount: US$ 0.590m　**IDB contribution**: US$ 0.383,5m
Non-reimbursable technical cooperation
Applicant: The Trinidad and Tobago Chamber of Industry and Commerce (TTCIC)
Executor: The Trinidad and Tobago Chamber of Industry and Commerce
Objectives: Improve the environment for business transactions and private investment by strengthening the ability of the Dispute Resolution Centre (DRC) to promote and operate a reliable Alternate Dispute Resolution (ADR) system within the country and at a sub-regional level.
Components: To achieve the objectives the project will have the following sub-programmes: (a) technical assistance to carry out a review of the legal and regulatory framework for ADR in Trinidad and Tobago and in the Caribbean region; (b) institutional strengthening of the Dispute Resolution Centre (ADR) by financing physical infrastructure, operating systems, financial resources and technical capacity to provide high quality and cost effective ADR services; (c) design of a training plan and of selection mechanisms and training opportunities for professionals interested in becoming ADR practitioners; and (d) design of a marketing study to provide a basis for the design and implementation of a campaign to promote the concept of ADR and its advantages, the recognition of DRC as leading provider of these services, and the wide use of ADR and of the DRC services in Trinidad and Tobago and throughout the Caribbean.

2000 ARGENTINA
Programme to Establish a National Network of Commercial Mediation and Arbitration Centres

Total Amount: US$ 2.508m   **IDB contribution**: US$ 1.0m
Non-reimbursable technical cooperation
Applicant: Argentine Chamber of Commerce (CAC)
Executor: Argentine Chamber of Commerce
Objectives: To help Argentina's business sector become more competitive and economically efficient and to enhance the climate for private investment in the country, by establishing a National Network of Commercial Mediation and Arbitration Centres and strengthening the institutional capacity of network centres. Description: The programme would have four components: (i) establishment of a National Network of Commercial Mediation and Arbitration Centres; (ii) institutional strengthening of Network Centres; (iii) training of neutral third parties (arbitrators and mediators) to work in the Network; and (iv) strategic publicity on the merits of institutionalised mediation and arbitration, and market penetration initiatives.

Resolution of Property Conflicts

1995 NICARAGUA
Programme of Support for the Resolution of Property Conflicts

Total Amount: US$ 3.3m **IDB contribution**: US$ 2.8m
Non-refundable technical cooperation
Applicant: Ministry of Finance (MIFIN) of Nicaragua
Executor: Ministry of Finance, through office of the Deputy Minister for Property
Objectives: To collaborate with the Nicaraguan government in speeding up the administrative resolution of property- related conflicts and initiating a process for titling urban property.
Components: The programme has three components: (a) administrative and technical strengthening of the Office of the deputy Minister for Property, the Office of the Attorney General for Property (PGP) and the National Commission for the Review of Confiscations (CNRC); (b) installation of a pilot urban titling programme; and (c) training and a publicity programme for relevant agency personnel.

1997 DOMINICAN REPUBLIC
Programme to Support the Modernisation of Real Property Adjudication System.

Total amount: US$ 0.150m   **IDB contribution**: US$ 0.150m
Non-refundable technical cooperation
Applicant: Government of Dominican Republic
Objectives: To assist the Government of the Dominican Republic in analysing the legal, institutional, and infrastructure framework of the Comisión Nacional de Modernización de la Jusridcicción de Tierras, and in formulating guidelines and recommendations for the optimal functioning of the Programme to Modernise the Real Property Adjudication and Registration System (PMJT).
Components: The programme will finance the hiring of a specialised firm to analyse

the institutional and legal framework of the PMJT, to update its technological resources, and reorganise and strengthen its technical and human resources.

1999 NICARAGUA
Programme to Support Alternative Mechanisms for Settling Property Disputes

Total amount: US$1.669,662m **IDB contribution**: US$0.982,456m
Non-refundable technical cooperation
Applicant: Nicaragua
Executor: Supreme Court of Justice of Nicaragua
Objectives: To support Nicaragua in settling property disputes, particularly through the introduction of the new alternative mechanisms established in the law, to be coordinated with the existing property system.
Components: The programme includes four components: (a) establishment and start up of the Dirección de Resolución Alterna de Conflictos de la Propiedad (DIRAC) [Alternative Property Dispute Settlement Directorate] in the Supreme Court; (b) training programme to obtain suitable staff, mediators and arbitrators who will provide efficient and effective service for rapid settlement of disputes about property; (c) publicity programme to broadcast the benefits and advantages of mediation and arbitration for persons involved in property disputes and for the community in general; and (d) support for the Property Bureau. As a continuation of technical assistance project of 1995, the Supreme Court agreed that this operation would offer support for the Property Bureau to increase efficiency processing of property claims and to improve coordination between them and the DIRAC.

Technical Assistance for Development of Justice Reform Projects

1995 DOMINICAN REPUBLIC
Support for Community Initiatives to Enhance the Administration of Justice.

Total amount: US$ 0.125m **IDB contribution**: US$ 0.100m
Non-reimbursable technical cooperation
Applicant: Fundación Institucionalidad y Justicia (FINJUS)
Executor: FINJUS
Objectives: To support the Foundation for Justice and Institutionality (FINJUS) in its programme to promote modernisation of the administration of justice.
Components: The project is supporting the preparation of basic analytic studies and the design of an action strategy in the judicial sector; training for judges and civil servants; and improving the administration of legal departments. It also involves consensus building through the national forum for Improving the Administration of Justice in the Dominican Republic and capacity building for FINJUS through programmes of evaluation, training and equipment.

1995 EL SALVADOR
Programme to Support the Reform of the Justice System

Total amount: US$ 0.144m   **IDB contribution**: US$ 0.137m
Non-reimbursable technical cooperation
Applicant: Ministerio de Planificación y Coordinación del Desarrollo Económico y Social (MIPLAN)
Executor: Comisión Coordinadora para el Sector Justicia/Unidad Técnica Ejecutora
Objectives: To help the Salvadorean government with preparation and implementation of the programme to strengthen the Judicial System.
Components: The technical cooperation finances the following components: (a) institutional strengthening, (b) establishment of alternative dispute resolution mechanisms, (c) penitentiary system reform, (d) protection and reeducation of delinquent and at-risk youngsters, (e) support of technical aspects in the development of new facilities, and (f) training programmes for personnel of those institutions.

1996 DOMINICAN REPUBLIC
Support to Modernisation of the Justice System Programme

Total amount: US$ 0.180m   **IDB contribution**: US$ 0.148m
Non-reimbursable technical cooperation
Applicant: The Dominican Republic.
Executor: Comisión Nacional de Apoyo a la Reform Judicial (CONAR)
Objectives: To increase feasibility and efficiency of future reform efforts and investments in the judicial area.
Components: The programme is divided in two components: (a) support of the Permanent Forum for discussion of modernisation of the justice system, and (b) financing of consultants in a broad range of areas to support the drafting of the Justice modernisation programme.

1996 HONDURAS
Institutional Strengthening of the Judicial System

Total amount: US$ 1.5m **IDB contribution**: US$ 1.5m
Non-reimbursable technical cooperation
Applicant: The Government of Honduras
Executor: The Supreme Court of Justice of Honduras
Objectives: To support the implementation of some of the components of the Programme to modernise the Administration of Justice in Honduras (PR-2116)
Components: Institutional strengthening of the Judicial Branch and training for all institutions participating in the administration of justice process in order to improve access to justice.

1996 NICARAGUA
Programme to support the National Assembly and the Justice System

Total amount: US$ 1.945m   **IDB contribution**: US$ 1.7m
Non-reimbursable technical cooperation

Applicant: The Government of Nicaragua.
Executor: The National Assembly of Nicaragua (NA) and the Supreme Court of Justice (SCJ)
Objectives: To support the process of consolidating the rule of law in Nicaragua by improving the country's labour legislation and setting the stage for reform of the justice system.
Components: The programme will (a) ensure the quality and consistency of existing legislation by conducting a selective review of the country's laws, (b) strengthen the rules and regulations governing the National Assembly and improve its technical capacity to carry out its legislative agenda, (c) support the process of judicial reform and consolidation through consensus-building and by paving the way to reform of the justice system and increasing spending on the sector, (d) draft improved ethical standards and enhance the professional ethics of court officials, judges and trial lawyers; and (e) lay the groundwork for programmes in the areas of office management and alternative dispute settlement mechanisms.

1997 ECUADOR
Modernising the Judicial System (Support programme for judicial reform)

Total Amount: US$ 2.4m **IDB contribution**: US$ 2.4m
Non-reimbursable technical cooperation
Applicant: Supreme Court of Justice
Executor: PROJUSTICIA
Objectives: To support the reform process for the judicial system, strengthening judicial independence, upgrading human resources and judicial administration, and facilitating access to justice.
Components: The project includes legislative development, i.e. supporting constitutional, regulatory and legal changes that will facilitate the reform now underway; it also contains a capacity building component that will set up a disciplinary system to strengthen the independence of the judiciary and a permanent, decentralised training system. The project will also strengthen the administration of justice, promote access to justice, and reinforce civil society through support for initiatives by citizen organisations.

1998 DOMINICAN REPUBLIC
Support for the Reform Programme of the Justice System for Minors

Total amount: US$ 0.120m **IDB contribution**: US$ 0.100m
Non-reimbursable technical cooperation
Applicant: the Dominican Republic
Executor: Comisionado de Apoyo a la Reforma y Modernización de la Justicia (CAMJ)
Objectives: To assist the government in the assessment of the legislation, institutions, infrastructure, equipment and personnel involved in the treatment of minors and to propose a programme for the administration of justice and protection of minors.
Components: Finance consultants in the areas of general diagnosis of the law on minors; design of institutional administrative mechanisms and training programmes;

development of court management and planning strategies; and drafting of the financing proposal for programme for the Administration of Justice and protection of minors.

1998 BOLIVIA
Support for the preparation of the Programme for Civil Society and Access to Justice

Total amount: US$ 0.150m   **IDB contribution**: US$ 0.150m
Non-reimbursable technical cooperation
Applicant: Ministry of Justice and Human Rights
Objectives: To assist the government in the assessment and design of the Programme for Civil Society and Access to Justice.
Components: Finance consultants in the areas of project design, judicial reform and alternative dispute resolutions, evaluation and design of the fund to be established to finance civil society participation, and institutional strengthening of the Ombudsman's office (Defensoría del Pueblo).

Regional Technical Cooperation

1993 – Regional – Costa Rica
I Seminar 'Justice in Latin America and the Caribbean in the 1990s. Challenges and Opportunities'

Total amount: US$ 320,000 **IDB Contribution**: US$ 300,000
Non-reimbursable technical cooperation
Applicant: IDB
Executor: IDB and the Government of Costa Rica.
Objectives: To promote dialogue on and analyse the situation of justice in the region and related reforms, and to examine the challenges in this area, given the phenomena of globalisation in the economy and law as a basic element of development.
Components: A seminar on five core topics in the areas of the administration of justice, legal training and the legal profession, justice and new approaches to development, the globalisation of law, and international cooperation. In addition, specialised studies and the results of the seminar were published and disseminated.

1995 Regional
Washington Conference on Judicial Reform in the Western Hemisphere

Total Amount: US$ 0.130m   **IDB contribution**: US$ 0.65m
Non-refundable technical Cooperation
Applicant: IDB
Executor: The Institute for the Study of the Americas (ISOA)
Objectives: To give a select group of high level judicial officials and specialists from Latin America, the Caribbean and the United States the opportunity to share experiences and exchange views on judicial reform.

Components: The Bank hired the ISOA as a professional services firm to render technical and logistical support for the two-day conference in Washington DC. Through presentations and workshops discussions, the conference allows evaluation of several of the reforms already implemented in the administration of justice in the Western Hemisphere, enabling participants to formulate future reform projects based on these evaluations.

1995 Regional – Uruguay
II Seminar 'Justice in Latin America and the Caribbean in the 1990s. Challenges and Opportunities'

Total amount: US$ 0.420m   **IDB contribution**: US$ 0.390m
Non-reimbursable technical cooperation.
Applicant: IDB
Executor: IDB
Objectives: To promote cooperation among Judicial and economic authorities, business community and potential donors to the process of reform of the justice systems with the aim of obtaining greater efficiency and efficacy in the economy.
Components: IDB borrowing countries participated in a seminar via representatives from Finance Ministries, Justice Ministries, Supreme Courts and other representatives of the public sector, private sector and international or specialised agencies. Leading specialists participated as panellists, with conference papers distributed prior to the seminar.

1996 Regional
Analysis of Best Practices in Judicial Reform

Total amount: US$ 0.350m   **IDB contribution**: US$ 0.1m
Non-reimbursable technical cooperation
Applicant: IDB
Executor: National Centre for State Courts and IDB
Objectives: To help consolidate the development, expansion and replication of best practices in reforming Latin America's judicial systems, based on a thorough analysis of experience to date.
Components: The Bank collaborated with USAID and the National Centre for State Courts to finance studies, analysis and the preparation of reports, and to support the holding of a Second Roundtable on Judicial Reform to examine the results of reform programmes carried out to date.

1996 Regional – Brazil
Seminar on State Reform in Latin America and the Caribbean

Total amount: US$ 0.400m   **IDB contribution**: US$ 0.340m
Non-reimbursable technical cooperation
Applicant: The Ministry of Public Administration and State Reform of Brazil (MARE) and the National School of Public Administration (ENAP) of Brazil.
Executor: National School of Public Administration (ENAP)
Objectives: To provide an ample opportunity for discussion and reflection on state

and government apparatus reform programmes.

Components: The seminar is organised as a series of panel discussions, followed by a discussion session moderated by the host country minister. The experiences in judicial reform of Great Britain and New Zealand were presented as well as a comparative study on state reform trends in the region, a paper on changes in the model of state throughout the world and a report by the IBDR and the IDB on their experience in support of the implementation of state reform projects.

1996 Regional
Judicial Education: Towards a Jurisprudence of Equality

Total amount: US$ 0.750m   **IDB contribution**: US$ 0.650m
Non-reimbursable technical cooperation
Applicant: Brazilian and Argentinean local chapters of the International Women Judges Foundation (IWJF).
Executor: BID and Local Chapters of the IWJF in Brazil and Argentina.
Objectives: To provide those involved in the administration of justice and/or judicial education with the knowledge and skills needed to apply international standards of human rights for women within their respective institutions.
Components: A programme of workshops and seminars entitled 'Towards a Jurisprudence of Equality', aimed at judges, academics and other persons and institutions involved in the process of administering justice.

1997 Regional
Globalisation and Urban Justice

Total amount: US$ 0.152m   **IDB contribution**: US$ 0.087m
Non-reimbursable technical cooperation.
Applicant: Tribunal de Justicia del Estado de Río de Janeiro
Executor: Tribunal de Justicia del Estado de Río de Janeiro
Objectives: To examine methodologies, tools and systems used by urban courts throughout the hemisphere in developing best-practice models and action plans for confronting the challenges facing justice in urban areas.
Components: There are three main components to this programme: (i) preparation of case studies by experts involved in innovations currently underway in urban courts; (ii) presentation of reports at a three-day workshop; (iii) preparation and publication of the workshop conclusions. The workshop topics relate to: access to justice, use of alternative dispute settlement methods, and administering information technology systems.

1997 Regional
Fundamental Rights Education and Training Workshop

Total Amount: US$ 0.250m **IDB contribution**: US$ 0.150m
Non-reimbursable technical cooperation
Applicant: IDB, OEA, Argentina
Executor: IDB and American University.
Objectives: To train judiciary officials from Latin America in the international

instruments and legal obligations of the Inter-American system of fundamental rights in the countries of the Region

Components: Prior to the training programme, consultants prepare bilingual legal materials that included fundamentals of international protection mechanisms including their structure, function, and their standards for state responsibility in key areas of fundamental rights, together with analysis of domestic implementation of international fundamental rights obligations. Judges were trained in an intensive weeklong seminar and practicum format, conducted by practitioners and scholars in the field. Participants attended lectures at the American University and the Inter-American Commission on Human Rights.

1997 Regional – Caribbean
Study on Improvements of Justice System in the Caribbean

Total Amount: US$ 0.055m   **IDB contribution**: US$0.055m
Non-reimbursable technical cooperation
Applicant: IDB
Executor: IDB
Objectives: To assess the current status of justice administration and judicial education in the Caribbean with a view to determining the technical assistance and other needs required to support the development of a modern judiciary which promotes principles of independence, impartiality, competence, efficiency and effectiveness. To assist in the establishment of the necessary institutional systems to improve the administration of justice.

Components: The IDB will hire consultants to undertake a comprehensive diagnostic of the justice administration and judicial education in the region and based on their findings develop an action plan. The diagnostic study will (a) inventory recent and ongoing technical assistance programmes and their output, and identify key players in the sector (including NGOs public, private, local and grassroots organisations with the expertise and willingness to be part of a revitalised judicial system); (b) summarise the current judicial systems, including enumeration of resources; identify key obstacles hindering the efficient operation of the court system; assess current judicial education systems and programmes; assess feasibility of establishing sustainable institutions and systems; and (c) consider interaction between national and regional bodies within the sector, resulting from policies, institutions and the regulatory framework. The action plan developed from the findings will provide a sense of priorities for proposed activities to be included in a technical assistance to be funded by the IDB with three sub-programmes: (a) improvement of court administration, (b) strengthening of judicial education, and (c) alternative dispute resolutions mechanisms.

1998 Regional
Strengthening Access to Judiciary Systems

Total amount: US$ 0.220m   **IDB contribution**: US$ 0.200m
Non-reimbursable technical cooperation
Applicant: Bolivia, Ecuador, El Salvador, Guatemala, Haiti, Nicaragua and Dominican Republic

Executor: Instituto Interamericano de Derechos Humanos
Objectives: Analysis of working experiences of public and private services of access to justice for the traditionally excluded sectors of society, to orient the establishment of programmes for the improvement of the access to justice.
Components: Analysis of obstacles impeding access to justice, identification of best practices among public and private services in the area of access to justice, preparation of lines of action according to those experiences, and organisation of a regional forum about access to justice.

CITIZEN SAFETY
I. Loan Operations

1998 COLOMBIA
Support of Peaceful Coexistence and Citizen Security

Borrower: The Republic of Colombia, the Capital District of Santafé de Bogotá and the Municipalities of Santiago de Cali and Medellín.
Executing Agency: National Planing Department (DNP); The Fondo Nacional de Desarrollo (National Development project Fund) (FONADE); The Capital District of Santafé de Bogotá; and the Municipalities of Medellín and Santiago de Cali.
Total amount: US$ 95.6m   **IDB contribution**: US$ 57.0m
Cofinancing: Local counterpart total: US$ 95.6m (Republic of Colombia: US$ 14.0m; Bogotá: US$ 6.6m; Medellín: US$ 10.0m; Cali: US$ 8.0m
Financial terms: Loan, with a 20 years amortisation period, and a 48 months' grace period, disbursed over 54 months.
Objectives: To reduce levels of violence and insecurity in several Colombian cities by strengthening efforts to prevent, counteract and control factors associated with criminal acts and violence.
Components: The programme finances principally consulting services and some equipment for national and municipal institutions in two sub-programmes. A national sub-programme will finance a series of initiatives to evaluate, develop, and consolidate a set of activities to be handled by national institutions: (a) development of a system to gather reliable and up-to-date data concerning the most representative incidents of crime in Colombia; (b) support for Ministry of Justice Programmes to bring the judicial system closer to the people and develop alternative pre-judicial methods for the administration of justice; (c) research on such topics as the impact of legal action and of certain legislative acts, justice and gender, and the peaceable reintegration of young people into society; (d) development of a national communication strategy to prevent violence; and (e) support for curriculum development and police education programmes to improve relations between the police and the communities they serve. Three additional components promote the exchange of experience among cities, evaluate results, support cities that cannot receive direct loans from the Bank and promote, administer and monitor the project. The municipal sub-programmes will support actions which may be new initiatives or successful experiences already

undertaken in the following generic categories: (a) establishment of local crime reporting stations; (b) programmes to improve access to justice; (c) programmes targeting youths; (d) educational programmes for the general public such as peaceful dispute resolution, arms control, etc.; (e) police education programmes to improve relations with community, foster respect for human rights; (f) citizens watch programmes; and (g) institutional strengthening of government departments.

1998 URUGUAY
Programme for Citizen Safety: Crime and Violence Prevention

Borrower: Eastern Republic of Uruguay
Executing Agency: Ministry of the Interior.
Total amount: US$ 25.0m   **IDB contribution**: US$ 17.5m
Cofinancing local counterpart funding US$ 7.5m
Financial terms: loan with a 20 years amortisation period, and a 5 years grace period, disbursed over 4.5 years.
Objectives: To prevent and deal with interpersonal violence and to reduce the perception of insecurity in Uruguay.
Components: The project is divided into three sub-programmes: 1) Building Institutional Capacity. Establish an institutional base from which to expand capacity to design and implement policies and programmes concerned with crime and violence, as part of a multisector strategy that will bring civil society organisations into the process. It will finance technical assistance for the institutional development of (a) Dirección Nacional de Prevención del Delito [National Department of Crime Prevention] (DNPD) and other key agencies; (b) prevention policing and (c) domestic violence prevention and assistance. 2) Young People as Prevention Agents. To lay the groundwork for developing a sound culture of violence prevention, recognising that early intervention through preventive activities is more cost effective and produces a greater impact. It will finance two subcomponents: a) Training and instruction programme for young people in high-risks areas; and b) National Juvenile Rehabilitation Centre. Implementation of a halfway house and the design of a model for services for the inmate population to make it easier for offenders to reintegrate effectively into society. 3) Community Crime Prevention initiatives. It will set up two Pilot Prevention Centres (PPC) and a fund for Local Crime Prevention Activities, to encourage civil society to become actively involved in crime prevention.

II. Non- Reimbursable Technical Cooperation

1996 BRAZIL
Comunidade Solidária Programme

Total amount: US$ 11.0m   **IDB contribution**: US$ 8.3m
Non-reimbursable technical cooperation
Applicant: Presidency of the Republic of Brazil (Casa Civil)
Executor: Foundation Banco do Brasil
Objectives: By improving the legal and regulatory framework, promoting

volunteerism and partnerships between the Federal government and the private sector, as well as facilitating information dissemination among civil society organisations, the Programme will help to create an enabling environment for these organisations to become more involved in the delivery of social services and the fight against poverty.

Components: (1) Strengthening Civil Society. The project will finance the preparation of alternatives for improving the legal and regulatory frameworks which govern civil society organisations; the development of a nationwide information network, including a home page to disseminate information and facilitate interaction among public, private and civil society organisations; the promotion of volunteerism through the creation of a national network of Regional Volunteer Service Centres; and the promotion of partnerships between the government at all levels and civil society in the fight against poverty and social exclusion. (2) Social Marketing. Through seminars, workshops, informational television programmes and general media campaigns, the programme will stimulate public dialogue among various social actors and disseminate information about successful experiences of civil society participation in social programmes and then encourage the duplication of these best practices.

1999 COSTA RICA
Justice Centres and Citizen Safety

Total amount: US$ 0.240m   **IDB contribution**: US$ 0.075m
Non-reimbursable technical cooperation
Applicant: Costa Rica
Executor: Ministry of Justice
Objectives: To support the Government of Costa Rica's strategy to a) promote the utilisation of non-violent measures as a way to resolve community and individual conflicts; b) provide alternative mechanisms to the formal justice sector for conflict resolution; and c) develop the institutional capacity within the community for duplicating mediation and arbitration centres.
Components: The programme will establish Justice Centre, a pilot programme in a representative municipality that will promote and provide low cost and accessible citizen conflict resolution. The programme has the following sub-components: (a) institutional design of the centre, studies that will include organisational and staffing assessment, as well as the informational and statistical requirements for the centre; (b) design and execution of mediation and arbitration courses, as well as the preparation of training material and videos as well as publicity brochures; (c) Financing the hiring of the director and staff of the centre; and (d) financing the evaluation, lessons learned and the replicability of the centre.

1999 COSTA RICA
Violence and Crime Prevention

Total amount: US$ 0.066m   **IDB contribution**: US$ 0.054m
Non-reimbursable technical cooperation
Applicant: Costa Rica
Executor: Ministry of Justice
Objectives: To provide the informational and analytical bases for supporting the

policy framework, strategy and action plan of the governmental authorities and civil society in the area of crime reduction.

Components: The project will fund consulting services that will: (a) identify institutional data sources and gather statistics with respect to crime and violence, identifying the legal and policy framework as well as ongoing governmental and civil society initiatives that impact on this issue; (b) develop a preliminary proposal to be presented to the Ministries of Justice and National Security as well as the Commission for Crime and Violence Prevention — the study will include an assessment, strategies that identify timetables, costs and priorities for governmental actions; (c) discussions and workshops with the authorities and civil society, to develop the final proposal; (d) discussion of the final outcome of the report with the bank and other possible donors.

Regional

1998 Regional – El Salvador
Forum on Learning to Live in Peace – Coexistence and Citizens safety in Central America and the Caribbean

Total amount: US$ 0.120m   **IDB contribution**: US$ 0.120m
Non-reimbursable technical cooperation
Applicant: LAC countries with violence-related problems
Host : The Government of El Salvador
Executor: IDB
Objectives: To promote a dialogue among Central American countries, enhance community participation and collaboration between the public and private sectors, and review best practices to combat different types of violence, as a direct follow-up on the results of the Cartagena Seminar, held on 14 March 1998.
Components: Conduct a regional meeting in San Salvador to focus on violence that affects specific sectors (justice, health, education, urban development, business, communications and media) and geographical areas (urban centres vs. rural communities).

1999 Regional Support for Prevention of Violence: National Prevention Plans and Mayor's Network

Total amount: US$ 0.350m   **IDB contribution**: US$ 0.300m
Non-reimbursable technical cooperation
Applicant: LAC countries with violence-related problems
Executor: IDB
Objectives: To support efforts to prevent urban violence in the countries of the region.
Components: The following activities will be financed: (1) support for the development of working plans for violence prevention in three countries (Chile and two other countries to be selected) through a) preparation of a diagnostic study on the magnitude and cost of violence in each country; b) survey and description of existing

programmes in each country for combating social and domestic violence; and c) establishment of a consulting group to review these documents and refine national violence-prevention strategies, and prepare draft working plans for reduction of violence in the respective country; and (2) support for networks of mayors in Latin America and the Caribbean for the identification, systematisation and information of successful practices to reduce violence at the municipal level. The component will also provide support for setting up a web page and the creation of a database on the levels and features of violence in the region.

1999 Regional Programme for Decentralisation and Effective Citizen Participation.

Total amount: US$ 0.665m   **IDB contribution**: US$ 0.605m
Non-reimbursable technical cooperation
Applicant: IDB
Executor: IDB
Objectives: To identify the links between decentralisation and increased citizen participation, bringing government closer to constituents so it will be more responsive to their needs.
Components: The programme works with borrowing member countries to produce six case studies which illustrate the conditions under which civil society has been able to successfully organise and improve community effectiveness and equity in a decentralised setting. The studies will include: (a) health/education studies in Guatemala and Jamaica; (b) social development policy in Peru and Bolivia; and (c) civil rights in Costa Rica (ability of local authorities to partner with communities to enhance personal safety) and Nicaragua (ability of women to organise at the national and local levels to promote legislation that address domestic violence).

CHAPTER 6

Conclusions: Promoting the Rule of Law in Latin America

Pilar Domingo and Rachel Sieder

The chapters in this volume record the experience, successes and failures of judicial reform processes funded by the main international donor organisations in Latin America. International interest and financial input in legal reform are not new phenomena for developing countries. Development and modernisation were the terms that underpinned the law and development movement in the 1960s; currently, rule of law and judicial reform are promoted under the remit of promoting democracy and market reform. Judicial reform is in itself a complex proposition, which may include or affect a wide range of aspects of the legal process, with different social and political consequences. Moreover, judicial reform initiatives are part of the wider political and developmental, if also ambiguous and all encompassing, process of 'state reform'. This endeavour projects a range of domestic and international agendas, represented through a variety of reform initiatives.

The preceding chapters have focused on the experience of international donor organisations and their role in the development of judicial reform processes in Latin America. Their involvement in these processes is neither linear nor always coherent, but it is important to reflect on their successes and failures given the impact of the rule of law on democracy and development. We hope that this volume contributes to a better understanding of the way in which international organisations rationalise and prioritise their reform proposals and agenda in Latin America. Many of the contributions also shed light on how reform agendas are implemented and followed up (or not). They indicate how international donor organisations relate to national governments and civil society, how they relate to each other and what factors account for the successes and failures of their reform initiatives.

In this concluding chapter we highlight some recurring themes that emerge from the preceding chapters. We also address the question of the connection between rule of law reform and broader processes of regime consolidation and state building, from both a 'state-centred' and a 'society-centred' perspective.

Recurring themes

i) How new is judicial reform on the international donor organisation agenda?

The first striking feature about reform initiatives funded by international donor organisations is the fact that they are not a new feature of external aid. As the chapters by Carothers, Salas and Sarles indicate, the conceptual link between law and development is an old concern. In the 1960s it was developed through the Law and Development movement, (with an emphasis on legal training, and on exporting the principles of the US legal tradition to developing countries, generally with little regard for or understanding of the national juridical tradition and social and economic context). The formalistic approach and naïvety of the Law and Development movement led to both a misreading of the role of law in the political and economic processes in developing countries, and seemingly, a disregard for informal aspects of conflict resolution. As military rule swept across Latin America, advocates of the Law and Development movement admitted defeat, and legal reform disappeared temporarily from the international agenda. Interest in the law on behalf of international donor agencies reemerged in the 1980s, firstly in the form of administration of justice reforms, primarily reflected in the aid packages of USAID to Central America. In part this was linked to an acknowledgement of the appalling human rights situation in Central America. Reform projects were aimed more at criminal justice, the police and law-enforcement agencies — albeit with limited results. By the 1990s legal reform was increasingly framed in terms of rule of law, under the broad remit of promoting market rule *and* democracy. Concerns here increasingly revolved around governance, understood as the state's capacity to provide good government in the form of an enabling environment of predictability, efficiency and transparency for market rule purposes; and legitimacy, stability and rights protection in the pursuit of democratic advancement.[1] Governance, then, encompassing both market rule and democracy as necessary partners which require rule of law and an effective justice system, became a widely used term of reference for reform projects. Rule of law concerns initially revolved primarily around issues of economic legal security, contract law and property rights, particularly as far as the World Bank and IDB were concerned. However, as the 1990s wore on, the discourse behind legal reform (and state reform more generally) increasingly took on board broader 'social' concerns. An additional issue that impacts, needless to say controversially, upon the reform agenda is the question of organised crime and the drugs war.

Thus, in various forms, and with varying degrees of intensity and financial commitment, law has been present on the agenda of donor institutions for several decades. The scope and amount of money spent on judicial reform programmes increased substantially in the 1990s. Virtually every country in the region is currently engaged in aspects of legal and judicial reform, often with the financial backing of a major international organisation.

ii) Multiplicity of reform agendas

As judicial reform has become a major area of international sponsorship, a second recurrent theme that emerges from the chapters is the problem of

---

[1] See Julio Faúndez, (1997) pp. 1–25, and Patrick McAuslan (1997) pp. 25–44.

conflicting agendas. The existence of a multiplicity of agendas does not necessarily mean that they contradict one another; they can be mutually re-enforcing as complementary parts of a broader process of state reform. However, reform objectives may conflict, as Carothers duly points out. For instance, reforms designed to enhance court efficiency may conflict with reforms which seek to improve access to justice; or human rights reforms may be undermined by measures aimed at improving international law-enforcement and curbing organised crime.

The multiplicity of agendas, then, can be problematic. To some extent contradictions *within* donor organisations are avoided in as far as a specialisation of reform areas and concerns can be discerned. Until recently, World Bank reforms centred mostly on enhancing court efficiency and case management. The Bank has always been constrained by its Articles of Agreement, which limit its scope of action to economically relevant aspects of policy, although, as Dakolias suggests, there appears to be an important shift towards more social considerations of rule of law issues. The IDB has followed a similar remit, but possibly voicing democratic considerations more explicitly in its reform objectives. USAID has traditionally been more involved in criminal law and police reform initiatives.

iii) Inter-organisation relations and co-ordination efforts

A related problem area acknowledged by most of the authors is that of the relationship between donor organisations. Judicial reform is hampered not only by the contradictions arising from multiple and at times conflicting agendas, but also from a lack of inter-organisational co-ordination. Often, donor organisations are simply not aware of the areas of reform that they are each addressing. Better transparency in the design and management of reform programmes as well as more readily accessible information would doubtlessly improve the prospects for a more coherent reform strategy. Organisations are called upon to improve information flows and cooperation between them in an effort to rationalise reform strategies at a regional level, avoid duplication of effort and enhance co-ordination rather than competition.

iv) Coherence and transparency in the design and implementation of reform initiatives

The problem of co-ordination and coherence is not only a matter for inter-organisational links, but also has to do with the internal distribution of work and funding *within* these organisations. This is also linked to the problem of multiple reform concerns. It is not only the case that reforms may be in tension with one another as a result of contradictory objectives, but also that they appear to be disjointed and disconnected. Reform projects in the past seem to have been designed in an ad hoc manner, lacking long-term planning and coherence with broader objectives of state reform agendas. Salas,

Biebesheimer and Carothers particularly stress the need for greater transparency and co-ordination, and better information both within and between donor organisations.

Coherence and transparency would also be better served by putting in place benchmarking criteria and more rigorous mechanisms by which to monitor and evaluate the progress of reform projects. Moreover, it is not evident that projects are carefully followed up in their implementation phase.

v) Learning by doing

Despite the contradictions that may arise from different and perhaps uncoordinated reform agendas, it is also the case that donor organisations have undergone major shifts in focus and approach in terms of how reform objectives are developed and how projects are implemented. This is evident from the chapters by Dakolias, Sarles and Biebesheimer. Learning by doing has an impact on judicial reform projects at two levels: firstly, there are lessons learnt from the practical and logistic side of project design and implementation. Consultation practices are being revised to broaden the range of actors involved in the design phase of reform projects. But also there is growing awareness that reforms which are not monitored and followed through risk not being properly implemented, and becoming isolated and disjointed policy prescriptions which are not embedded in broader social and political processes.

Secondly, the experience of judicial reform has informed current ways in which rule of law issues are considered and defined within the international organisations. For instance, early reform projects limited to case management and court-room administration, attractive precisely because of their somewhat 'apolitical' nature, are increasingly seen to be insufficient to address more structural problems of rule of law in the region. The chapters by Dakolias, Sarles and Biebesheimer reflect important developments in how their respective organisations see rule of law in terms of broader state reform objectives. A consequence of this is the expansion of the judicial reform agenda as international organisations venture timidly towards reform objectives which may appear to be more politically and socially sensitive than in the past. However, it still remains to be seen how learning from past misjudgements is currently informing reform projects both in their design and implementation phase, and with regard to how they fit into the larger picture of political and economic development.

vi) Relations between organisations and national/local contexts

A connected area of improvement identified as necessary by the authors is that of the degree to which reform projects are imported prescriptions rather than policy proposals which reflect specific local needs and power relations.[2] International donor organisations often are seen to be too far removed and distant from the political and social context of the countries where they sponsor reform projects. This top-down and technocratic approach to some extent accounts for the failings of reform initiatives. In addition to not necessarily being suited to local problems, reforms which are brought in from outside may lack legitimacy and a sense of national ownership. Moreover, they may inspire resentment at the local level, especially if they are perceived as part of a package of donor conditionality at the expense of national sovereignty. Under the label of neutral technocratic expertise, international donors' policy proposals can fail to take into consideration not only specific national political and social conditions, but also the complexity of power relations at the level of policy makers and within the particular agency which is targeted for reform. Without sensitivity to national contexts reform designs are likely to be faulty and, perhaps more importantly, they will not benefit from a broader process of legitimation and acceptance.

vii) Broadening consultation processes

It is the acknowledgement of these weaknesses which has prompted international donor organisations to rethink their relations with national actors. Notably, the chapters by Dakolias, Biebesheimer and Sarles all stress the need for donor organisations to engage in more open and participative consultation processes with 'civil society', and to work more closely with grass-roots organisations and NGOs (discussed below). This indicates a recognition that reform processes will only have meaningful impact if they are sufficiently rooted in society. The difficulty comes, surely, in defining how consultation processes are to take place, who is to be consulted, and at what stage.

'Ownership' of reform projects is important at various levels. If they are not publicly debated — at least through the appropriate legislative channels, then it is unlikely that society will develop a sense of identification with and support for reform projects, which will otherwise appear as isolated technocratic policy directives. Secondly, it may be the case that those targeted by the reform need to be consulted in order to assure their commitment for the implementation phase of reform projects. And finally, there is a problem of political will and ensuring a sufficient level of commitment on the part of the political elites to ensure that legislation is passed and reform processes are implemented. Without these three levels of some form of consultation or tendering, reform projects risk being perceived as purely imported models that might be seen not to be suited to local or national needs and conditions.

---

[2] See Javier Ciurlizza (2000) for an insightful discussion of the role of international organisations in judicial reform.

viii) Issues on the reform agenda

It is evident from all five chapters that judicial reform comprises a broad range of areas that are listed as reform-worthy. Carothers identifies four clusters of rule of law reform, all of which generally fall within the rubric of supporting market reform and (or) democracy: reform of criminal justice; reforms concerned with improving economic legal security, with an emphasis on property rights and commercial law; human rights, social justice and access to justice. In fact, the range of issues that need to be addressed to make rule of law possible seems immeasurable. It is notable that the donor organisations appear to be increasingly willing to undertake new areas of reform in recognition of the extreme weakness of rule of law institutions and the debilitating effect that this has both on democracy and market rule. The challenge lies in the degree to which comprehensive reform strategies can be designed which will effectively rise to the occasion of strengthening rule of law.

Rule of Law, State and Society in Latin America

Political democratisation advanced apace in Latin America throughout the 1980s. However, by the end of the 1990s many countries in the region appeared 'stuck' in a state of incomplete or unconsolidated democratisation. Some can be described as 'illiberal democracies', to borrow Zakaria's term, where political rights are broadly respected but civil rights weakly upheld, and socio-economic rights almost non-existent — a state of affairs which applies to most of Central America and Colombia, but also to many rural areas across the continent.[3] Others have moved towards some kind of semi-authoritarian variant of rule, as in the cases of Venezuela and Peru.[4] Even in those countries where electoral democracy appears to have been secured as 'the only game in town', such as Argentina, state institutions — and particularly the judiciary — remain marked by inefficiency, corruption and resistance to reform. It is in this context that rule of law is of crucial importance for democracy to progress. A definition of rule of law could include the following components:

- respect for political and civil rights (protection for individuals from arbitrary actions by government or by other citizens)
- equality of treatment before the law (irrespective of gender, social class, etc.)
- effective due process guarantees
- accountability of holders of governmental office to the law

---

[3] Fareed Zakaria (1997) pp. 22–43.
[4] Semi-authoritarian regimes may display many of the institutional features of democratic rule, such as national multi-party elections, but are structured in such a way that those institutional features never seriously threaten the hold of power by the regime. For a discussion of democracy assistance to semi-authoritarian regimes see Thomas Carothers (2000).

- the efficient administration of justice
- equal access to the law (which implies due attention to culturally sensitive mechanisms for conflict resolution)
- a clear regulatory framework for economic activity (guarantees of property rights, arbitration etc.)

'Rule of law', then, is a broad notion, which encompasses more than simply institutional dimensions of the law (which are often referred to under the narrower rubric of 'judicial reform').

In the following section we discuss the insertion of judicial reform projects within the broader remit of rule of law and democratic advancement. It is important to unpack the notion of judicial reform in the pursuit of good government. Firstly, at the level of the state there are two parallel dynamics in how public sector reform, including judicial reform, is approached; economic liberalisation and democratic advancement. Secondly, as 'civil society' increasingly becomes an important term of reference for reform processes, judicial reform at the societal level is aimed at making the law socially relevant in order for democratic citizenship to be possible.

Rule of law and state reform

The challenge that has been set for Latin American countries over the last twof decades is that of achieving democratic consolidation combined with long-term sustainable economic growth and development. As the reform agenda of multilateral donor organisations has expanded, increasingly the terms 'democracy', 'market rule' and 'state reform' have been wound together in the pursuit of 'governance'. As mentioned above, governance is identified as the desired goal of state reform and refers to the state's capacity to engage in governmental decision-making within an institutional environment of 'accountability, transparency, probity and rule of law'.[5] Governance is understood in the world of international donor organisations as the process by which responsive government and democracy is enhanced, but also market economics is facilitated, thus enabling growth and development.[6]

Throughout the 1980s newly established democracies struggled to survive the severity of economic crisis as well as the political and institutional uncertainties of transition processes. On the political side, in the best of cases, and with varying degrees of 'smoothness', institutional reform and gradual accommodation of the different social and political actors involved led to a relative stabilisation of electoral politics. Democratic institutions, however, remained precarious and debilitated. Peru and Venezuela are noteworthy

[5] Patrick McAuslan (1997) p. 27.
[6] See the chapters in Julio Faúndez (1997) for in-depth discussions of 'governance' and state reform, and their usage by donor organisations.

examples of democratic fragility; and Mexico is perhaps only now really engaging with the realities of democratic political outcomes after over a decade of economic liberalisation. On the economic front, the hardships of debt crisis, combined with the exhaustion of import-substitution-industrialisation (ISI) and state-led capitalist development, led to a re-consideration of development alternatives. Prompted by the IMF and World Bank, notably, the countries in the region converged towards the imple-mentation of structural adjustment, fiscal austerity and, eventually, economic liberalisation, under the premise that market rule would lead to long-term growth and development.

The sequence and timing of political liberalisation and the implementation of neo-liberal measures have varied considerably throughout the region. Also, both processes of political change and economic transformation inevitably involved a fundamental redefinition of the state in terms of its insertion in the economy and in society, along with a realignment of political forces and sectoral interests. Although there has been an apparent routinisation of democratic procedures, democratic institutions lack credibility and face serious problems of legitimacy and societal embeddedness. In economic terms, neo-liberal reforms have not resulted in sustainable patterns of growth and stability. In a bid to rebuild a sense of regime legitimacy and economic viability, policy makers, encouraged by international organisations, have increasingly adopted the language of 'state reform'. This assumes that political and economic processes of change can be made to converge towards a common goal of good governance where liberal democracy and market rule will be mutually re-enforcing.[7]

Within the international organisations, especially the World Bank, the complexities of economic reform in social and political terms have increasingly been internalised in their own approach to governance and development. Whereas the first generation of internationally funded reform projects revolved around structural adjustment, by the early 1990s it was increasingly evident that growth was limited, and the promised 'trickle-down' effects of economic liberalisation were not happening quickly enough. Then it was argued that market rule was hindered by institutional factors resulting from inefficient, unreliable and unaccountable state institutions. Consequently the international reform agenda expanded from purely economic concerns to taking on an interest in public sector modernisation. Amongst other things, notions of institutional predictability, legal security and reliability in the workings of rule of law became a focus of attention for those organisations concerned with promoting an enabling environment for market economics.[8] Yet the emphasis was still on top-down reform directives. However, by the end

---

[7] See Philip Oxhorn and Pamela Starr (1999a). See also Laurence Whitehead (1993).
[8] See World Bank (1999)

of the 1990s, governance increasingly came to include more participatory and inclusive notions of reform, where the state's responsiveness to demands from below was seen to be a necessary element of good government, along with it's capacity to address issues of poverty and social marginality. These are important shifts in attitude and approach within international organisations, especially the World Bank. In the rule of law debate, the shift is expressed in terms of a more explicit concern for the 'democracy' aspect of rule of law, and also the effort to open up channels of consultation and participation.

Thus, state reform has been increasingly conceived in terms of both supporting democracy *and* promoting market rule, presented as two mutually reinforcing processes. At this point it is important to stress that they are essentially two separate objectives which have a distinctive conceptual logic of their own.[9] Although there may be areas of overlap and indeed, convergence, they are distinct, parallel processes. Democratic procedures can yield political outcomes that may in fundamental ways conflict with the imperatives of market rule. The winners and losers of both processes may not necessarily coincide, thus leading to a build up of social tensions, which can exert tremendous pressure on democratic institutions. Here, long-term structural factors come into play, combined with conjunctural (and changing) correlations of social and political forces. Oxhorn and Starr even suggest that to the extent that convergence has taken place, this is more the result of coincidence than compatibility. Certainly it would appear to be the case that the social and political consensus which emerged around earlier economic stabilisation packages was possible within a democratic context because of the severity of economic instability and in some cases hyperinflation. This created a situation in which the immediate benefits of stabilisation cut across all social sectors. However, as poverty and social exclusion remain unresolved, the memory of economic instability fades, and the earlier consensus around the model comes under strain. Yet at the same time the neo-liberal model has also had the effect of atomising society and weakening channels of opposition to this apparent consensus around market economics — at least temporarily. Those that are marginalised or excluded from the benefits of market rule are socially and consequently politically disempowered so that the economic model generally remains unchallenged. Venezuela provides a telling example, nonetheless, of the fragility of democratic institutions strained by economic hardship.

It is evident that throughout the region the state faces a crisis of legitimacy, in varying degrees of intensity. In economic terms, the model at best has

---

[9] Philip Oxhorn and Pamela Starr (1999a) conclude that not only are the two processes separate; they may also indeed conflict. Laurence Whitehead (1993) discusses the complexity of this dual process, underlining that there is no reason to assume that a convergence between economic and political liberalisation is inevitable. See also G. Hawthorn (1993) and Leila Frischtak (1997).

yielded stability, but the problems of poverty and social exclusion delegitimise and weaken democratic institutions of representation, increasingly seen to be far removed from the harsh experience of large sectors of society. In political terms, democratic institutions are discredited through widespread practices of self-enrichment, corruption and a pervasive culture of impunity in public office. Government officials are seen as neither responsive to electoral demands, nor accountable for their actions. Finally, in social terms, the state not only fails to protect civil rights (political rights being fairly well established throughout the region), but in some cases is complicit with outright human rights violations at the hands of law-enforcers.[10] Moreover, what Guillermo O'Donnell refers to as the 'brown areas' of society, where the state lacks the capacity to assert an authoritative presence of law and order, do not appear to have diminished with economic and political liberalisation.[11]

From a state perspective, rule of law is about a territorially bounded institutional network of rules and regulations that are legally binding upon state and society. Rule of law reforms, as they are taking place in Latin America, essentially reflect the response by power-holders, prompted either by electoral competition, or encouraged and indeed financed by donor organisation, to confront this deep crisis of legitimacy. They reflect a necessary re-evaluation of the role of the state in terms of its relationship to society.

Law is ultimately about norms and values and the interaction between citizens and institutions. Latin America is marked by a general lack of internalisation of rights and obligations throughout society and high levels of mistrust and dissatisfaction with the judicial system. Evidently what citizens expect and demand of the law and the state varies according to country and historical context, but the widely perceived gap between 'el derecho' (norms) and 'el hecho' (practice) is a generalised phenomenon. Three factors in particular contribute to negative perceptions of the justice system. First, historical legacies of arbitrary behaviour by the state, such as military repression under authoritarian regimes or corrupt and brutal policing under democratic rule. Constitutional guarantees have often provided little or no protection in practice for weak and vulnerable groups. Second, powerful elites tend to operate 'above' or 'outside' the law; impunity is widespread and powerful wrongdoers are rarely made accountable through legal means. In some instances prosecutions for human rights violations or corruption have occurred and these have had a positive impact on popular perceptions of the judiciary. However, this can easily be dissipated if judicial propriety and activism declines (as, for example, in the case of Argentina, where support for the judiciary increasing following the prosecutions of the junta in the 1980s, but subsequently declined under Menem). Third, the inability of post-

---

[10] See Guillermo O'Donnell (2000).
[11] Guillermo O'Donnell (2000). See also Guillermo O'Donnell (1993).

transitional state institutions to tackle the problem of violence and organised crime has had a corrosive effect on the population's perceptions of the law and the justice system. This is exacerbated when entrenched corruption within the judiciary often facilitates the operations of organised criminal groups. In response to widely perceived public insecurity, certain sectors of the population call for tough 'law and order' policies which are often injurious to due process and human rights guarantees. In addition, the inability of the state to provide basic guarantees of public security has also encouraged private forms of 'justice', such as vigilantism, paramilitarism and lynchings of suspected criminals. Efforts to strengthen the rule of law must be located within a much broader, more holistic process whereby ordinary citizens come to believe in the impartiality and effectiveness of the justice system. Evidently this involves more than international assistance to fund institutional reform and 'strengthen civil society' (see below): it implies hard trade-offs between those who manipulate the law to protect their own interests and those who wish to promote greater access to justice.

In sum, the reform agenda grows and develops in accordance with the diversity of demands and expectations that are increasingly placed upon the weak democratic states of Latin America. As Carothers reminds us, the reform agenda reflects a variety of interests and aspects of rule of law enhancement.

i) Promoting market economics

The economic agenda of rule of law reform has been driven by the notion that the market requires an institutional environment where the rules of transaction are minimally predictable and impartial. In recent years there has been growing academic interest in the linkages between law and economics, developing increasingly around the contention that in the absence of legal security, market economics will not yield optimal and sustainable long-term growth.[12] At a general level, the argument holds that institutional incentives or obstacles, in the form of legislation, regulation and law-enforcement, shape the economic opportunities and choices available to individuals in society, thus determining patterns of economic development. In the context of market economics, the issue at hand is the state's institutional capacity to secure guarantees around property rights, and to provide a framework of predictability and reliability in how rules and laws are applied, especially in those areas of the law which affect economic transactions.

The connection between economic performance and legal security has thus increasingly been the object of academic research. While the general propositions around the relationship between law and economics are highly suggestive, scholarly work has yet to provide strong and conclusive empirical

---

[12] See Douglas North (1990) for a neo-institutional approach to understanding economic development

evidence regarding the specific impact of law and adjudication on economic development.[13] Further research on the relationship between law and economics in the region should be encouraged.

Recurrent themes in the literature are the following: corruption increases transaction costs for business, representing a form of informal taxation for the private sector through the payment of bribes to public officials. In the banking sector, the problems of collecting bank obligations, and the corresponding high costs of inefficient litigation increases the price of credit to the detriment of business. Where property rights are not effectively protected, property assets are unlikely to be put to efficient use — for instance, the cost of rental leases are increased as property owners must insure themselves against eviction costs.[14] Linked to this, the problem of securing intellectual property rights can have a discouraging effect on technological progress. Recent research suggests that the state's incapacity to deal with soaring crime rates in Colombia has had a detrimental effect on national economic performance. Business ventures and general investment is discouraged in an environment where judicial rulings lack predictability in the application of the law. And finally, inefficiency and court delays add to the general transaction costs of economic activity where conflict arises.[15]

There are, then, diverse and complex ways in which the market is potentially affected both by how the judiciary operates, and also by the nature of the regulatory and legal framework that touches upon economic transactions in society. Of interest is that much of the international donor sponsored legal reforms concerned with economic efficiency are designed primarily to stream-line court administration, and improve case-management. Other areas of rule of law reform on the economic agenda deal with taxation, rules for foreign investment, competition and commercial law, and specialised training in these areas, and alternative dispute resolution mechanisms for business, but progress remains patchy.[16] And then there is an expressed interest in generally promoting transparency and accountability in the public sector, with a view to enhancing the credibility of the institutional environment and attracting foreign investment.[17]

---

[13] See Patrick McAuslan (1997) pp. 28–34.

[14] Nestor Humberto Martinez (1998) pp. 3-15, p. 5.

[15] Robert Sherwood (1998) pp. 31–9.

[16] Javier Ciurlizza (2000) pp. 165–88. On recent legislation regarding competition law in Latin America see Malcolm Rowat (1997).

[17] It is important to note that the business sectors of Latin America, and indeed foreign investment in the past, have not consistently favoured greater transparency and accountability. Under state-led capitalism, business interests thrived in the murky waters of state patronage, clientelism and bureaucratic obscurity which allowed for such practices as suspect access to state credits or tax evasion. As the state has 'down-sized', and the private sector exposed to the realities of market competition, predictability and transparency in the rules of transaction have become more attractive.

ii) Promoting democracy

The connection between rule of law and democracy is complex. This is not the place to engage with the long-standing theoretical debates about the role of law in democratic processes. It is important, however, to point to the various levels at which rule of law supports democracy. Within democratic government, rule of law acts as the normative background to the process of government. At one level, it presumes government by consent, within the boundaries of a constitutional arrangement that establishes the normative and legally binding criteria of limited, responsible and accountable government and public office. At another level, through a regime of rights protection - civil and political - rule of law establishes a positive connection between state and society, and provides the legal space for the development of citizenship. Both dimensions of rule of law (rights protection and accountable government) are critical within democratic rule for the construction of regime legitimacy. And rule of law has become particularly prominent in the political discourse in recent times in Latin America, especially as other arenas of regime and government performance remain weak — for instance, the persistently unabated levels of poverty and social exclusion.

The judiciary is one of the principal institutional mechanisms for the establishment of rule of law. The judicial function resolves conflict which arises between state and society, and between individuals in society, it administers criminal justice, it acts as guardian of the law against the abuse of power by public officials,[18] and it acts as the principal agent of rights protection.[19]

Judicial reforms, then, are aimed at addressing in part those aspects of rule of law that support democratic consolidation. Firstly, the legitimacy of public officials and state institutions rides on the extent to which they are effectively subjected to a regime of legal accountability.[20] Accountability and transparency have become important criteria by which to measure good government. Persistent and widespread corruption and impunity in public office damage the credibility of democratic institutions and can threaten regime viability, as in the cases of Peru and Venezuela. There are two areas of reform which would directly address this problem of 'horizontal accountability' and enhance the principle of separation of powers: judicial independence of the courts; and the extent of judicial review powers vis à vis the other branches of the state. As these are overtly political questions, international donor organisations have generally been shy of pursuing reform initiatives that engage with these two questions. The principal contribution to enhanced judicial independence has taken place through the establishment of more merit based promotion systems within the ranks of the judicial hierarchy,

---

[18] Jerome L. Waltman (1988) pp. 216–34, p. 216.
[19] Guillermo O'Donnell (1999c) pp. 303–38.
[20] See Guillermo O'Donnell (1999b).

and the creation of judicial councils in charge of the administration (including appointments) and management of the judicial branch.

The other level at which democracy is legitimated through rule of law revolves around the state's capacity to make good its promise of human rights protection and effective due process. Without this aspect of rule of law, democracy is unlikely to achieve broad societal acceptance and a minimum level of civic trust in public institutions. It is through the protection of rights that a positive relationship between state and society can develop. Access to justice for citizens (discussed below) will also strengthen democratic values and a societal attachment to rule of law, as the law can then become a potential tool of empowerment from below. Pro-democracy judicial reforms will typically include human rights training, enhancing judicial independence, criminal law reform, prison reforms, legal aid, the establishment of ombudsman institutions and improving access to justice. Here also, though, there may be conflicting agendas. For instance, there is a likely tension between the criminal justice priorities of reducing crime in a region where crime rates have soared and public security has become a major social issue, and the concern with addressing the human rights dimension of the criminal justice system.

Promoting democracy, then, is a major objective of the rule of law reform agenda. It reflects and responds to a pressing need to bolster regime legitimacy in the fragile democracies of the region. However, the issues involved are complex and very diverse. For reforms to be effective, they must be part of an integrated and coherent project of state reform. Moreover, they must be seen to be more than top-down or internationally driven policy directives. Otherwise they risk remaining as piecemeal and misguided reform processes which are disconnected from the broader political and social context. Increasingly throughout the 1990s the language of 'ownership' and the need for broader social consultation has been taken on board as civil society becomes a relevant actor.

Rule of law and civil society

During the 1980s international aid to strengthen the rule of law in Latin American focused almost entirely on reforming judicial institutions. However, by the 1990s, reflecting broader trends in international democracy promotion assistance, efforts to secure and consolidate the rule of law adopted a dual approach. This involved a continuation of *top down* strategies, focusing on reform of state institutions such as the judiciary and public security forces; but also the inclusion of *bottom up* initiatives, encompassing a range of activities aimed at 'strengthening civil society'.[21] These two dimensions were generally held to be mutually reinforcing in the process of rule of law reform.

Throughout the decade, the term 'civil society' was laden with expectations and much imprecision existed within academic and policy circles as to its precise meaning and content. However, as Pearce notes, it was invariably used to signal an aspirational inclusionary project in which 'the economically poor and marginalised can access the institutions and structures of the newly democratised polities and make them work for them'.[22] Having previously organised to oppose authoritarian rule, it was now hoped that civil society groups could make under-performing state institutions in the new democracies more responsive to the populace.[23] This was fundamentally about 'deepening' or 'consolidating' democracy; transforming the formal political rights of citizenship achieved through transition from authoritarian regimes into a more substantive practice of citizenship, which included civil and perhaps even socio-economic rights. This aspirational notion of civil society was taken up in the 1990s by the international donor organisations, which advanced 'civil society strengthening' as part of a broader agenda of modernising the state, strengthening democratic governance and cementing economic liberalisation across the region. Carothers refers to a neo-Tocquevillian ideal of civil society on the part of donors that is 'diverse, active, and independent...that articulates the interests of citizens and holds government accountable to citizens'.[24] Civil society then, was to be the watchdog that would act as a check on the state to ensure representative and accountable governance in the flawed and fragile new democracies.

Yet civil society has always been a contested term. Quite who or what it was understood to refer to across Latin America was very often unclear. Was it NGOs, social or 'popular movements' and civic associations? Did it include private sector and business associations? This is not the place to get tied down in lengthy theoretical debates.[25] However, if civil society is understood in a broad sense as associational life which exists outside of, although in a relationship with, 'political society' (political parties) and institutions of the state, it is clear that it is highly divided, fragmented and stratified. Different elements of civil society are frequently in direct conflict or competition with each other,

---

[21] For a comprehensive and incisive overview of democracy assistance see Thomas Carothers (1999); see also Peter Burnell (ed.) (2000).

[22] Jenny Pearce (1997) pp. 57–83, p. 66.

[23] During the 1980s and 1990s, large donor organisations such as the World Bank also hoped that 'civil society organisations' would ameliorate the high social costs of economic policies of structural adjustment. Throughout Latin America NGOs assumed service delivery tasks as the social infrastructure of the state was reduced. See Paul J. Nelson (1995).

[24] Thomas Carothers (1999) p. 87.

[25] For useful summaries see Jenny Pearce (1997); Gordon White (1993); and Alison Van Rooy (1998) chapter one.

and as Whitehead has rightly indicated, some parts are downright 'uncivil' in their behaviour, such as organised criminal networks or religiously or ethnically intolerant groups.[26]

Civil society, then, is not an unproblematic given. Its nature in any one country is shaped by its political and socio-economic historical development. Latin America as a region has a long tradition of grass-roots movements organised in opposition to the state, such as peasant movements and workers' organisations. However, it is also marked by a strong historical legacy of corporatist relations, wherein the modernising state organised and coopted civic interest groups, and of clientism, where hierarchical patronage reward relations structured relations between politically powerful sectors and subordinate individuals and groups. The pervasiveness of these overlapping phenomena of corporatist legacies, cooption tactics and clientelist practices necessarily problematises the notion that civil society can act as a watchdog to ensure the accountability of a less than democratic state. Some elements of what might be defined as civil society (for example, some business or trade union associations) might better be understood as existing in a symbiotic, even parasitic relationship with authoritarian elements of the state and political elites. That is, they may have interests that are directly threatened by greater openness, transparency and access: the very values and practices that a stronger civil society supposedly promotes. Just as many political parties in the new democracies are decidedly undemocratic in their internal organisation, operating more as clientelistic associations for the private economic advancement of their members than as vehicles for the representation of their members' interests, so too civil society has its uncivil and anti-democratic components. In addition, the process of economic liberalisation which Latin America has undergone in the last two decades, has favoured and strengthened some groups and disadvantaged and weakened others. The economic rigours of structural adjustment and the slashing back of what were, at best, weak and uneven forms of state social provision have prompted some civil groups, such as indigenous people to 'associate and organise'.[27] However, they have equally contributed to privatised behaviour, anomie and apathy amongst many other sectors, whose members now focus their energies almost exclusively on the daily struggle for material survival. Discussion of institutional reform that relies on the notion of civil society strengthening cannot, therefore, be separated from a broader analysis of the modernisation of political structures and shifts in prevailing models of political economy and development. A more nuanced understanding of 'civil society' is essential if its 'strengthening' is proposed as a means to secure the rule of law. As Van Rooy has stated, 'civil society must be empirically portrayed in all its conflictual, relational aspects before we can

---

[26] Laurence Whitehead (1997).
[27] See Deborah Yashar (1999).

make judgements about its relationships to either development or democracy'.[28] Treating civil society as an ethical and moral goal, rather than an objective and complex reality, only serves to muddy the analytical waters.

In practice, international assistance to strengthen civil society and further the rule of law in Latin America has tended to be focused almost exclusively on advocacy NGOs.[29] However, although they can play an important role, such advocacy NGOs are not a substitute for a vibrant, autonomous associational life. They are rather just one part of broader, complex, country-specific civil societies and need to be approached and analysed as such. How do advocacy NGOs fit into a country's civil society as a whole? What are the power relationships at play between different elements of civil society, political society and the state? And how do these interact with international actors and market forces?

In sum, we need to explore what *kind* of 'civil society' exists in relation to given kinds of political society, state and model of economic development and what elements or interplay of elements will further the rule of law. This implies three things. First, accepting that civil society is necessarily divided and that conflict exists between its constituent parts. Second, that not all that is civil society is necessarily 'civilising' in its impact. Third, historically locating 'civil society' within a range of distinct political and socio-economic contexts. As Fox has stated, we need to develop analytical frameworks to determine how, when and in what circumstances certain civil society actors can contribute to the construction and effectiveness of institutional checks and balances and greater governmental accountability.[30] Brysk has advocated a focus on the *function* of civil society actors, which she defines as mobilisation, contention and institutionalisation, to examine the democratising impact of civic organisations. As she notes, these functions play different roles in democratisation: raising awareness and developing a sense of citizenship, shaping the public agenda, or changing institutions through collective action.[31] In addition to more attention to types and functions of civic actors, approaches that pay greater attention to local context must be developed if the effectiveness of rule of law assistance that emphasises the strengthening of civil society is to be properly gauged. The challenge is how to achieve positive synergy between

---

[28] Alison Van Rooy (1998) p. 69.

[29] Such advocacy NGOs are involved in a wide range of activities: election monitoring, civic education, parliamentary transparency, human rights, anti-corruption, the environment, women's rights and indigenous rights: Carothers (1999) p. 210; see also Julie Hearn and Mark Robinson (2000). For a thorough and clear survey of international donors' approaches to 'civil society' see Alison Van Rooy (1998).

[30] Jonathan Fox explores the relationship between vertical accountability (power relations between the state and its citizens) and horizontal accountability (the checks and balances within the state itself), analysing the role of civil society in advancing these two dimensions and the effect of both kinds of accountability on framing civil society itself: Jonathan Fox (2000).

[31] See Alison Brysk (2000). Brysk's focus is on *democratic* civil society.

reform efforts focused on state institutions and support to certain civic groups in order to advance the rule of law in different political and socio-economic circumstances.

Access to justice and 'informal justice'

Earlier judicial reform assistance in Latin America tended to focus on top-down institutional and technical features. In a positive development, international support for the rule of law is now beginning to take account more generally of the users of the judicial system and, specifically, is being focused on securing greater access to justice for the poor and underprivileged.[32] Many of these efforts involve support for legal services NGOs, which work on behalf of particular marginalised sectors of the population, such as indigenous people or poor urban settlers. Such organisations raise individuals' awareness of their rights and support them in their recourse to the legal system, for example through training para-legals to offer alternative sources of legal aid or through public interest litigation.[33] Another positive development for increasing access to justice and changing popular attitudes towards the law is the growing support among donors for alternative dispute resolution mechanisms or ADR. In most developing countries only a small fraction of the population has direct access to the court system for dispute resolution, and that system is beset by backlogs and inefficiency. Resort to non-judicial mechanisms such as local mediation and arbitration has therefore long been seen by many as a necessary element of building the rule of law. In theory, informal dispute resolution processes offer a number of advantages: they are more accessible in terms of the language employed and feature simpler, cheaper procedures; they are more flexible and deliver a speedier resolution than the courts; and they also involve a greater degree of participation by the parties to a conflict, who are encouraged to reach a consensual outcome. Such elements ('alternative remedies') were strengthened in new penal procedures codes introduced throughout Latin America in the 1980s and 1990s.[34]

However, while ADR holds out the prospect of making justice more accessible, both in economic and cultural terms, it also raises a number of complex questions. First, there is the difficult issue of how to guarantee respect for individuals' rights in the informal system.[35] Alternative legal orders can be highly authoritarian; exercising social control in ways which are abusive of individual

---

[32] Alejandro M. Garro (1999); José Thompson (1999). For current World Bank thinking on this question see World Bank (2000) pp. 91–115.

[33] On para-legals and their contribution to securing greater citizen access and governmental accountability see Ford Foundation (2000) chapter ten.

[34] The introduction of oral trial proceedings throughout Latin America during the last fifteen years has also contributed to making the formal court system more accessible.

[35] Richard Abel (1982).

human rights and liberties or intolerant of gender and ethnic differences or differences of sexual orientation. Informal, alternative justice systems, therefore, cannot be reduced to majoritarian 'justice' and must include adequate due process guarantees if they are not merely to embody the arbitrary exercise of local power. This in turn raises the question of how alternative dispute resolution forums are linked to the formal judicial system: some form of judicial review is evidently necessary, but if appeal to higher courts is used simply as a means to overturn local decisions, then ADR mechanisms will be undermined. Second, concern exists that alternative resolution based on consensus outcomes may, in practice, mean resolution in favour of the more powerful party. In particular, alternative and 'traditional' justice forums tend to be male dominated and problems of intra-familial violence are often not addressed or dealt with in such a way that they systematically disadvantage women. Current international assistance places much more emphasis on redressing women's unequal access to justice than previously. It is therefore to be hoped that attempts to strengthen ADR will be more gender-sensitive than in the past. Third, there is the question of whether such informal justice mechanisms can ever really tackle problems such as violence and organised crime. Attempts have been made, for example the *rondas campesinas* in Peru, formed to deal with petty crime, cattle rustling and minor civil disputes in the late 1970s and 1980s.[36] However, while success stories exist, the dangers of vigilantism are also present. Perhaps the most extreme example of this is the phenomenon of lynchings of suspected criminals being registered throughout rural and urban Latin America, particularly in Guatemala, Peru and Mexico.[37]

The central paradox is that, ultimately, tackling violence and organised crime requires a stronger state, not a decentralisation of justice. Previously 'strong' states in Latin America meant dictatorial or coercive regimes, but in fact many Latin American states were and continue to be weak, in the sense that they do not exercise effective control or legality over large swathes of national territory and state institutions.[38] A strong state is a one that provides effective protection for its citizens against arbitrary acts by both private and state actors. However, many states in the region do not have a monopoly on the use of force (Colombia, Peru, Mexico, Guatemala, El Salvador) or have a less-than-transparent relationship with coercive non-state actors — such as paramilitaries in Colombia and Central America. And across the region arbitrary and illegal acts by those who exercise state power, for example within the armed forces, police and the judiciary, remain unpunished. Strengthening ADR is a positive development but it cannot be separated from the question of

---

[36] See Orin Starn (1999).

[37] See Eduardo Castillo Claudett (2000).

[38] Guillermo O'Donnell's (1999a) aforementioned 'brown' areas: territories and institutions where neither reasonably effective bureaucracies nor properly sanctioned legality operate.

institutional strengthening at national and local levels, which contributes to a strong state respectful of the rule of law.

One important dimension of informal justice which is gaining ground throughout Latin America is that of 'indigenous justice'. Demands for ethnic recognition within the law gained force throughout the 1980s, a response to both domestic and international developments. Liberal constitutionalism had long failed to protect the interests of indigenous people, indeed the introduction of the liberal ideology of legal equality in the nineteenth century was used to expropriate indigenous community lands and abolish the limited protections that had existed under colonial and conservative rule. Indigenous people, some of the poorest sectors of the population, had little access to formal, state justice which was costly, punitive and invariably conducted in a language other than their mother tongue. In practice, indigenous, community-based dispute resolution mechanisms continued to exist alongside state justice. By the end of the twentieth century international legislation, such as the International Labour Organisation's Convention 169, favoured a greater formal recognition of the de facto legal pluralism which existed in many Latin American countries. Such reforms were increasingly demanded by organised indigenous peoples and their supporters, resulting in a series of constitutional reforms in the 1990s which recognised Latin American countries as multicultural and promised political, administrative and legal reforms to facilitate greater representation and participation of indigenous people in the body politic.[39] Commitments were made to respect indigenous political and legal autonomy, strengthen local indigenous authorities and respect culturally specific forms of dispute settlement. Advances in country-specific secondary legislation and jurisprudence vary, Colombia currently having advanced furthest in this respect.[40] During the 1990s some efforts were made to incorporate indigenous authorities and practices into the national legal system as courts of first instance. For example, in Peru a programme of non-lawyer justices of the peace was promoted following the 1993 Constitution (many of these justices of the peace used mechanisms of conciliation and mediation and spoke Quechua). Bolivia's decentralisation initiative, the 1994 Ley de Participación Popular, officially recognised indigenous customary legal practices that had previously existed 'outside the state'.[41] In Guatemala, following the 1996 peace settlement, international donors supported a pilot programme of Conflict Resolution Centres in rural, indigenous areas, which included indigenous lay-judges and which aimed to incorporate culturally specific conciliation mechanisms. Such developments, which essentially treat indigenous customary

---

[39] See Donna Lee Van Cott (2000); Willem Assies, Gemma van der Haar and André Hoekama (eds.) (2000).
[40] See Esther Sánchez Botero (2000).
[41] See Donna Lee Van Cott (2000).

law as a form of ADR, hold out the prospect of 'building the rule of law' in a way that reaches poor rural inhabitants. In a best case scenario they will help the law to become more accessible and representative for indigenous people. Certainly such initiatives to strengthen civil society go beyond support for urban-based NGOs and focus on rural civil society writ large (where the presence of NGOs may be minimal). It is also an approach to legal reform that dovetails with current donor preferences for democratic decentralisation and the strengthening of representative and responsive local government.

The problems of ADR mechanisms outlined above also apply to indigenous legal norms and practices; mechanisms must be found which guarantee indigenous rights to autonomy at the same time as guaranteeing the individual rights of indigenous people. However, such regulatory and supervisory mechanisms linking indigenous dispute resolution fora and the national judicial system must operate in culturally sensitive fashion, so that local indigenous autonomy is not simply repressed by the non-indigenous state under the banner of protecting universal human rights.[42] The challenge ahead is how to link greater space for local legal practices to a transformative *national* project for the rule of law. This will not be an easy task. In general national judicial systems remain distant from and mistrusted by most indigenous people.[43] Across the continent the judiciary is almost universally hostile to the idea of legal pluralism and indigenous customary law, a consequence both of positivist legal traditions and of the economic interests of legal professionals in monopolising the law. Nonetheless, the recognition of indigenous customary law, together with initiatives such as strengthening justice of the peace programmes, providing court translators for indigenous plaintiffs and defendants, providing legal defence services and educating judicial personnel in emerging international legal norms towards indigenous people and examples of good practice in other countries are important developments. They hold out the prospect of narrowing the distance between state law and indigenous citizens, improving access to justice for the poorest, most disadvantaged sectors of the population.

Conclusion: The Politics of Rule of Law Reform

The economic, political and social concerns with rule of law construction are by no means necessarily the same. There may be conflict in the reform agendas; there may indeed also be a degree of overlap and compatibility. But whatever the reform agenda, its passage and implementation is necessarily a political process despite the intention, or even mandate, of international organisations to remain outside the political. The *politics of reform* is an important aspect that therefore needs to be considered.

---

[42] For development of this argument see Jane Collier and Shannon Speed (2000).
[43] Shelton Davis (1999) Juan Méndez et al. (2000) pp. 152–59, p. 156.

Firstly there is the question of how reforms are prioritised both at a national and international level. These are inherently political decisions. For instance, are equal amounts of resources spent on reforms targeted at improving access to justice relative to reforms regarding economic legal security? Does the national logic of prioritisation of reforms take its cue from the international agenda? How does this balance out against domestic pressures and demands?

Secondly, reform agendas cannot be politically or socially neutral, precisely because specific political and sectoral interests will be affected by their implementation. Reform processes take place within complex social and political contexts where their acceptance and likelihood of success will depend on several factors. Reform projects require the support of the ruling coalition, and this will depend on the particular correlation of forces and the degree to which political actors feel they stand to gain from a particular reform. The failure of many reforms often is strongly linked to the lack of sufficient political will and commitment on behalf of the ruling coalition to ensure their successful implementation, even when legislation has been passed (albeit reluctantly). On the other hand, every political actor throughout the region seems to be jumping on the band wagon of rule of law construction because, as Carothers points out, this is a convenient 'post-ideology' which, in an abstract sense, suits all political parties and is well-received by the electorate. Reform legislation may be passed, but difficulties also arise at the moment of implementation. There may be powerful resistance amongst social sectors that are affected by the reform and have sufficient political or economic clout to escape its effects. Public officials, such as judges or police officers, may obstruct the implementation of reforms that they feel threatened by. Then there is the question of how rooted reform projects are in the national context, with all its complexities. Without a sense of national 'ownership', reform projects risk remaining abstract blue prints and dead letters. The effectiveness of reforms will necessarily depend on the degree to which they correspond to the diverse interests and needs of society.

Strengthening the rule of law is no longer a strictly national question. The erosion of state sovereignty which has resulted from globalisation raises larger questions about the nature, direction and efficacy of rule of law assistance, particularly that which aims to strengthen civil society as a means to ensure greater responsiveness and accountability. The transnational influences on the kind of demands civil groups make on their states have increased in the last two decades. Alliances of domestic and transnational civil groups increasingly engage in what Sikkink has termed 'boomerang strategies' to influence nation-states from above and below, and from outside.[44] While the direct impact of

---

[44] Margaret Keck and Kathryn Sikkink (1998); Thomas Risse, Stephen C. Ropp and Kathryn Sikkink (eds.) (1999).

such strategies on state behaviour has often been quite limited, the diffuse effects should not be under-estimated. In particular, the universalisation of human rights, and the notion that foreign actors and governments can intervene to prevent or punish the transgression of rights in other countries, has gained ground. Many human rights advocates would argue that domestic accountability for gross violations and effective due process guarantees should be a benchmark by which to measure the effectiveness of rule of law assistance to any given country.[45]

As Carothers observes in his introductory essay, 'rule of law', like democratisation, can mean all things to all people. However, if the rule of law means greater access to justice for the underprivileged, accountability and an end to impunity, and the provision of culturally appropriate mechanisms for dispute resolution then it will imply tough trade-offs. As the World Bank states in its 2000/2001 *World Development Report*, 'Making laws and their interpretation more sensitive to the needs of the disadvantaged requires building coalitions to this end'.[46] While powerful interests are stacked against greater accountability through the law, the increasing recourse of domestic civil groups to international norms and regulatory orders (such as indigenous rights or human rights legislation) should and could be strengthened by appropriate donor strategies. This implies a deep understanding of the local political, social and economic context on the part of donors. Formulaic, technocratic fixes divorced from the local context are doomed to failure, but appropriate, engaged and politically sensitive support can help advance a rule of law agenda.

The progression towards rule of law construction will depend not only on the accumulation of reforms, but also on the ways in which they are received and evolve within the intricate web of state, and state and society relations, in all its complexity. Here the interplay between formal institutions and informal networks of rules and relationships is also important. Political culture and long-standing habits of impunity are hard to kick and constitute an intangible factor which will determine the implementation of reforms. At the same time, though, institutional change and piecemeal reforms do have a gradual impact on political behaviour, and old forms of political and social interaction will eventually be transformed. However, the rate of change is likely to be frustratingly slow. Although current developments are to be welcomed and encouraged, ultimately it is by no means clear that the long-term outcome of current endeavours of state reform will result in the consolidation of rule of law, democratic stability and economic viability.

---

[45] Margaret Popkin (2000).
[46] World Bank (2000) p. 103.

Bibliography

Abel, Richard (1982) 'The contradictions of informal justice' in R. Abel (ed.), *The Politics of Informal Justice* (New York: Academic Press).

Adelman, Sammy and Paliwala, Abdul (eds.) (1981) *Law and Crisis in the Third World* (New York: Hans Zell).

Alvarez, Irma (1999) 'La evaluación de los jueces está en las leyes', *El Universal*, Bogotá, 18 August.

Alvarez, Irma (1999a) 'Fiscal avala emergencia judicial', *El Universal*, Bogotá, 26 August.

Alvarez, José (1991) 'Promoting the "Rule of Law" in Latin America: Problems and Prospects', *George Washington Journal of International Law and Economy*, vol. 25, pp. 287–332.

Annis, Sheldon (1987) 'Can Small-scale Development be a Large-scale Policy? The Case of Latin America', *World Development Report*, vol. 15, pp. 129–34.

Apter, David E. (1987) *Rethinking Development: Modernization, Dependency and Post-Modern Politics* (Newbury Park, CA: Sage Publications).

Assies, Willem, van der Haar, Gemma, and Hoekama, André (eds.) (2000) *The Challenge of Diversity: Indigenous Peoples and Reform of the State in Latin America* (Amsterdam: Thela Thesis).

Bernbaum, Marcia (1999) *Weaving Ties of Friendship, Trust, and Commitment to Build Democracy and Human Rights in Peru* (Lima: IPEDEHP).

Blair, Harry and Hansen, Gary (1994) *Weighing in on the Scales of Justice: Strategic Approaches for Donor-Supported Rule of Law Programmes* (Washington, DC: US Agency for International Development).

Brown, Robert Jr. (1995) 'Order from Disorder: The Development of the Russian Securities Markets', *University of Pennsylvania Journal of International Business Law*, vol. 15, pp. 509–58.

Brysk, Alison (2000) 'Democratising Civil Society in Latin America', *Journal of Democracy*, Vol. 11, no. 3, pp. 151–65.

Burg, Elliot M. (1977) 'Law and Development: A Review of the Literature and a Critique of "Scholars in Self-Estrangement"', *American Journal of Comparative Law*, vol. 25, pp. 492–530.

Burnell, Peter (ed.) (2000) *Democracy Assistance: International Co-operation for Democratization* (London: Frank Cass).

Buscaglia, Edgardo (1997) 'Obstáculos de la reforma judicial en América Latina', in Jarquin, Edmundo and Carrillo, Fernando (eds.) (1997) *La economía política de la reforma judicial*, pp. 42–3.

Buscaglia, Edgardo and Dakolias, Maria (1996) 'Judicial Reform in Latin American Courts: The Experience in Argentina and Ecuador', World Bank Technical Paper No. 350, World Bank.

Call, Charles T. (2000) *Sustainable Development in Central America: The Challenges of Violence, Injustice, and Security* (Hamburg: Institut für Iberoamerika-Kunde).

Cameron, Maxwell A. (1997) 'Political and Economic Origins of Regime Change in Peru: The Eighteenth Brumaire of Alberto Fujimori', in Cameron and Mauceri (eds.), *The Peruvian Labyrinth: Polity, Society, Economy*, pp. 37–69, (Pennsylvania: Pennsylvania State University Press).

Cameron, Maxwell A. (1998) 'Self-Coups: Peru, Guatemala, and Russia', *Journal of Democracy*, vol. 9, pp. 125–39.

Carothers, Thomas (1991) *In the Name of Democracy: US Policy Toward Latin America in the Reagan Years* (Berkeley: University of California Press).

Carothers, Thomas (1998) 'The Rule of Law Revival', *Foreign Affairs*, March-April 1998, pp. 95–106.

Carothers, Thomas (1999) *Aiding Democracy Abroad: The Learning Curve* (Washington, DC: Carnegie Endowment for International Peace).

Carothers, Thomas (2000), 'Struggling with Semi-Authoritarians', in Peter Burnell (ed.), *Democracy Assistance: International Co-operation for Democratization* (London:Frank Cass) pp. 210–25.

Carty, Anthony (ed.) (1992) *Law and Development* (New York: New York University Press).

Castillo Claudett, Eduardo (2000) 'La justicia en tiempos de la ira: linchamientos populares urbanos en América Latina', paper presented to XII International Congress of Customary Law and Legal Pluralism, Chile.

Chinchilla, Laura (1998) 'Seguridad ciudadana y consolidación democrática en América Latina', paper presented at the Woodrow Wilson Center Latin America Program.

Ciurlizza, Javier (2000) 'Judicial Reform and International Legal Technical Assistance Latin America', in *Democratization*, vol. 7, no. 2, pp. 211–30.

Clark, Ann Marie, et al. (1998) 'The Sovereign Limits of Global Civil Society,' *World Politics* no. 51, pp. 1–35.

Collier, Jane and Speed, Shannon (2000) 'Limiting Indigenous Autonomy in Chiapas, Mexico: The State Government's use of the Discourse of Human Rights', in *Human Rights Quarterly*, vol. 22, no. 4, pp. 877–905.

Committee on Legal Services to the Poor in the Developing Countries (1974) *Legal Aid and World Poverty – A Survey of Asia, Africa, and Latin America* (New York: Praeger).

Conference on Security and Cooperation in Europe (1990) Document of the Copenhagen Meeting of the Conference on the Human Dimension, June 29, reprinted in *International Legal Materials*, vol. 29, pp. 1305–6.

Crohn, Madeleine and Davis, William E. (eds.) (1996) *Lessons Learned: Proceedings of the Second Judicial Reform Roundtable held in Williamsburg, Va., May 19– 22, 1996*, (Williamsburg: National Center for State Courts).

Dakolias, Maria (1995) 'A Strategy for Judicial Reform: The Experience in Latin America', *Virginia Journal of International Law*, vol. 36, pp. 167–231.

Davis, Shelton (1999) 'Comments on Dandler' in Méndez, Juan et al. (1999) *The (Un)Rule of Law*, pp. 152–9.

DeLisle, Jacques (1999) 'Lex Americana?: United States Legal Assistance, American Legal Models, and Legal Change in the Post-Communist World and Beyond', *University of Pennsylvania Journal of International Economic Law*, vol. 20, 1999, pp. 179–308.

Development Associates, Inc. (1988) *A Framework for Supporting Democratic Development in Latin America and the Caribbean*, (Arlington, VA: USAID/Bureau for Latin America and the Caribbean).

Dias, C. J. et al. (eds.) (1981) *Lawyers in the Third World: Comparative and Developmental Perspectives* (New York: International Center for Law in Development.

Douglas, Justice William O. (1962) 'Lawyers of the Peace Corps', *American Bar Association Journal*, vol. 48, 1962, pp. 909–13.

Fatton, Robert Jr. (1999) 'The Impairments of Democratization: Haiti in Comparative Perspective', *Comparative Politics*, vol. 31, no. 2, pp. 209–21.

Faúndez, Julio (ed.) (1997) *Good Government and Law: Legal and Institutional Reform in Developing Countries* (London: Macmillan).

Faúndez, Julio (1997a) 'Legal Technical Assistance', in Faúndez, Julio (ed.), *Good Government and Law: Legal and Institutional Reform in Developing Countries* (London: Macmillan) pp. 1–25.

Ford Foundation (2000) *Many Roads to Justice: The Law-Related Work of Ford*

Foundation Grantees around the World (New York: Ford Foundation).

Fox, Jonathan (2000), 'Civil Society and Political Accountability: Propositions for Discussion', draft paper presented at the conference 'Institutions, Accountability and Democratic Governance in Latin America', University of Notre Dame, May 2000.

Franck, Thomas M. (1992) 'The Emerging Right to Democratic Governance,' American Journal of International Law, vol. 86, pp. 46–91.

Frischtak, Leila (1997) 'Political mandate, institutional change and economic reform', in Faúndez, *Good Government and Law,* pp. 95–119.

Gardner, James A. (1980) *Legal Imperialism: American Lawyers and Foreign Aid in Latin America* (Madison: University of Wisconsin Press).

Garro, Alejandro M (1999) 'Access to Justice for the Poor in Latin America', in Méndez, Juan, O'Donnell, Guillermo and Pinheiro, Paolo Sergio (eds.), *The (Un)Rule of Law and the Underprivileged in Latin America* (Notre Dame: University of Notre Dame Press).

Hammergren, Linn (1998) *Institutional Strengthening and Justice Reform* and *Judicial Training and Justice Reform* (Washington, DC: SAID/Centre for Democracy and Governance).

Hammergren, Linn (1998a) *The Politics of Justice Reform in Latin America: The Peruvian Case in Comparative Perspective* (Boulder, CO: Westview Press).

Hammergren, Linn (1998b) 'Code Reform and Law Revision', US Agency for International Development, PN-ACD-022, August.

Hawthorn, G. (1993) 'Liberalisation and 'Modern Liberty': Four Southern States', in *World Development,* vol.21, no. 8, pp. 1299–312.

Hearn, Julie and Robinson, Mark (2000) 'Civil Society and Democracy Assistance in Africa', in Burnell (ed.) (2000) *Democracy Assistance*, pp. 241–62.

Heymann, Philip B. (1990) *Options for United States Policy Toward Guatemala: Hearing Before the Subcommittee on Western Hemisphere Affairs of the House of Rep.* 101st Cong., 2nd Sess., pp. 59–60 (Harvard: Harvard University Law School).

Humberto Martinez, Nestor (1998) 'Rule of Law and Economic Efficiency' in Jarquín, Edmundo and Carrillo, Fernando (eds.) *Justice Delayed: Judicial Reform in Latin America* (Washington, DC: Inter-American Development Bank).

Huntington, Samuel (1991) *The Third Wave,* (Norman, OK: University of Oklahoma Press).

IDB (1994) IDB Document, 'Eighth General Increase in Resources'

(Washington, DC: IDB).

IDB (1996) IDB Document GN-1883-4, March 'Frame of Reference for Bank Action in Programs for Modernization of the State and Strengthening of Civil Society' Washington, DC: IDB).

IDB (1996a) *IDB Resource Book on Participation*, DPP, SDS, DPA/DEV (Washington, DC: IDB).

Jarquín, Edmundo and Carrillo, Fernando (eds.) (1998) *Justice Delayed: Judicial Reform in Latin America* (Washington, DC: Inter-American Development Bank).

Johnson, Tim (1999) 'Venezuelan panel takes control from Congress', *Miami Herald*, 31 August.

Johnson, Tim (1999a) 'La presidenta del Supremo venezolano dimite y da por enterrado el Estado de derecho', *El País*, 25 August.

Kaufman, Daniel, Kraay, Aart and Zoido-Lobaton, Pablo (1999) 'Governance Matters', unpublished manuscript (Washington, DC: World Bank).

Keck, Margaret and Sikkink, Kathryn (1998) *Activists Beyond Borders: Transnational Advocacy Networks in International Politics* (Ithaca, NY: Cornell University Press).

Korten, David C. (1991) 'The Role of Nongovernmental Organizations in Development: Changing Patterns and Perspectives', in Paul, Samuel and Israel, Arturo (eds.) *Nongovernmental Organizations and the World Bank: Cooperation for Development*, pp. 20–44.

Kritz, 'Neil J. (1996) 'The Rule of Law in the Postconflict Phase: Building a Stable Peace', in Crocker, Chestar A. and Hampson, Fen Osler with Aall, Pamela (eds.) (1996) *Managing Global Chaos: Sources and Responses to International Conflict*, (Washington, DC: United States Institute for Peace Press) pp. 587–606.

Lawyers Committee for Human Rights (1989) *Underwriting Injustice: AID and El Salvador's Judicial Reform Programme* (New York: Lawyers Committee for Human Rights).

Lawyers Committee for Human Rights and Programa Venezolano de Educación-Acción en Derechos Humanos (1995) *Halfway to Reform: The World Bank and the Venezuelan Justice System* (New York: Lawyers Committee for Human Rights).

Lawyers Committee for Human Rights, (2000) *Building on Quicksand: The Collapse of the World Bank's Judicial Reform Project in Peru* (New York: Lawyers Committee for Human Rights).

Levitsky, Steven (1999) 'Fujimori and Post-Party Politics in Peru', *Journal of Democracy*, No. 3, vol. 10, pp. 78–92.

Lindblom, Charles E. (1990) *Inquiry and Change* (New Haven: Yale University Press).

Lynch, Dennis O. (1981) *Legal Roles in Colombia* (Uppsala and New York: Scandinavian Institute of African Studies, International Center for Law and Development).

McAuslan, Patrick (1997) 'Law, Governance and the Development of the Market: Practical Problems and Possible Solutions', in Julio Faúndez (ed.), *Good Government and Law: Legal and Institutional Reform in Developing Countries* (New York: St Martin's Press).

McClintock, Cynthia (1996) 'La voluntad política presidencial y la ruptura constitucional de 1992 en el Perú', in Tuesta Soldevilla (ed.), *Los enigmas del poder: Fujimori 1990–1996* (Lima: Fundación Friedrich Ebert), pp. 60–6.

Méndez, Juan, O'Donnell, Guillermo and Pinheiro, Paolo Sergio (eds.) (1999) *The (Un)Rule of Law and the Underprivileged in Latin America* (Notre Dame: University of Notre Dame Press).

Merryman, John H. (1977) 'Comparative Law and Social Change: One the Origins, Style and Revival of the Law and Development Movement', *American Journal of Comparative Law*, vol. 25, pp. 457–91.

Merryman, John Henry, Clark, David S. and. Friedman, Lawrence M (1979) *Law and Social Change in Mediterranean Europe and Latin America: A Handbook of Legal and Social Indicators for Comparative Study* (Stanford: Stanford Law School).

Mertus, Julie (1999) 'From Legal Transplants to Transformative Justice: Human Rights and the Promise of Transnational Civil Society', *American University International Law Review*, vol. 14, 1999, pp. 1335–89.

Messick, Richard E. (1999) 'Judicial Reform and Economic Development: A Survey of the Issues', *World Bank Research Observer*, vol. 14, no. 1 (February 1999), pp. 117–36.

National Bipartisan Commission on Central America (1984) *The Report of the President's National Bipartisan Commission on Central America* (Washington, DC: Government Printing Office).

Neild, Rachel (1998) 'Themes and Debates in Public Security Reform' (Washington DC: Washington Office on Latin America).

Nelson, Paul J. (1995) *The World Bank and Non-Governmental Organizations* (Basingstoke: Macmillan Press).

Nichols, Philip M. (1997) 'The Viability of Transplanted Law: Kazakhstani Reception of a Transplanted Foreign Investment Code', *University of Pennsylvania Journal of International Economic Law*, vol. 18, pp. 1235–79.

North, Douglas (1990) *Institutions, Institutional Change and Economic Performance* (Cambridge: Cambridge University Press).

O'Donnell, Guillermo (1993) 'On the State, Democratisation and Some Conceptual Problems: A Latin American View with Glances at Some Post-communist Countries', in *World Development*, vol. 21, no. 8, pp. 1355–71.

O'Donnell, Guillermo (1999) *Counterpoints: Selected Essays on Authoritarianism and Democratization* (Notre Dame: University of Notre Dame Press).

O'Donnell, Guillermo (1999a) 'On the State, Democratization, and Some Conceptual Problems: A Latin American View with Glances as Some Postcommunist Countries', pp. 133–57 in O'Donnell, Guillermo *Counterpoints: Selected Essays on Authoritarianism and Democratization* (Notre Dame: University of Notre Dame Press).

O'Donnell, Guillermo (1999b) 'Horizontal Accountability in New Democracies' in Schedler, Andreas, Diamond, Larry and Plattner, Marc (eds.) (1999) *The Self-restraining State: Power and Accountability in New Democracies* (London: Lynne Rienner Publishers) pp. 29–52.

O'Donnell, Guillermo (1999c) 'Polyarchies and the (Un)rule of Law in Latin America", in Mendez, Juan et al, *The (Un)rule of law and the Underprivileged*, pp. 303–338

O'Donnell, Guillermo (2000) 'Democracy, Law and Comparative Politics', Kellogg Institute Working Paper No. 274.

Orth, John V. (1998) 'Exporting the Rule of Law', *North Carolina Journal of International Law and Commercial Regulation*, vol. 24, pp. 71–82.

Oxhorn, Philip and Pamela Starr (eds.) (1999) *Markets and Democracy in Latin America: Conflict or Convergence?* (London: Lynne Rienner Publisher).

Oxhorn, Philip and, Pamela Starr (1999a) 'The Logics of Liberalization', in Oxhorn, Philip and Starr, Pamela (eds.), *Markets and Democracy in Latin America: Conflict or Convergence?* (London: Lynne Rienner Publisher) pp. 241–53.

Paul, James C. N. (1995) 'The United Nations Family: Challenges of Law and Development: The United Nations and the Creation of an International Law of Development', *Harvard International Law Journal*, 36, Spring, p. 307.

Paul, Samuel and Israel, Arturo (1991) *Nongovernmental Organizations and the World Bank: Cooperation for Development* (Washington, DC: World Bank).

Pearce, Jenny (1997) 'Civil Society, the Market and Democracy in Latin

America', *Democratization*, Vol. 4, No. 2, pp. 57–83, p. 66.

Popkin, Margaret (2000) *Peace Without Justice: Obstacles to Building the Rule of Law in El Salvador* (Pennsylvania: Pennsylvania University Press).

Raustiala, Kal (1997) 'The "Participatory Revolution" in International Environmental Law', *Harvard Environmental Law Review*, 21, p. 537.

Risse, Thomas, Ropp, Stephen C., and Sikkink, Kathryn (eds.) (1999) *The Power of Human Rights: International Norms and Domestic Change* (Cambridge: Cambridge University Press).

Rodriguez, Marcela (2000) 'Empowering Women: An Assessment of Legal Aid Under Ecuador's Judicial Reform Project', (Washington, DC: World Bank).

Rose, Carol V. (1998) 'The "New" Law and Development Movement in the Post Cold War Era: A Vietnam Case Study', *Law and Society Review*, vol. 32, pp. 93–140.

Rosenn, Keith (1969) 'The Reform of Legal Education in Brazil', *Journal of Legal Education*, vol. 21, pp. 251–83.

Rosenn, Keith (1987) 'The Protection of Judicial Independence in Latin America', *University of Miami Inter-American Law Review*, vol. 19, pp. 1–36.

Rowat, Malcolm (1997) 'Competition Policy in Latin America: Legal and Institutional Issues'in Faúndez, Julio (ed.) (1997) *Good Government and Law: Legal and Institutional Reform in Developing Countries* (New York: St. Martin's Press), , pp. 165–88.

Salman, Lawrence F. and Eaves, A. Paige (1991) 'Interactions between Nongovernmental Organizations, Governments, and the World Bank: Evidence from Bank Projects', Paul, Samuel and Israel, Arturo (eds.) *Nongovernmental Organizations and the World Bank: Cooperation for Development.*

Sánchez Botero, Esther (2000) 'The *tutela*-system as a means of transforming the relations between the State and the indigenous peoples of Colombia' in Assies et al., *The Challenge of Diversity*, pp. 223–241.

Schedler, Andreas, Diamond, Larry and Plattner, Marc (eds.) (1999) *The Self-Restraining State:Power and Accountability in New Democracies* (London: Lynne Riener Publishers).

Seidman, Ann and Seidman, Robert (1996) 'Drafting Legislation for Development: Lessons from a Chinese Project', *American Journal of Comparative Law*, vol. 44, pp. 1–44.

Seligson, Mitchell, Cruz, José Miguel and Cordova Macias, Ricardo (2000)

Auditoría de la democracia: El Salvador 1999 (Pittsburgh: University of Pittsburgh).

Sherwood, Robert M., et al. (1994) 'Judicial Systems and Economic Performance', *Quarterly Review of Economics and Finance*, Vol. 34, Summer, p. 101.

Sherwood, Robert (1998) 'Judicial Systems and National Economic Performance', in Jarquín, Edmundo and Carrillo, Fernando (eds.) *Justice Delayed: Judicial Reform in Latin America* (Washington, DC: Inter-American Development Bank).
Sieder, Rachel (forthcoming, 2002), *Multiculturalism in Latin America: Indigenous Rights, Diversity and Democracy* (Basingstoke: Palgrave)

Starn, Orin (1999) *Nightwatch: The Politics of Protest in the Andes* (Durham, NC, and London: Duke University Press).

Tamanaha, Brian Z. (1995) 'The Lessons of Law and Development Studies (reviewing Carty and Adelman)', *The American Journal of International Law*, vol. 89, pp. 470–86.

Theobald, Robin (1990) *Corruption, Development, and Underdevelopment* (Durham, NC, and London: Duke University Press).

Thompson, José (1999), 'Access to justice and the underprivileged in Latin America', preliminary summary of Inter-American Development Bank consultancy on access to the rule of law for the underprivileged, mimeo (Washington, DC: IDB).

Tome, Joseph (1997) 'Comment', in Julio Faúndez (ed.) (1997) *Good Government and Law: Legal and Institutional Reform in Developing Countries* (New York: St. Martin's Press) pp. 45–50.

Trubeck, David M. (1990) 'Back to the Future: The Short Happy Life of the Law and Society Movement', *Florida State University Law Review*, vol. 18, pp. 4–55.

Trubeck, David M. (1996) 'Law and Development: Then and Now', Paper Presented to the American Society of International Law, Washington, DC.

Trubeck, David M., Dezalay, Yves, Buchanan, Ruth and Davis, John R. (1994) 'Global Restructuring and the Law: Studies of the Internationalization of Legal Fields and the Creation of Transnational Arenas', *Case Western Reserve Law Review*, vol. 44, 1994, pp. 407–98.

Trubek, David M. and Galanter, Marc (1974) 'Scholars in Self-Estrangement: Some Reflections on the Crisis in Law and Development Studies in the United States', *Wisconsin Law Review*, vol. 1974, pp. 1062–102.

United Nations (1993) *The Fifth United Nations Survey of Crime Trends and Operations of Criminal Justice Systems*, (New York: United Nations).

United Nations (1999) *Global Report on Crime and Justice* (New York: Oxford University Press).

United Nations Development Programme (1995) *Good Governance and Sustainable Human Development* (New York: United Nations).

United Nations Development Programme (1999) 'Regional Justice Project of the Bureau for Latin America and the Caribbean, Semi-Annual Report', January–June.

United States Department of State (1999) 'Peru Country Report on Human Rights Practices for 1998', (Washington, DC: Bureau of Democracy, Human Rights, and Labour).

US Agency for International Development, 'Democracy', http://www.info.usaid.gov/democracy/

US General Accounting Office (1996) 'Promoting Democracy: Progress Report on US Democratic Development Assistance to Russia' (Washington, DC: GAO).

US General Accounting Office (1999) 'Foreign Assistance: Rule of Law Funding Worldwide for Fiscal Years 1993–1998', General Accounting Office, GAO/NSIAD-99-158 (Washington, DC: GAO).

US General Accounting Office (1999) 'Foreign Assistance: US Rule of Law Assistance to Five Latin American Countries' (Washington, DC: GAO).

US General Accounting Office (1993) 'Foreign Assistance: Promoting Judicial Reform to Strengthen Democracies' (Washington, DC: GAO).

Van Cott, Donna Lee (2000) 'A Political Analysis of Legal Pluralism in Bolivia and Colombia', *Journal of Latin American Studies*, Vol. 32 (1), pp. 207–34.

Van Cott, Donna Lee (2000a) *The Friendly Liquidation of the Past: The Politics of Diversity in Latin America* (Pittsburgh: University of Pittsburgh Press).

Van Rooy, Alison (1998) *Civil Society and the Aid Industry: The Politics and Promise*, London: Earthscan/North-South Institute).

Waltman, Jerome L. (1988) 'The Courts and Political Change in Post-Industrial Society, in Waltman, Jerome L. and Kenneth M. Holland (eds.) *The Political Role of Law Courts in Modern Democracies* (London: Macmillan Press).

Washington Office on Latin America (1990) *Elusive Justice: The U.S. Administration of Justice Program in Latin America* (Washington, DC: Washington Office on Latin America).

White, Gordon (1993) 'Civil Society, Democratisation and Development (I): Clearing the Analytical Ground', *Democratization*, vol. 1, no. 3 (Autumn), pp. 375–90

Whitehead, Laurence (1993) 'On "Reform of the State" and "Regulation of the Market"', in *World Development*, vol. 21, no. 8, pp. 1371–92.

Whitehead, Laurence (1997) 'Bowling in the Bronx: The Uncivil Interstices between Civil and Political Society', *Democratization*, vol. 4, no. 1, pp. 94–114.

Wood, Ellen Meiksins (1995) *Democracy Against Capitalism* (Cambridge: Cambridge University Press).

World Bank (1988) 'Ethical Guide for Bank Staff Handling Procurement Matters in Bank-Financed Projects', http://www.worldbank.org/publicsector/anticorrupt/ethicalguide.htm

World Bank (1995) *The World Bank and Legal Technical Assistance: Initial Lessons* (Washington, DC: World Bank).

World Bank (1996) *Staff Appraisal Report: Ecuador Judicial Reform Project* (Washington, DC: World Bank).

World Bank (1997) Press Release, 'World Bank Helps Pioneer Judicial Reform in Peru', News Release No. 98/1555/LAC, 7 December (Washington, DC: World Bank).

World Bank (1997a) *The State in a Changing World, World Development Report 1997* (Washington DC: World Bank).

World Bank (1998) 'The Bank's Relations with NGOs: Issues and Directions', Social Development Papers, Paper Number 28, August 11 (Washinton, DC: World Bank).

World Bank (1999), *Reforming Public Institutions and Strengthening Governance* (Washington, DC: World Bank).

World Bank (1999), 'Procurement Guidelines http://www.worldbank.org/html/opr/procure/guidelin.html

World Bank (2000), *World Development Report 2000/2001: Attacking Poverty* (New York: Oxford University Press/World Bank).

World Bank Anti-Corruption Knowledge Resource Center, 'Preventing Corruption in Bank Projects and Keeping our House in Order' http://wwww1.worldbank.org/publicsector/anticorrupt/prevent.htm

World Bank Legal Department (1995) 'The World Bank and Legal Technical Assistance,' Initial Lessons Policy Research Working Paper, No. 1414, p. 9.

World Bank Listing of Ineligible Firms,

http://www.worldbank.org/html/opr/procure/ debarr.html

World Bank Wolfensohn, James D. (1998) 'New Measures to Combat Fraud and Corruption',
http://www.worldbank.org/publicsector/anticorrupt/newmeasures.htm

Yashar, Deborah (1999) 'Democracy, Indigenous Movements, and the Postliberal Challenge in Latin America', *World Politics*, Vol. 52, no.1, pp. 76–104.

Zakaria, Fareed (1997), 'The Rise of Illiberal Democracy', *Foreign Affairs*, Vol. 76, no. 6, pp. 22–43.